D0487669

THE IMPERIAL
WAR MUSEUM
BOOK OF

VICTORY IN EUROPE

THE IMPERIAL
WAR MUSEUM
BOOK OF
VICTORY IN EUROPE

JULIAN THOMPSON

BCA

LONDON   NEW YORK   SYDNEY   TORONTO

Previous page: **British infantry and armour advancing along the main road to Vassy, 4 August 1944.**
(B8603)

First published 1994 by Sidgwick & Jackson Limited

a division of Pan Macmillan Publishers Limited
Cavaye Place London SW10 9PG
and Basingstoke

Associated companies throughout the world

CN 2800

Copyright © Julian Thompson and the Imperial War Museum 1994

The right of Julian Thompson to be identified as the
author of this work has been asserted by him in accordance
with the Copyright, Designs and Patents Act 1988.

All rights reserved. No reproduction, copy or transmission
of this publication may be made without written permission.
No paragraph of this publication may be reproduced, copied or
transmitted save with written permission or in accordance with
the provisions of the Copyright Act 1956 (as amended). Any
person who does any unauthorised act in relation to
this publication may be liable to criminal prosecution
and civil claims for damages.

9 8 7 6 5 4 3 2 1

A CIP catalogue record for this book is available from
the British Library

Photoset by Parker Typesetting Service, Leicester
Printed and bound in Great Britain by
BPC Hazell Books Ltd, Aylesbury, Bucks

CONTENTS

ACKNOWLEDGEMENTS

Without the letters, accounts and taped interviews of the people I have quoted, this book would not have been possible to write. My first acknowledgement must be to them. Their names are listed in the Index of Contributors. I am equally indebted to the photographers, film cameramen and artists whose pictures I have used to illustrate the book.

Next my thanks must go to the senior members of the staff of the Imperial War Museum whose support was invaluable. Dr Christopher Dowling, Keeper of the Department of Museum Services, introduced me to the project and encouraged me throughout. Roderick Suddaby, Keeper of the Department of Documents, was an unfailing source of help and 'points to march on'. I am also deeply grateful to Margaret Brooks (Keeper of the Department of Sound Records), Jane Carmichael (Keeper of the Department of Photographs), Angela Weight (Keeper of the Department of Art), Roger Smither (Keeper of the Department of Film) and Gwynn Bayliss (Keeper of the Department of Printed Books). Space precludes naming the host of those in the Museum Departments to whom I repeatedly turned for help: for their sound advice and priceless nuggets of information, my warmest thanks. I must however make mention of Michael Moody, Jenny Wood and Pauline Allwright (Department of Art); Paul Sargent, Jane Fish and Kay Gladstone (Department of Film); Peter Hart and Conrad Wood (Department of Sound Records); Paul Kemp (Department of Photographs); and the foursome in the Department of Documents, Phil Reed, Simon Robbins, Nigel Steel and Steven Walton, and latterly Penny Goymer, not only for help and moral support, but also for allowing me to join their 'coffee boat'.

My thanks are also due to Peter Simkins of the Research and Information Office for reading the complete typescript, and for his invaluable comments and suggestions.

I am indebted to General Sir John Hackett for reading and commenting on the Arnhem chapter, and for his advice and encouragement. General Hackett followed distinguished service in the Western Desert by command of 4th Parachute Brigade in Italy and at Arnhem. He was wounded during the battle, taken prisoner, and escaped thanks to the bravery of the Dutch people.

I must also mention Brigadier Bryan Watkins who kindly spared time from a busy life to read two of the chapters. Bryan fought in the campaign as a troop leader in 1st Royal Tanks. This experience, and much study of the campaign over the years since 1945, enabled him to cast a critical eye over those two chapters from a perspective ranging from tank turret to high level strategy. Linda Kitson, War Artist and friend, gave many hours which she could ill spare, while enduring the added pressure of moving house, to help me with the selection of pictures from the rich art collection in the Museum.

I am especially grateful to the present Viscount Montgomery of Alamein for making an exception in my case, by lifting the temporary ban he had placed on research on his father's papers in the Imperial War Museum, while he and Alistair Horne were writing a book about the Field Marshal.

I must also thank the Tank Museum for allowing me to reproduce the leaflet on page 13.

My warm thanks are due to William Armstrong of Sidgwick & Jackson, for suggesting that I write this book, and for steering me along in a most tactful way. I am also grateful to Helen Gummer of Sidgwick & Jackson for her forebearance and patience, and to Peter Ward the designer.

As always, Jane Thompson's comments and criticisms of the work as it unfolded were of inestimable value. Without her support, in this and in many other ways, the book would not have been written.

CHRONOLOGY

For reasons explained in the Prologue, the majority of events in this Chronology are those covering the activities of Montgomery's 21st Army Group.

1944

General Sir Bernard Montgomery arrives in England and takes command of the Allied Land Forces for the invasion of France, under overall command of General Dwight D. Eisenhower, the Supreme Commander.	2 January
Landings in Normandy by Montgomery's 21st Army Group consisting of Lieutenant-General Bradley's United States 1st Army and Lieutenant-General Dempsey's British 2nd Army.	6 June
Severe gale destroys the American Mulberry (artificial harbour), and damages the British Mulberry.	19–22 June
Capture of Cherbourg by United States 1st Army.	27 June
Capture of Caen by Canadian and British troops of British 2nd Army.	9 July
Invasion of South of France by General Devers's 6th Army Group consisting of United States 7th Army and French 1st Army.	15 August
The Battle of Normandy ends with the closing of the Falaise Pocket. The advance to the River Seine by 21st Army Groups begins.	20 August
Paris liberated by French and American troops of Bradley's 12th Army Group.	25 August
Eisenhower assumes overall responsibility for land operations with Field Marshal Montgomery commanding 21st Army Group, General Bradley commanding 12th Army Group, and General Devers commanding 6th Army Group, as his principal subordinate land commanders.	1 September
Brussels liberated by British 2nd Army.	3 September
Antwerp liberated by British 2nd Army.	4 September
Operations by British 2nd Army and Canadian 1st Army, to clear the Scheldt Estuary and south-west Holland.	12 September to 5 November
Operation Market Garden, including the Battle for Arnhem.	17–26 September

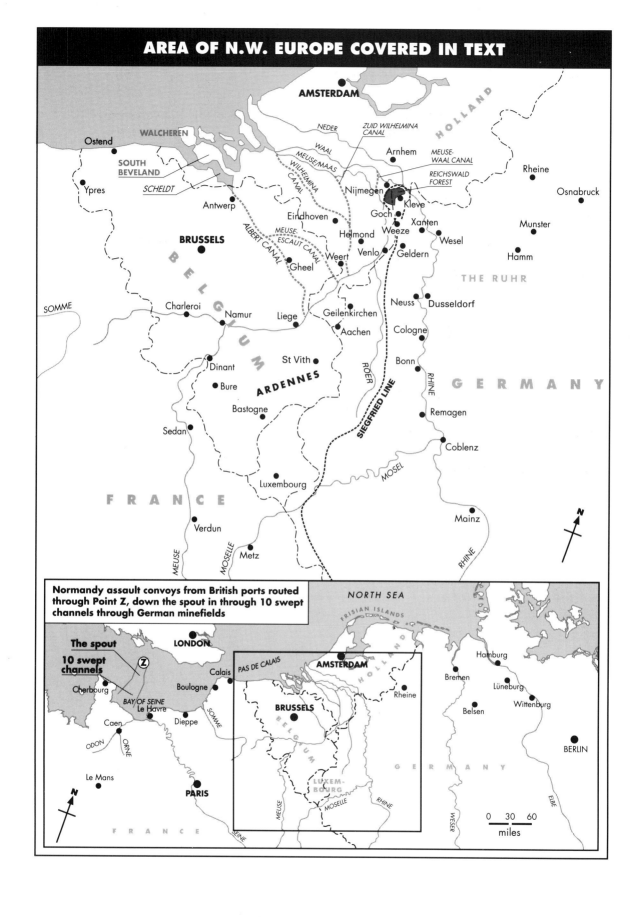

AREA OF N.W. EUROPE COVERED IN TEXT

AMSTERDAM

HOLLAND

WALCHEREN

Ostend

NEDER

ZUID WILHELMINA CANAL

SOUTH BEVELAND

WAAL

MEUSE-MAAS

Arnhem

MEUSE-WAAL CANAL

Rheine

Ypres

WILHELMINA CANAL

REICHSWALD FOREST

Osnabruck

SCHELDT

Antwerp

Nijmegen

Kleve

Eindhoven

Goch

Xanten

Munster

BRUSSELS

MEUSE-ESCAUT CANAL

Helmond

Weeze

Hamm

ALBERT CANAL

Weert

Venlo

Geldern

Wesel

BELGIUM

Gheel

THE RUHR

Charleroi

Namur

Liege

Geilenkirchen

Neuss

Dusseldorf

Dinant

Aachen

Cologne

SOMME

St Vith

ROER

Bonn

RHINE

GERMANY

Bure

ARDENNES

SIEGFRIED LINE

Bastogne

Remagen

Sedan

Coblenz

Luxembourg

MOSEL

FRANCE

Verdun

Mainz

N

MEUSE

MOSELLE

Metz

RHINE

Normandy assault convoys from British ports routed through Point Z, down the spout in through 10 swept channels through German minefields

NORTH SEA

FRISIAN ISLANDS

The spout

LONDON

HOLLAND

Hamburg

10 swept channels

Z

Calais

PAS DE CALAIS

AMSTERDAM

Bremen

Lüneburg

Cherbourg

Boulogne

Rheine

Wittenburg

BAY OF SEINE

Le Havre

BRUSSELS

Belsen

Caen

Dieppe

BELGIUM

ODON

ORNE

SOMME

BERLIN

Le Mans

LUXEM-BOURG

GERMANY

PARIS

RHINE

N

FRANCE

SEINE

MEUSE

MOSELLE

WESER

ELBE

0   30   60
miles

Operations to clear the West Bank of the River Maas.	12 October to 3 December
Landings on the island of Walcheren as part of operations to clear the Scheldt estuary and open the port of Antwerp.	1 November
Germans launch counter-offensive in the Ardennes.	16 December

1945

Ardennes battle ends.	16 January
Battle by British 2nd Army to clear the Roermond Triangle (the area bounded by the Rivers Roer, Wurm and Meuse).	15–28 January
Battle of the Rhineland, operations under command of 21st Army Group, by Canadian 1st Army and United States 9th Army to clear the west bank of the River Rhine in preparation for the crossing by 21st Army Group north of the Ruhr.	8 February to 5 March
The Rhine crossing by 21st Army Group. Crossings by United States and French Armies at Remagen, Mainz, Wurms and Philippsburg.	23 March
Advance to the River Elbe, northern Holland, and the Baltic by 21st Army Group. United States Armies advance into western Czechoslovakia and Austria.	27 March to 4 May
German forces in Holland, north-west Germany and Denmark surrender to Field Marshal Montgomery on Lüneburg Heath.	4 May
General Jodl signs act of military surrender of all German Forces at Eisenhower's Headquarters at Rheims.	7 May
In Berlin, Field Marshal Keitel signs formal ratification of surrender.	8 May

PROLOGUE

Field Marshal Archibald Wavell wrote to Basil Liddell Hart:

> I think I should concentrate entirely on the actualities of war – the effects of
> tiredness, hunger, fear, lack of sleep, weather, inaccurate information, the
> time factor and so forth.[1]

[1] Letter to Liddell Hart, 13 July 1935.

Using the Imperial War Museum archives that is what I have set
out to do against the broad backcloth of the British involvement
in the Allied invasion of north-west Europe in June 1944 and the
subsequent campaign which took the Allies across France, Belgium and
Holland and into Germany, culminating for the British on Lüneburg
Heath on 4 May 1945. As far as possible I have let the participants tell the
story, providing linking text to set the scene where necessary, or to
explain the overall picture. There is a minimum of coverage of the
strategic and operational level of war, and little more at the tactical level.
I have included few senior 'voices', because I wanted the reader to get
the feel for what the campaign was like for those who did the actual
fighting, or were as near to it as possible.

Accounts of the land campaign are overwhelmingly in the majority.
Only the soldiers could finish the job. The navies and air forces, having
borne the major share of the burden for so long, were in a supporting
role, none the less vital for all that. Had the Battle of the Atlantic been
lost, all planning for assaulting, let alone maintaining a campaign in,
north-west Europe would have been academic. By early 1944 the
strategic air offensive by Royal Air Force Bomber Command and the 8th
United States Air Force was beginning to pay dividends, particularly in
its impact on the Luftwaffe. New methods, such as marking techniques
pioneered by Group Captain Leonard Cheshire, improved the accuracy
of Bomber Command's night offensive. Thanks to the P-51 Mustang,
which was able to escort the American bombers all the way to the target
and back, the 8th Air Force was winning the daylight battle. The outcome was the Luftwaffe's almost total dedication to defending Germany. As a result 2nd Tactical Air Force and 9th United States Air Force
had little competition in the skies over Normandy. The crucial part
played by the tactical air forces in support of the Allied armies in
Normandy and throughout the campaign cannot be overemphasized.

The reader should know what this book does not do. It does not set
out to be a comprehensive history of the north-west European Campaign of 1944-45. Many have already been written, and no doubt there
are more to come. It does not cover American, Canadian, French and

other Allied participation other than in passing. Without American participation, which on land in north-west Europe hugely outnumbered all the other Allies combined, the Campaign would never have begun, let alone been concluded successfully. American air power, shipping, landing craft and equipment, such as tanks, jeeps and guns in their own and all Allied armies, played an indispensable part. Without the Red Army which, from 1941 to the end, engaged the major part of the German Army in one of the bloodiest campaigns in history, it would have been impossible for the Western Allies to contemplate embarking on the campaign in north-west Europe at all. (The Soviets lost over 13 million dead and missing. The Battle of Berlin alone from 16 April to 8 May 1945 cost the Russians 305,000 casualties.) Finally the book does not cover the vital work of the Resistance Movement, SOE or Special Forces. These merit a book on their own.

Some readers, particularly those with no experience of war, may be shocked by some of the views expressed in the accounts. For the British, the fifth anniversary of the War fell three months after the Normandy landings. The whole country, to a greater extent than in 1914–18, had been involved for five long years, which had seen the blitz, losses at sea, in the air and on land. For a long time, the survival of Britain was at stake. There had been disasters: Dunkirk, Greece, Crete, Singapore, to name but a few. There was little sympathy for the Germans, but respect for the fighting qualities of the Wehrmacht and even the Waffen SS, however vile the cause for which they were fighting. They were arguably the best army the world has ever seen. Few members of the British public had any doubts about the rightness of their cause. Anti-war protest was muted.

In September 1944, Lieutenant-General Sir Miles Dempsey, commanding the British 2nd Army, finished an order to his Army on non-fraternization with the Germans with the words:

> We must remember always that these are the people who, twice in the last thirty years, have deliberately brought us to war.

Few of his soldiers would have needed reminding. Most of those over forty-five years old, of whom there were plenty, particularly in senior positions, had fought in the previous contest; as had the fathers, uncles and elder brothers of those in this round too young to have participated in the preceding one. The strength of feeling about the need to defeat the regime which held power in Germany is borne out by the substantial number of conscientious objectors who served as medical orderlies in the Second World War in all theatres. It was unnecessary, as in the First World War, for the Allied press to invent stories of the Hun raping nuns, or bayoneting babies. As the Allies were to discover, atrocities, beyond the comprehension of the British newspaper proprietors of 1914–18, were there for all to see when the armies arrived in Germany and the occupied territories.

An officer who fought in north-west Europe has written:

It was an amazing campaign – the quality of the staff work has probably never been rivalled (people were so experienced by then) and the expertise of the old hands who had survived the war so far too was unrivalled (although many of them were pretty 'cagey' – and rightly so!), whilst the overall quality of the lower ranks (many very, very young and flung into battle with little real preparation) was very variable. The best were super, but too many were not really up to the demands of the tougher parts of the fighting.

The deficiencies cannot be laid at the door of the young men. As the last winter of the War approached, there was a serious shortage of well-trained manpower available to the British. There were all too few remaining, particularly in the infantry, of those who had trained together in the battle camps in the years before D-Day. Individual reinforcements need training as part of the team. Unless formations were withdrawn from the battle for protracted periods, there was no opportunity for this. On the job training is a poor substitute for thorough preparation. Infantry casualties were heavy. There is a perception in the public mind that the casualty rate in this campaign was substantially lower than in France and Belgium in 1914–18. Two examples may correct this impression, at least as far as the infantry is concerned; they were not much lower. In nearly four and a half years on the Western front, starting in August 1914, a particular regular battalion[1] lost 5,110 killed and wounded, giving a monthly loss rate of 98.26, which over a period of eleven months would have resulted in 1,080 casualties. The 2nd East Yorkshires, one of the D-Day assault battalions, lost a total of 1,072 dead, wounded and missing in the eleven months between Normandy and reaching Bremen. This was not exceptional. Indeed over a shorter period, the 4th Somerset Light Infantry lost 1,313 killed or wounded. The 4th Somersets landed in Normandy with the 43rd Wessex Division on 23 June 1944. On 5 July three officers and 62 other ranks were required as reinforcements. Between 14 and 18 July, a further twelve officers and 479 other ranks arrived and even then the Battalion was still below its full strength of 36 officers and nearly 700 soldiers.[2] The 3rd Infantry Division suffered 6,000 casualties in the first two months of fighting in Normandy. In the battle of Arras in 1917, over a period of six weeks, the same Division had 5,400 casualties.

When the campaign ended, the prospect of further fighting in the Far East was very real. We know now that the Japanese were to surrender only three months later, and few, if any, of those who soldiered on to the end in Europe were to get nearer to the Japanese than India. But even at the highest level, August 1945 was by no means the anticipated finishing date for the Japanese war. At the Allied conference in Quebec in August 1943, the date for the invasion of Japan was set at summer 1946 at the earliest. The dropping of the two atomic bombs ended the

[1] John Terraine, *The Smoke and the Fire*, Sidgwick & Jackson, p. 210.

[2] Sidney Jary, *18 Platoon*, Sydney Jary Ltd, p. 2.

war before two vast amphibious operations, immediately followed by two potentially protracted land campaigns, Malaya and mainland Japan, could be prosecuted.

Finally, I have tried to tell the story 'warts and all', not least because of my admiration for what Field Marshal Wavell called, 'The indomitable figure of the British soldier . . . whose humorous endurance of time and chance lasts always to the end.'

Quotations The text contains many direct quotations from written documentary material and interview tapes. These are reproduced verbatim where possible, but obvious errors have been corrected and minor confusions clarified. It has not been thought necessary to indicate where quotations have been abridged.

Photographs All the illustrations used in this book have come from the Imperial War Museum, and have been listed with their reference after the appropriate caption.

Chapter headings All the quotations in the chapter headings with two exceptions are phrases taken from the 21st Army Group Order of the Day issued by Montgomery relevant to operations described in that chapter. The exceptions are Chapter One, where the heading is a phrase lifted from a minute from Montgomery to Churchill, dated 1 January 1944, after seeing the existing plans for the invasion of Normandy for the first time; and Chapter Six, where the heading is taken from 21st Army Group Directive dated 9 October 1944.

'My first impression is that the present plan is impracticable'

PREPARATION AND PLANNING FOR THE NORMANDY INVASION

'It was wonderful to watch the quiet steady stream of craft slipping out past the Portsmouth Forts, so silent and orderly.'
CAPTAIN JOE PATTERSON,
Number 4 Commando

Landing craft passing through the boom at Spithead, 5 June 1944. (A23838)

Monty's appointment was a popular one since he seemed to be on a winning streak. Not all senior officers would be equally happy, as he had a reputation for sacking those he disapproved of. But this did not reach our humble level, and we merely got a spectator thrill out of the possibility that heads could roll . . .

LIEUTENANT SIDNEY ROSENBAUM
33rd Field Regiment Royal Artillery
3rd British Infantry Division

The invasion of north-west Europe, to which the Americans and British now bent their minds and energies, was the most stupendous enterprise in the history of warfare. To assault Fortress Europe was daunting enough, but having gained a foothold, their only way out of the beachhead lay in defeating the most formidable army in the world. This could only be achieved by a ruthlessly sustained, well coordinated and increasing concentration of violence upon the field of battle. There were times when the difficulties loomed so large that, before the arrival of General Sir Bernard Montgomery to command all Allied Land Forces, some of the stoutest hearts quailed at the prospect, including Churchill himself.

Under Lieutenant-General Frederick Morgan, the Chief of Staff to the Supreme Allied Commander (COSSAC), planning for landing in north-west Europe had been under way for well over a year before the appointment of General Eisenhower as Supreme Allied Commander. Although Montgomery poured scorn on the COSSAC plan, the work done by Morgan and a host of others was invaluable. The selection of the beachhead area, reconnaissance, and the designing and construction of an array of specialized equipment, were all in hand before Montgomery grasped the reins. His greatest contribution before D-Day, within days of arriving, was insisting on radically changing the plan by expanding the size of the initial beachhead and the number of assault divisions; his total professionalism and clarity of thought; and imbuing everybody with his enthusiasm and confidence in the outcome.

An operation on so vast a scale and of such complexity depended on a multitude of techniques and equipment conceived and refined by some of the best brains in the Allied camp.

Among the many brilliant ideas devised by the planners was the artificial harbour, Mulberry. As early as 1942, Churchill had minuted Vice-Admiral Lord Louis Mountbatten, then Chief of Combined Operations, telling him to devise piers that would float up and down with the tide, concluding: 'Don't argue about it, the difficulties will argue themselves.' Vice-Admiral John Hughes Hallett wrote, in 1947, to a civil engineer:

> You overestimate the part played by Lord Mountbatten at the particular
> period in question (1943). The project was decided upon at a stage when an
> Operational Staff, headed by General Morgan, had been established to plan

The Allied High Command Team for North-West Europe
Front row (from left to right): **Air Chief Marshal Sir Arthur Tedder** (Deputy
Supreme Commander), **General Dwight D. Eisenhower** (Supreme Commander),
General Sir Bernard Montgomery (Commander 21st Army Group and overall land
commander initially).
Back row (from left to right): **Lieutenant-General Omar N. Bradley**
(Commander United States 1st Army for the invasion and subsequently 12th Army
Group), **Admiral Sir Bertram Ramsay** (C.-in-C. Allied Naval Forces), **Air Chief
Marshal Sir Trafford Leigh-Mallory** (C-in-C Allied Expeditionary Air Forces),
Lieutenant-General Walter Bedell Smith (Chief of Staff Supreme Headquarters
Allied Expeditionary Force). (NYT13625)

the invasion. It was this staff, of which I was the Naval Head, which had the
responsibility for deciding and advising on such matters.

A few days later he wrote:

Happening to be at Home this week end, I have taken the opportunity to
look through my rather scanty diary, to refresh my memory on one or two
points.

Here they are:–

It was either 13.6.43. or 20.6.43. (probably the former) that I decided to rely on an artificial port of some magnitude. (The idea came to me oddly enough during the singing of the Anthem at the Abbey!)

. . . . between that date and 27th June (1943) the Port was a cardinal point of the COSSAC Plan.

Hughes Hallett proposed that an artificial harbour be constructed by sinking blockships off the Normandy Coast. To his direction a harbour plan was drawn up by Lieutenant-Commander I. G. Steele RN, who selected a site at Arromanches.

From the first day of the landing, the intention was to land as much as possible of the stores for the army over the five assault beaches, using an array of craft ferrying from merchant ships anchored off shore. To give some protection to these craft it was decided to establish five craft shelters code-named Gooseberries. At each beach twelve old merchant ships were to be sunk in a line in about fifteen feet of water (at low tide), giving about a mile of breakwater. Under the lee of the Gooseberries, craft ferrying stores ashore could be fuelled, watered, repaired and serviced, and meals provided for their crews. Without the Gooseberries, if a gale blew from the north, the craft would be driven ashore and damaged beyond repair, thus cutting the life-line of the armies ashore.

Eventually, two of the Gooseberries would grow into Mulberries, 'no mean agricultural feat', one senior naval officer commented. The Gooseberries were to be positioned as follows:

Gooseberry 1	Varreville	Utah Beach	
Gooseberry 2[1]	St Laurent	Omaha Beach	US
Gooseberry 3[2]	Arromanches	Gold Beach	
Gooseberry 4	Courcelles	Juno Beach	British
Gooseberry 5	Ouistreham	Sword Beach	

[1] became Mulberry A
[2] became Mulberry B

The Mulberries were to consist of a breakwater made up of large concrete boxes, code-name Phoenix, sunk in deep water, up to thirty-three feet at low tide. Outside each harbour it was intended to place one mile of floating breakwater, code-name Bombardon, to give additional protection to the harbour. There was also to be an arrangement of piers capable of taking a 25-ton load, and one capable of berthing a landing ship tank (LST) and bearing a load of 40 tons, the weight of a Cromwell tank.

The ingenious ideas spawned by the forthcoming invasion were not limited to artificial harbours. To speed up the provision of fuel ashore, two pipelines were planned to pump fuel direct from England to the beachhead. Nicknamed Pluto (pipeline under the ocean), they would be towed across, unwinding from giant cotton-reels. Drawing on the lessons of other landings, including the abortive Dieppe raid, a range of armoured vehicles was produced. Their purpose was to support the assaulting infantry across the beach and inland after the naval bombardment lifted, and to clear gaps in minefields and other obstacles. Duplex

The large concrete boxes known as Phoenix, were built on the South coast of Britain, and launched sideways as shown in this film still. Many were sunk to conceal them from prying German air reconnaissance, before being refloated and towed across to Normandy for the two artificial harbours known as *Mulberries*. (FLM2373)

Armoured Vehicle Royal Engineers (AVRE), Churchill Tank with petard mortar. The projectile used for blasting gaps and holes in buildings and defences is standing by the mortar. (H38002)

drive (DD) tanks, with a propeller for propulsion and high canvas screens for flotation, would swim into the beach from landing craft off shore. Other tanks would land direct from landing craft. Armoured Vehicles Royal Engineers (AVRE) would carry fascines to fill anti-tank ditches, and blast concrete obstacles with a mortar known as a petard.

Amphibious Sherman DD tanks come ashore. These pictures were taken during the Rhine crossing in March 1945, but DD tanks were used on D-Day in Normandy.
Top: **like floating hip baths.** (BU2172)
Centre: **canvas flotation screen still up.** (BU2173)
Bottom: **canvas screen lowered, and showing propellers at the back.** (BU2175)

Crab Sherman Flail Tank for clearing a lane through anti-tank minefields. (H38079)

AVRE Carpet-Laying Churchill Tank. The tank can lay the carpet while under fire by rolling forward unwinding the strip from the roller. Once the carpet is laid, the tank uncouples leaving it for following vehicles. Very useful for boggy ground or soft sand. (H37859)

There were bridge-layers, and Crab mine-clearing flail tanks. Others would lay track-way. Some were equipped with a flame-thrower. All had been developed and their crews trained under Major-General Percy Hobart's 79th Armoured Division. Known as 'Hobo's Funnies', they were not to fight as a Division, but deployed with the assaulting British divisions, and on many occasions throughout the ensuing campaign.

Some of the troops who were to take part in the forthcoming campaign had been training for years. Captain M. A. Philp, the brigade signals officer of 185th Infantry Brigade, part of 3rd Infantry Division, described his impressions on joining in June 1943:

> There was nothing unusual about the Brigade to distinguish it from any
> other except that it had been recently earmarked to take part in the assault
> on the Continent and had so far done no Combined Operations training. I

found it typical of many in the United Kingdom at that time which had never seen action. Adequately trained but managing on old and worn-out equipment. The men browned off after a string of, to them, not very purposeful exercises.

Other units had been in Divisions that had seen plenty of fighting, and had been brought back to the United Kingdom by Montgomery to leaven the largely inexperienced Home Army with some battle-hardened troops. One such was the 2nd Battalion the Devonshire Regiment, in 50th Infantry Division. Diana Holdsworth, the young wife of a recently joined subaltern, who had not been in battle, was acutely aware that:

> For some of the women whose husbands had been in action through Sicily and Italy it was a period of great stress. They felt their men could not possibly live through another series of battles. Some of the men felt the same.
>
> Men who had become disturbed by their battle experience were whisked out of sight and said in medical circles to be suffering from 'Battle Fatigue'. But their colleagues in the Battalion cheerfully labelled them 'Bomb Happy'. Nevertheless stress was present. It was an emotion, unnamed, to be subdued. The symptoms were there with foolish squabbles and the feeling of compulsive, urgent gaiety which engulfed the Battalion with its endless parties and dances.
>
> Those who had the courage to express feelings of doubt or fear about their fate found themselves the cause of acute embarrassment.

Major C. K. ('Banger') King, commanding A Company the 2nd Battalion the East Yorkshire Regiment, due to be the left assault battalion in 3rd Infantry Division, wrote to reassure his batman's mother:

> This is a short note to thank you very much indeed for your kindness in doing my washing. Your son looks after me in the way that I imagine you look after him. We are both very lucky.
>
> I hope you are not worrying too much about him. As a bachelor I haven't any (family) worries, but I feel that it's up to me to get as many of my company through this business as I can. The men take the place of a family in my estimation. I have never cared very much for what the higher authorities think (which is probably why I am only a major!) And you can be sure that I won't lead your son or any of my Company into any damn suicide act.
>
> We are a very happy Company – and quite efficient too, which is the best protection your son can have. It's the inefficient lazy crowd that suffers the heaviest casualties – as I saw in the Middle East.

Units and formations usually began their Combined Operations training with simple exercises. Philp's Brigade Signals Section

> studied the special communication lay-outs necessary, the extra and new

equipment, we learnt how to waterproof vehicles and considered how to reconstitute it (the headquarters) on landing. We began some Combined Operations exercises, pretty primitive at first, known as 'dryshod exercises'. A road or some other suitable landmark represented the coast line and if you were on one side of it, you were technically afloat and on the other side on land again. Men and vehicles were fed across the 'coastline' at specified intervals to represent landing craft discharging their contents. As events moved on so we gradually became more sophisticated and made acquaintance with landing craft and experienced the exhilaration or misery of the sea depending upon individual ability to cope with a floor that was never still. Eventually all this training grew and grew over the months until we were able to take our place in a full seaborne divisional large scale exercise.

The exercises were spartan to put it mildly. After embarking the 'fleet' would mow [sic] around the Moray Firth during the night to simulate the cross channel journey and then decant us on various beaches on the south side of the Firth, as a very cold bleak winter's dawn was breaking. We would wade ashore catching our breaths at the cold and hopping about trying to keep our more vulnerable parts out of the water. More often than not there was a rime of ice along the water's edge. Brigade Headquarters would embark in the HQ ship specially fitted out for Combined Operations including extra wireless communications for the three services and an operations room where the battle was plotted on maps as the reports came in. When the bridgehead had been secured the Brigadier would give the word for Brigade HQ to go ashore and we would clamber down the side of the ship into a small landing craft. On one celebrated occasion when it was particularly cold and unpleasant the landing craft grounded rather far out and we had a long waist-deep wade to get ashore. The Brigadier stood in the bows and watched us all plunge in and then made the coxswain pull off and go alongside a tank landing craft discharging nearby, whose vehicles were going into only a foot or so of water. The Brigadier transferred to this, walked along to its ramp and, as a vehicle was going out at that moment, didn't step off the end of the ramp, but to one side, right into a hole up to his neck. None of us dared laugh.

As D-Day approached, new equipment began to arrive. Philp's signal section received new four-wheel-drive vehicles, followed by other equipment.

It was a joy to get brand new vehicles after struggling along with old clapped-out ones necessitating a constant battle to keep them on the road.

Many of the pre-D-Day exercises were limited to landing and rehearsing the sequence of events immediately following the landing, vital to the smooth execution of the operation on the day. But in many cases it was done at the exclusion of training for the weeks and months of fighting after D-Day in some very testing terrain and circumstances. This training was not omitted in all units, but certainly in enough for it to have an effect on subsequent performance.

Major David Warren, commanding C Company 1st Battalion the Hampshire Regiment:

> On our return from Italy, we were not earmarked for the assault. But that changed, and from then on the whole of our training was geared to the actual landing in Normandy. Perhaps this was a mistake, because after the landing we had to fight the war ashore like everybody else. Also we had carried out landings in Sicily and Italy, so we knew about landing craft. We felt confident that having done it before, we could do it again. But there was also a feeling that as this was the third time, something might go wrong. At the same time everyone was one hundred per cent sure that the operation would work, whatever happened personally or to one's unit. We wanted to get on with it – it was the green light for the end of the war, or so we thought.

Trooper Philip Pritchard, in 6 Commando in Brigadier Lord Lovat's 1st Special Service Brigade (later in the War the Special Service Brigades were redesignated Commando Brigades, thus avoiding the initials SS, with their Nazi connotation):

> We went on several warm-up exercises which consisted of leaving Newhaven by LCI(s) (landing craft infantry – small) and landing (always wet) at a point between Lancing and Worthing. From here we went to the River Arun as it passed through Arundel. We always chose a spot away from the bridge, and used rubber boats to cross the river in the dark. We then marched for a further distance and dug in to await the dawn. Thereafter we returned to our billets.

Second Lieutenant Sidney Rosenbaum was a troop officer in a regiment of self-propelled (SP) artillery, equipped with American 105mm howitzers in tanks from which the turret had been removed. These vehicles were nicknamed Priests. The guns were designed to fire from the armoured vehicle; artillery on tracks could keep up with armoured formations, whereas towed artillery did not have the same mobility. As the time for the invasion drew near, final exercises took place,

> but without the guns, which were now having their final waterproofing and welding done. The waterproofing was done with the aid of a sealing compound, new to most of us, called Bostik. The kits had to be cut to shape, and with scissors thoughtfully provided. The most bizarre feature of the waterproofing was a kind of square (or, rather oblong in section) chimney or funnel that stuck up like a wren's tail out of the rear of the SPs (and likewise tanks) just above the engines so that water should not be able to flood them. Drivers, who were also sealed in, had been trained to drive with water up to their ears – or thereabouts. But the funnels were a good deal taller than that, possibly in case waves splashed over the top [*Rosenbaum's surmise is correct*]. After landing, the funnels, or shutes, as they were also known, were to be

blown off with an explosive charge; otherwise the engines would have overheated.

Major Warren remembered:

> Security was very tight. My brigade commander told me after the war, that after attending a briefing in London for all brigadiers, he went to the flat his wife had up there. When he arrived, she said she would like him to tell her where the landing would be, because she might be able to help with information. She said that her family had always spent their holidays near Arromanches. He had to keep a straight face and say nothing. Our beach was nearby.

Throughout the period of planning and preparation leading up to D-Day, it was important to convince the German High Command that the Allied assault would fall on the Pas de Calais; and after D-Day that the Normandy landings were a diversion to draw German reserves away from north of the Seine, as a prelude to the main attack in that area. To this end an elaborate deception plan, code-name Fortitude, was hatched. For such a plan to be successful, it must accord with the preconceived ideas of those whom it is designed to deceive. Fortunately, von Rundstedt, the German C.-in-C. West, commanding all armies from Holland to the Mediterranean, was firmly convinced that the main landings would be in the Pas de Calais.

The pattern of Allied air activity was shaped to support Fortitude. For every reconnaissance over Normandy, two were flown over the Pas de Calais. Twice the number of bombs were dropped on coastal batteries north of Le Havre, compared with those to the west. Ninety-five per cent of attacks on railways took place north and east of the Seine.

To reinforce the perception that the main invasion force was poised in eastern England, a radio deception operation was mounted. Montgomery's headquarters was just north of Portsmouth, but the radio traffic was carried by land-line to Kent before being transmitted. First Canadian and 3rd US Armies, follow-up formations, were formed into a bogus army group under Patton with appropriate radio traffic.

Another deception operation played to one of Hitler's obsessions, that the Allied plans included invading Norway. Colonel Roderick Macleod, a gunner with a distinguished record from the First World War, was summoned in early March 1944 and told by the Signal Officer in Chief of Home Command

> to operate a deception plan to cover the invasion of Normandy which would take place about the end of May. I was to go to Scotland and represent an Army about to invade Norway with the object of pinning down the 9 German divisions known to be there and prevent them interfering with the landings. This would be done by means of wireless traffic which the Germans in Norway and France would pick up. The Germans would be able to plot our various HQ within an accuracy of 5 miles and could tell the type

of HQ by the signals from the sets being used. The dispositions of the troops was left to me, and I could ask Scottish Command for anything I wanted. Care would be taken that officers representing various commanders and staffs stayed in those appointments because the Germans would recognise their voices. For example, a man could not be say, a Corps commander one day and a brigade major the next, nor vice versa, so careful records must be kept of each officer's work on the R/T.

As a result of Macleod's work, the Germans sent three more divisions to Norway. These divisions remained there until the end of the War.

On 20 May, Macleod was told to reshape his deception operation to cease posing a threat to Norway and, with Patton's Army, switch the threat to the Pas de Calais. 'The Normandy landings were to appear as a feint, and ours, some time later, as the main invasion.'

This time Macleod made up convincing plans to land at Etaples, Calais and Dunkirk with objectives inland. He asked that bridges over the Somme be bombed as if to prevent reinforcements from the south coming into the Pas de Calais. The destruction of these bridges would hinder reinforcements moving in the opposite direction, which fitted the real plan.

When, after the landings on 6 June, a German map was captured it showed

> our dispositions in Scotland. It was extraordinarily accurate. It showed the Army, Corps and Divisional HQs in their correct locations (except for the 3rd Division near Nairn) and even with their proper numbers. Their direction finding must have been excellent.

February 1944, Rommel shakes hands with Lieutenant-Colonel Priller, the German fighter ace, who would be one of only two Luftwaffe pilots to strafe the beaches in daylight on D-Day. (HU63666)

Meanwhile across the Channel, preparations had been in hand to repel the invasion. Under Field Marshal von Rundstedt, Field Marshal Rommel, commanding Army Group B from Holland to the Loire, devised a plan to fortify the coastline with underwater obstacles. These would, he hoped, take a heavy toll of landing-craft before they reached the minefields on the beaches. To hinder airborne landings, all open areas within seven miles of the coast were planted with heavy posts, some tipped with shells initiated by trip-wires connecting the posts. Low-lying areas were flooded and wired. Gaps between the flooded areas were mined.

Coastal artillery and anti-tank gun positions were built of concrete with overhead protection. New batteries, minefields, pill-boxes and wire entanglements were constructed. These improvements were not only made north of the Seine, but between Le Havre and Cherbourg, which had previously been neglected.

To achieve his aim of defeating the Allies on the beaches, Rommel was prepared to sacrifice depth. He argued that in the face of Allied air power, there was no point in holding back a strong armoured reserve, because it would never reach the battlefront in time to be effective. General Geyr von Schweppenburg, the commander of Panzer Group

CAPTURED DIAGRAMS SHOWING ANTICIPATED·

CAUSE

AND

EFFECT

OF BEACH DEFENCES

"I have expressed my deep appreciation of the well-planned and well executed work performed in so few months.

The main defence zone on the coast is strongly fortified and well manned; there are large tactical and operational reserves in the rear areas. Thousands of pieces of artillery, anti-tank guns, rocket projectiles, and flame-throwers, await the enemy; millions of mines under water and on the land lie in wait for him. In spite of the enemy's great air superiority, we can face coming events with the greatest confidence."

(signed) ROMMEL, Field Marshal   22. May 1944

Diagrams originally in a leaflet issued, on Rommel's orders, to show his soldiers how the obstacle belt on the beaches was intended to inflict such serious damage on the Allies that the landings would fail. First published in *The Story of 79th Armoured Division*, in the Department of Printed Books, Imperial War Museum, and reproduced by kind permission of the Tank Museum.
(Negative number 63697)

West, comprising all von Rundstedt's armoured formations, was so concerned at Rommel's unconventional plan that he eventually appealed to Hitler. The outcome was a compromise that divided the armour, and satisfied no one.

Rommel, deceived by re-routed radio messages indicating that Montgomery's headquarters was located south of London, continued to believe that the main blow would fall in the Pas de Calais, or mouth of the Somme, with a strong diversion in western Normandy. Hitler ordered the strengthening of the coast defences in the Bay of the Seine and reinforcements to be sent to this area, because he also insisted that

German heavy guns dominated the approaches to the Pas de Calais. A still from a captured German film.
(FLM2371)

the whole of France must be defended; fortunately for the Allies, only eighteen out of a total of C.-in-C. West's sixty divisions were deployed between the Seine and the Loire.

Nevertheless, the estimated build-up rate of German divisions to face the invasion began to rise to the point where by the end of the first ten days there could be twenty-seven German divisions facing eighteen Allied. This made the railway interdiction plan, conducted by the Allied Air Forces since February, even more important.

Captain Charles Sherrington of the Railways Research Service pointed out to Air Marshal Sir Trafford Leigh-Mallory, the Air C.-in-C. of the Allied Expeditionary Force, that merely cutting lines would be inadequate. Attacks on railway yards, locomotives, rolling stock, signalling systems, points and repair facilities would be needed.

Sherrington, who probably knew more about French and Belgian railways than anyone else in Britain, wrote to Leigh-Mallory:

> To refresh my memory on rail routes from the Rhine to the Atlantic coast, I designed a little diagram.
>
> Since 1916 I have made a special study of Western European railways and their working; in fact, it has been my official job for the British railways for the last 20 years, consequently one knows most lines intimately and many little stations and junctions provide vivid memories, M. David Chef de Gare at Laon with his 'Grande Barbe', the filthy engine round house at Quimper, the all electric signal box at Rennes, the dock sidings at Bordeaux or the control office at the Gare de l'Este, etc.
>
> But to others it must be difficult to envisage the railway network which is so complex, as I spin off routes and junctions, and therefore it occurred to

TRAINS WITHOUT JANES
**Cover of booklet
illustrated by the
cartoonist Giles to
assist Allied pilots in
recognizing the
different types of
German trains.**
(Negative number
HU63709). From the
Sherrington papers in the
Department of Documents
(P218)

me that you might find useful the little diagramatic chart enclosed. The
difficulty was to compress it for the pocket and yet make it comprehensible.

The question of casualties to civilians caused General Pierre Koenig, the
Commander of the FFI (Les Forces Françaises de l'Intérieur), to protest
to Eisenhower. He offered to disrupt the railway system by sabotage
alone. Eisenhower refused. He could not accept that such an important
plan should rely entirely on what amounted to a gamble. Churchill too
was concerned about the number of civilian casualties, and how German
propaganda might paint the British and Americans in an unfavourable
light. According to the minutes of a Cabinet meeting on 3 May 1944:

> THE PRIME MINISTER then turned to the question of attacks on railway
> centres and asked if Air Chief Marshal Tedder would be content with a
> plan governed by the restriction that the number of civilian casualties in
> such attacks up to D-Day was not to exceed 10,000.
> SIR ARTHUR TEDDER said it was extremely difficult to make an accurate
> estimate of the casualties inflicted from the reports available. These were
> often conflicting and varied from day to day. He thought the number
> killed so far was probably between 3,000 and 4,000.

Eventually Tedder was invited to ensure that the number of civilians
killed up to D-Day did not exceed 10,000.

In the three months before D-Day only four of the eighty rail targets
escaped serious damage. Rail traffic throughout France dropped by 70
per cent. The pattern of railway layout allowed the object to be achieved
with the main weight of attacks north and east of the Seine.

These sorties over France and Belgium were not always perhaps the
welcome change from attacks into the heart of Germany that one might
think. The words 'grim trip' appear in the logbook of Flight Lieutenant
Easton, an Australian Lancaster bomber navigator.

Typhoons also took part in the attacks on railways. Sergeant Pilot
John Golley:

> The Typhoon was a big aircraft, with armour plate, and very fast. When I

Page from Flight Lieutenant Easton's log book; he was the navigator of Lancaster F for Freddie, which is in the Imperial War Museum. His comments on a sortie to bomb the Lille railway yards before D-Day are revealing, as is the loss rate of 20 out of the 74 aircraft which took part. (Negative number HU3705). From the papers of Flight Lieutenant Easton (77/26/1)

Date	Hour	Aircraft Type and No.	Pilot	Duty	Remarks (including results of bombing, gunnery, exercises, etc.)	Time carried forward — 175.45	206.40
						Flying Times Day	Night
9.5.44	1513	Lancaster 'F'—DV372	F/L Marshall	Navigator	High Level Bombing WAINFLEET	1.40	
10.5.44	2210	Lancaster 'F'—DV372	F/L Marshall	Navigator	OPERATIONS :— LILLE (Loco sheds & Rlwys)		
SORTIE 14		Fuel load : 1300 gls			ROUTE:— BASE — CLACTON — 5110N 0245E —		
		Bomb load : 12,000 lbs			5045N 0310E — 5038N 0305 — 5037N 0255E		
		Bombed at : 0000			5110N 0245E — CLACTON — 5252N 0030E — BASE		
		Height : 8800'			REMARKS :— Grim trip. Lost 6 crews from		
		Distance : 500			Station including S/L's Smith & Powell, F/L Scott		
		No a/c : 74			& F/O Ward. George Jones — best pal gone.		
		Missing : 20			Chased by 2 eng. E/A. Saw a/c down in flames		
					over △ — 'chute seen to open. A/c down on port		
					on way home — Orbited sth. of △		3.20

first took one off, it felt like controlling a charging bull. It could take a lot of punishment. In the run-up to D-Day we attacked marshalling yards, airfields, bridges and gun positions. This was fun. Then we were equipped with rockets, four under each wing. A full salvo was the equivalent of a broadside from a light cruiser. Our job after D-Day was to be a tank busting outfit.

Throughout the period between his arrival in England in January 1944 and D-Day, Montgomery visited his troops to speak to them and 'put them in the picture'. Private Tom Tateson, 7th Battalion the Green Howards, in the British 50th Infantry Division, remembers:

> The inspection over, he took up his familiar position on the top of some army vehicle and called us to gather round in an informal manner. He then told us in his characteristic way, that we were going to land in France, knock Jerry for six, and finish the war off. There was absolutely no doubt about it – it was all planned and organised. We would just go in, do the job, and that was that. There was something so tremendously impressive, almost hypnotic in his performance, that it did inspire us with a confidence which in retrospect was not at all justified. It was the sheer matter-of-fact certainty of his message that was so much more effective than a high-flown Harfleur-type effort.

Most of those Montgomery addressed were impressed by his confidence and relaxed style. Usually the troops loved it, although some officers thought there was too much showmanship about it all. Not every soldier was enthused; some of the more hardbitten troops, brought back for the invasion, were hostile. Sergeant George Self of 8th Battalion the Durham Light Infantry, a battalion which had seen much hard fighting in North Africa and Sicily:

> Montgomery visited us and told us that 50 Div would be one of the leading divisions in the invasion. Morale dropped for a few moments. After he had gone, there was a lot of discussion about divisions lying about in the country that had never been on active service, and how it was not right that

General Montgomery visits 6th Airborne Division in England before D-Day. From left to right: **RSM Parsons** (8th Parachute Battalion), **General Montgomery, Major Bill Collingwood** (Brigadier Major 3rd Parachute Brigade), **Brigadier James Hill** (Commander 3rd Parachute Brigade). (H36429)

we should do the invasion. People were bitter. We had done plenty of fighting; let someone else have a go. There were no problems with discipline, but a lot of moaning. About 50 per cent liked Montgomery and thought there was no one like him. The other 50 per cent didn't like him, although they accepted him as a leader.

When we moved to a camp near Romsey we had battles with the Yanks nearly every night in Southampton. The cause of the friction was money and their arrogant behaviour. Eisenhower came to see us and gave us a lecture about the American soldier. He agreed they were overpaid, over-sexed and over here, but when they got over the other side, they would show us the road home; how to fight. That was the worst thing he could have said. That night the blood flowed in Southampton.

Company Sergeant-Major Bill Brown, who had spent much of the war as an instructor and recently joined D Company 8th DLI, had a different opinion:

Eisenhower was great. He really looked immaculate and did more to lift my morale than anyone else. I felt very apprehensive. I didn't know what it would be like; you couldn't visualise it. Most of the company felt like sheep before the slaughter. They knew what was coming.

The switch from follow-up division to an assault role, generated something more than grousing in 50th Division; a great deal of staff work.

Major Peter Martin's A Company of 2nd Battalion the Cheshires was to be attached to 151 Infantry Brigade of 50th Division for the assault. The Battalion had fought in France in 1940, the Western Desert and Sicily. As the divisional machine-gun battalion, the 2nd Cheshire's companies were allocated in direct support of brigades, and unlike a rifle company commander in a standard infantry battalion, a machine-gun company commander was involved in planning at brigade level:

> All this time we were suffocated with paperwork: operation orders, intelligence summaries etc. There was also a feeling of unreality, surrounded by the beautiful, peaceful countryside. When you are living rough already, going into battle is much easier, than if you are having a really cushy life and suddenly thrust into it. For the first time I felt sorry for the RAF, who went straight into all that carnage from eating bacon and eggs in the mess.

The time came to move into the transit camps from which troops would embark in landing-craft and ships, or emplane in gliders or aircraft. Sometimes there was leave for the lucky ones. Private Tom Tateson:

> To my astonishment I was told that I was to go on immediate leave for 48 hours. While elated at the news, I was baffled as to why I had been given preference over the other, much longer-serving men. For a short time previously, letters home had been censored, with the exception of a limited number of 'green envelopes'. These could not be censored in the writer's unit, but could be opened further up the line. I had already used my limited quota when I received a letter from Olive telling me she was pregnant again and was very upset and worried. I had to use an ordinary envelope and just hoped it would not be opened. My letter was very tender and emotional, which I would not have sent through the 'open' post except for the urgency. Lt Wilson never mentioned it to me, nor did the NCOs, who must surely have enquired why I should be so favoured. But I feel it was because Lt Wilson had read that letter that he gave me a last chance to see Olive. The Army was not totally without sensitivity.
>
> I was very conscious that there was a real possibility of being killed. This meant leaving Olive widowed with a child not yet a year old and another on the way. Olive was to hear no more of me from that time in May until October when she received my printed postcard informing her that I was alive and a POW. This was one week before Robert was born.

To Diana Holdsworth, her husband's move to the transit camps came without warning:

> We were startled by the familiar roar of an army motor bike. The front door, which was never locked, was opened noisily and my husband's twin brother came banging up the stairs to the flat. He stood in the doorway in an embarrassed way. He looked so comic in his blue striped pyjamas over which he had thrown a battledress blouse and a pair of army boots. He spoke hesitantly without his usual assurance. 'This is it, we've got to get back to camp pretty damn quick.' David told his twin to wait for him

A woman hangs out her washing in a south coast garden on 5 June 1944, while vehicles stream down to one of the ports for loading. (NYT27247)

downstairs. Michael turned on his heels without a word of farewell and clattered down the stairs again.

David kissed me. Then using the same words as Michael, he said, 'This is it my darling, I have to go.' He went quietly and quickly down the stairs, the front door banged. I looked out of the window and watched them ride off together on the swaying motor bike into the night.

The next ten days seemed like an eternity. Suddenly one night the sky was full of aircraft and I knew the invasion had begun. It was almost a relief.

The transit areas to which units moved in late May, near their embarkation ports and airfields, were usually tented camps set up in fields, and where possible under trees to assist concealment. The whole of the south coast of England was one huge staging area, stretching inland for miles. Once in the camp, troops were sealed in and forbidden any contact with the outside world. Tom Tateson:

The closed area to which we moved was in the New Forest, near Southampton. There were innumerable American tanks and other vehicles parked under the trees at the side of the road, which gave perfect concealment from the air. I have a vivid memory of reveille being sounded over the Tannoy system; and emerging from the bivouac to a beautiful fresh May morning, the grass heavy with dew, and feeling that life was good. The bugle call sounded so clear, almost bell-like in the crystal clear early morning of an English meadow.

Some did not have to move; Sergeant Self:

One day a fence was put up round the camp. The NCOs were sent for and told that anyone caught outside would be court-martialled. Nobody got out.

Sherman crews carrying out last minute maintenance in a transit area before D-Day. These tanks will be landed on the beach direct from landing craft. The absence of screens shows that they are not DD tanks. (H38970)

We had the best briefing I have ever known in the forces; even the private soldiers were present. There were scale models, photographs of guns, minefields and so on. Our battalion as part of 151 Brigade was to land in the second wave of 50 Div.

The 4/7th Royal Dragoon Guards, equipped with Sherman tanks, were destined to be the first British armoured regiment ashore on D-Day. Trooper Austin Baker had been attached to C Squadron's armoured recovery vehicle (ARV):

A turretless Sherman fitted with gas welding equipment, towing bars and all kind of fitters' paraphernalia. It was intended to carry a kind of flying squad of fitters and I was to be its wireless operator.

The Camp was packed with troops and equipment of all kinds. The whole place was very well run by an American permanent staff. The food was much better than we had been used to for a very long time, and there were good NAAFIs and several cinemas. We all slept in tents.

Briefings were more comprehensive for those that needed greater detail, although actual places were concealed by giving them false names. Not everyone was taken in by the false maps. Captain Joe Patterson, the Medical Officer of 4 Commando, a veteran of the retreat to Dunkirk, and

Captain Patterson, RAMC, Medical Officer 4 Commando. From Patterson papers in the Department of Documents (66/192/1). (Negative number HU63704)

Royal Marine Commandos being briefed in a transit camp. H38949)

a founder member of 5 Commando with whom he had taken part in the Madagascar landings, was a more cynical observer of events:

> The air photographs were very clear, and it would not have taken much enterprise to pick out the place on a map of France. However, we were asked not to do so. The Free French troops in the Unit nearly all recognised the area at once. Some of them even lived in the area, and had been in the town less than a year before. One used to work the lock gates at the mouth of the canal before the war.
>
> The endless conferences were rather tedious, and to my mind a bit overdone. Anyone who had been in action before could feel that such detailed planning was rather a waste of time. Personally I refused to be tied down to much detail in my plans, knowing full well that things would look very different when the time came. When they tried to pin me down to which house I was to make my RAP (Regimental Aid Post), I drew the line completely.
>
> I distributed my final items of kit and lectured the troops on the uses of morphia etc. and soon we were absolutely ready. An extra six bottles of fluid plasma suddenly arrived, sent by mistake. I was very glad of it, and we managed to persuade the AMDS to get the Giving Sets for it. This plasma proved its worth in the early stages of the battle. It appeared later that the advice of the people who were in the Sicily landings, in which each RAMC man carried a bottle of plasma and a giving set, was not taken by the medical units following us, with disastrous results on the beachhead, as the blood and plasma stock were sunk, and none was available until late on D-Day.

The selection of the day and hour for the landings was the outcome of juggling many, often conflicting, requirements. The Army wanted to attack at dawn. But the Navy and Air Force wanted at least an hour of daylight to soften up the beach defences. The initial landings had to be made on the earliest possible high tide to allow a follow-up on the second high tide before last light. A further complication was presented by the underwater obstacles. To allow demolition teams to neutralize these, the first wave had to land three hours before high water. The time of high water was different on each beach. The airmen wanted a full moon the night before D-Day, but rising after midnight. Aircraft carrying the airborne divisions could approach in darkness, arriving as the moon rose to assist in the identification of dropping and landing zones. All these requirements could only be met on three days in any month. Finally the wind must not be above Force 4, the cloud base above three thousand feet and no thicker than five-tenths. The records for the past century showed that the chances of achieving this weather in Normandy in June were thirteen to one against. Based on all the factors, Eisenhower selected 5 June as D-Day.

Everything would depend on the safe and timely arrival of the armies off the coast of Normandy. This lay in the hands of the Royal Navy and United States Navy. The Naval forces for Operation Neptune, the code-name for the maritime part of Operation Overlord, the whole invasion operation, were commanded by Admiral Sir Bertram Ramsay. He brought to this task experience gained in the landings in North Africa and Sicily. He had commanded the Naval forces in the evacuation from Dunkirk, and was now charged with the safe passage of the Allied Armies to France, from which the British Army had been expelled so ignominiously in 1940.

Success depended on a host of factors: skilful staff work, joint training, rehearsals, loading plans at ports scattered from the Thames, through the southern and western coasts of the United Kingdom, right round to Belfast and the Clyde. Sailing and assembling the mass of craft and shipping, navigating through swept lanes to the correct offshore anchorages and lowering positions, vectoring craft down the boat lanes, and disembarking loads on the right beach; escorts, bombardment, and turn-round of craft; all this and much more was ultimately Ramsay's responsibility as Allied Naval Commander Expeditionary Force (ANCXF).

The Navies' problems would not end on D-Day. The break-out of the Allied Armies depended on a massive build-up of troops, tanks, guns, ammunition and fuel, and thousands of tons of other equipment and supplies landed over open beaches. The lack of ports would only be partly mitigated by the artificial harbours, themselves vulnerable to bad weather.

The eminent historian, Correlli Barnett, has commented:

These stupendous problems facing the Navies are sometimes ignored by

some historians of the land campaign in Normandy, who commence their narratives on the beaches, almost as if all that lay between southern England and Normandy were a No Man's Land swiftly and easily traversed by the attacking armies.

United States troops and vehicles loading on to LCTs. The vehicle backing on to the centre craft is a half-track. (PL25481)

The movement and loading of units at the ports in the United Kingdom had to be dovetailed into a complicated plan. Tactical loading ensured that the right loads came off the ships and craft in the correct order, designed so that units and sub-units who had to fight together on landing were either married up in the same craft, or could do so quickly on arrival on the beach or in the bridgehead. Philp describes the loading of 185 Infantry Brigade:

> The first to go were those vehicles due to land last. Those due to land early finally embarked at south coast ports on 3 June. To increase its prospect of survival Brigade HQ had been split in two. My section travelling with the Brigade Commander embarked in a destroyer.

Joe Patterson:

> The whole of Cowes roads and Southampton Water, as far as the eye could see, was packed with shipping. Thousands of ships and landing-craft of all

Landing craft massed at Southampton ready for D-Day. (A23731)

kinds filled the sea, and in the sky were serried ranks of balloons, hundreds and hundreds of them.

Petty Officer Frank Coombes, one of twin brothers who both served in Motor Torpedo Boats (MTBs) throughout the war and had seen a good deal of action:

> On Sunday (4 June 1944), the Flotilla paraded to attend a Flotilla church service. It was obvious from the shipping and assault craft in and around Portsmouth that the attempt to assault 'Fortress Europe' was imminent, and that Coastal Forces were to play an important part. The church service only confirmed that our Flotilla, the 55th, was allocated a specially prominent role. The parson did not help one little bit when he exhorted us to be 'valiant unto death'. We wanted to go, not only to the lav, but to get it over with. Everybody knew that this was it. That church service was better than any enema.

For the parachute and glider-borne soldiers of the airborne divisions, the full briefings took place in the sealed transit camps. D Company 2nd

Battalion the Oxfordshire and Buckinghamshire Light Infantry (52nd Light Infantry) was briefed by their company commander, Major Howard. The company, destined to be the first Allied sub-unit to land in Normandy, was to seize the bridges over the Caen canal and river Orne some five miles inland from Ouistreham, by *coup de main*. Six Horsa gliders, each carrying about twenty-five men, were to lift in the Company. Private Denis Edwards:

> Three Horsa gliders were allocated to each bridge. Each glider to be loaded with identical equipment, and each to include Royal Engineers to deal with the demolition charges on the bridges.
>
> We spent the entire afternoon being briefed in the different tasks of each 25-man platoon. Then the tasks of each 7-man section were considered and finally, in cases where individuals had special tasks, these were also looked at in detail since, working in darkness, it was essential that everyone knew what everyone else was doing at any given time, and to be in a position to carry out their job if the appointed individual was not available for any reason. Nothing could be left to chance, and split-second accuracy was vital for the success of the mission. My platoon was to fly in the first of the three gliders to go down on to the canal bridge.
>
> At around 22.00 hours we turned in for the night. It was hot in the small tent and I didn't feel much like sleeping. The task that had been allocated to us seemed so great and our force so small. Although it would hopefully only be for a short time, the prospect of initially being the only unit of the entire Allied force actually in France, and facing the might of the German Army, seemed to me to be a daunting proposition.
>
> Glancing round our 7-man-section tent, dimly lit by a hurricane lamp, I noted that although it was after 22.30 hours, and in the normal way since we always rose at the crack of dawn we would all be asleep by that time, several, if not all, were still awake. It was well into a restless night, and the best part of a packet of 20 cigarettes later, that I finally dropped off into a shallow sleep.

Although the weather in May had been perfect, by 2 June, when some of the Naval bombarding forces had begun moving south from Belfast, Scapa and the Clyde, the omens were bad. Worsening weather, rising to gale force on 4 June, caused a postponement. Joe Patterson:

> It was clearly impossible to start in such weather, and we got more and more depressed. The prospect of postponement for 14 days really appalled us, as it would mean returning to imprisonment in camp again. On Sunday 4 June, the spindrift was flying in scuds across the roadstead and people coming in duty craft arrived soaked to the skin. It was during the small hours in the blackness of the nights that I felt really chicken-hearted at times, but the foul weather always made me feel that 'it couldn't be today'.

One of the major problems facing Eisenhower and his planners, when contemplating a postponement of more than a day, was that the next

tide and time 'window' for landing was fourteen days off. Troops could not be kept cooped up in ships, often at anchor, for so long. They could not be allowed ashore now that many, although by no means all, had been fully briefed. The sealed camps were in many cases now occupied by follow-up units, so there was nowhere for them to go. On the evening of 4 June, with the gale still blowing, but with better weather forecast, Eisenhower made the decision to go ahead with the landing on 6 June; confirming it early on the morning of the 5th.

The last loads of troops embarked on 5 June, including 6 Commando into their LCI(s)s; Pritchard:

> The landing craft infantry (small) was a 110-ton craft, not unlike an MTB in looks. It could carry around 100 men, and had a crew of 17. It was, perhaps just as well that none of us knew the specification of these vessels and the fact that they were of wooden construction with large, unprotected petrol tanks, liable to explode should they be hit in that area.

Frank Coombes in 55th MTB Flotilla:

> The four boats led by Bradford in 617, quietly rumbled away from HMS

Soldiers of 6 Commando having a cup of tea while waiting to embark. Many commandos were parachute trained, hence the wings on three of the soldiers in the picture. The man in the foreground clasping a mug is a member of a 3-inch mortar detachment as shown by the barrel propped against his body. He would wade ashore carrying the 50lb barrel in addition to his bergen rucksack, personal weapon and ammunition, and the total would have probably exceeded his own body weight. (H39040)

Dolphin and down the buoyed channel. The thought that we were embarking on an operation of great importance, and knowing little of what it would entail, produced much gut churning. We hoped the walkers on Southsea Front admired our red and white shark's jaws painted on the bows. As we turned south by the Nab Tower, the Skipper passed the word that we were to guard some minesweepers, which, with a midget submarine already across the other side, was the only friendly force in front of us.

Joe Patterson thought the weather too rough:

It was teatime on Monday 5 June, when noticing the minesweepers beginning to creep out, I realised the show was on. I had been offering heavy odds that it would be cancelled again at lunchtime. I felt rather appalled, when I looked at the sea. It was blowing half a gale from the SW, and banking up black and beastly for what promised to be a thoroughly dirty night.

We were issued with real maps and real place names. Our job was to land on the left-hand edge of [Queen] Red Beach, that is to say the extreme left of

Commandos embark on LCI (Small) at Warsash. (H39041)

'It was perhaps just as well that none of us knew the specifications of these vessels, and that they were of wooden construction with large, unprotected petrol tanks, liable to explode should they be hit in that area.

TROOPER PRITCHARD
6 Commando

the whole Invasion; at the western part of Ouistreham, the mouths of the river Orne and Caen Canal.

The E. Yorks were going in at H-Hour to clear the beach defences, and to make gaps in the wire and minefields for us. We were to go in 30 minutes later, pass through the E. Yorks, dump our rucksacks, and crash into Ouistreham, taking the beach defences up to the canal mouth from the rear, and clearing the strong point round the Casino and the six-gun battery at the eastern end of town. The French troops were given the Casino job.

The rest of the Brigade, numbers 3, 6 and 45 (RM) Commandos, were to come in at about H plus 2 Hours, and make straight for the Orne and Caen Canal bridges, and link up with 6th Airborne Division. In the event of the Orne and Caen Canal bridges being blown we would have to cross the river and canal in rubber boats.

We were to follow the rest of the brigade into the Orne bridgehead with all speed as soon as we had cleaned up the Ouistreham defences. It was not our job to mop up Ouistreham. This fact gave me a considerable headache on D-Day as it turned out, as no one seemed quite clear who was to do the mopping up.

Now all the shipping was quietly and slowly filing out through the booms, the LCTs with their camouflaged loads of tanks and ammunition, the big LSTs packed with vehicles, the LSIs, all slung around with their LCAs, and the little LCIs with their troops sardined aboard. All the rest of the Brigade was in LCIs, and our French troops ranged up alongside us in theirs to give us a hail.

Besides all these hundreds of craft, were countless corvettes, and frigates, rows of destroyers, cruisers, and the monitor *Roberts*. It was wonderful to watch the quiet steady stream of craft slipping out past the Portsmouth forts, so silent and orderly, with no sirens or fuss, their balloons marking those already hidden by swarms of intervening craft.

Feeling rather small and chicken-hearted, I set about my final packing. I spliced my identity discs on string and gloomily hung them round my neck. I dished out anti-sea sickness tablets and morphine and talked to all the troops about my final medical plans. I had a heated tussle with the Brigade Major on the subject of the rum issue, finally settling that the troops could only have it 30 minutes before landing. To issue it as intended, before embarking in the LCAs, with two hours of cold and sea-sickness ahead would have been folly.

I had a bath. 'Washing off the B. Coli in case you stop one', as the Naval doctor said.

The wind howled and it rained in vicious scuds. As the skipper said in his speech to ship's company: 'The High Command must be counting heavily on surprise, for the Germans must surely think that not even Englishmen could be such fools as to start an invasion on a night like this.'

The bad weather on 4 June had reinforced German assumptions that the invasion was not imminent, certainly not within the next two weeks. The bad weather had also grounded the Luftwaffe reconnaissance aircraft and driven the German Navy into port. Satisfied that all would remain quiet for a time, Rommel left his headquarters for Germany. He wanted to persuade Hitler to release more troops, and in particular to allow him to move 12 SS Panzer Division to the St Lô-Carentan area.

That evening Allied airborne troops were also on the move to their airfields. Major Ken Darling, the second-in-command of the 12th Parachute Battalion, in Brigadier Poett's 5th Parachute Brigade of 6th British Airborne Division, wrote to his wife from the transit camp:

This letter is being written by me on the eve of battle; it will be held up for 48 hrs and then posted so that the Censor is not offended. By the time it reaches you we will no doubt be hard at it with the Boche and from the papers you will no doubt be able to see where we are operating. It is an extremely well laid on show and we all have complete confidence in the outcome of the battle which is going to be no ordinary one.

Must stop now as it is not long before we go to the airfield and roar into the sky.

CHAPTER TWO

'The time has come to deal the enemy a terrific blow in western Europe'

D-DAY: THE 6TH OF JUNE 1944

'If it hadn't been for the rope, we wouldn't have done it, wearing gas trousers and some of us carrying bikes.'
COMPANY SERGEANT-MAJOR BILL BROWN
8th Battalion Durham Light Infantry

Juno Beach: the Canadians come ashore. Like Bill Brown's Battalion which landed on Gold Beach they are in a follow-up wave landing from Landing Craft Infantry. (A23938)

BY AIR TO BATTLE

As the evening of 5 June approached, the 'Second Front' on which such high hopes were riding was irrevocably launched. The years of planning, hard work and training were to be put to the test. Of all the Allies, Britain was the most fearful and expectant. She had borne the brunt of the war against Germany until the entry of the Soviet Union and the United States, and then been an armed camp for two more years. Perhaps the end really was in sight.

The personal message issued by General Montgomery to all troops under his command, held by the Department of Documents. (Negative number MH4180)

21 ARMY GROUP

PERSONAL MESSAGE FROM THE C-in-C

To be read out to all Troops

1. The time has come to deal the enemy a terrific blow in Western Europe.

The blow will be struck by the combined sea, land, and air forces of the Allies—together constituting one great Allied team, under the supreme command of General Eisenhower.

2. On the eve of this great adventure I send my best wishes to every soldier in the Allied team.

To us is given the honour of striking a blow for freedom which will live in history; and in the better days that lie ahead men will speak with pride of our doings. We have a great and a righteous cause.

Let us pray that " The Lord Mighty in Battle " will go forth with our armies, and that His special providence will aid us in the struggle.

3. I want every soldier to know that I have complete confidence in the successful outcome of the operations that we are now about to begin.

With stout hearts, and with enthusiasm for the contest, let us go forward to victory.

4. And, as we enter the battle, let us recall the words of a famous soldier spoken many years ago :—

> " He either fears his fate too much,
> Or his deserts are small,
> Who dare not put it to the touch,
> To win or lose it all."

5. Good luck to each one of you. And good hunting on the mainland of Europe.

B. L. Montgomery
General
C.-in-C 21 Army Group.

1944.

Montgomery's plan, which formed the basis for plans at army, corps, division, brigade and down to every soldier, was as follows. Soon after midnight on the night preceding the seaborne invasion, three airborne divisions would drop and land by glider on the flanks of the bridgehead: the British 6th Airborne Division east of the River Orne and Caen Canal, the United States 82nd and 101st Airborne Divisions north and north-west of Carentan, at the base of the Cotentin peninsula. The tasks of these divisions was to protect the flanks of the bridgehead, silence selected German batteries and strong points, and seize key bridges and routes. Some bridges were to be destroyed to delay German counter-attacks, others held for future use by the invading armies.

Soon after dawn the seaborne assault would begin, starting in the west with Lieutenant-General Omar Bradley's First US Army landing on Utah and Omaha beaches. Lieutenant-General M.C. Dempsey's Second British Army was to land on three beaches: Gold, Juno and Sword. The British assault would be preceded by special assault teams of 79th Armoured Division, combat engineers, and DD tanks, all of which would touch down on the beaches before the infantry debouched from their landing craft. The Americans, having eschewed 'Hobo's Funnies', planned to have four tank battalions landing with their infantry.

Among the first away were the *coup de main* party of the 52nd Light Infantry in 6th Airborne Division; Private Denis Edwards:

Fully loaded up, we staggered off to nearby covered trucks to take us to the airfield, about a mile away. The staff, who had looked after us in the temporary camp, came out of their tents, waved and wished us good luck. Singing merrily, we waved back and whistled to the NAAFI girls.

At the airfield we clambered from the trucks and were given a cup of tea. We sat around the edge of the tarmac runway, smoking heavily and cracking corny jokes. While we all affected an air of total unconcern, I am sure that others like me, had churning stomachs.

The gliders were already in position behind their towing bombers. To pass the time and take our minds off other things, many of the lads exercised their artistic talents upon the fuselages of their gliders. Within a short time the gliders were covered in graffiti. In normal times we would not have dared deface any part of a glider, but this evening no one minded; these six gliders would never be coming back.

Time dragged, until at about 22.00 hours, the order rang out: 'Emplane'. I gave the earth by the runway a good stamp, in the hope that a little bit of English earth would accompany me on my journey. Once inside the glider the singing and the jokes continued, and on the surface there was an air of good humour; but this did not conceal a strong undercurrent of tension. While the jokers helped to ease the tension, I became increasingly scared as I strapped myself into seat number 13, which I always considered a lucky number for me. Major Howard, the Company and *coup-de-main* force commander, and Lieutenant Brotheridge, my platoon commander, were

Glider troops drawing graffiti on their glider before take-off.
(H39179)

travelling in our glider. We were to lead the way, and if all went well, would touch down first.

At 22.56 hours the steady hum of the bomber engines suddenly increased to a deafening roar. My muscles tightened, a cold shiver ran up my spine, I went hot and cold, and sang all the louder to stop my teeth chattering. There was a violent jerk and a loud twang, as the slack on the tow rope was taken up by the tug aircraft. The glider rolled slowly forward, and my throat tightened as the plywood flying box gathered speed. With a bump or two, the heavily laden glider gathered speed, left the ground, set down with a bump, a final jerk and roar of engines, and we were airborne. The other five gliders would be following at one minute intervals.

I experienced a psychological change during the last few minutes before and after take-off. Nothing I had experienced in training, could compare with the sheer panic that engulfed me as I sat in the dark glider waiting for take-off and my first trip into battle. I gripped my rifle between my knees so hard, that my knuckles must have shown white under the camouflage grease-paint. But at least the weapon stopped my knees knocking together.

At the moment the glider left the ground, I underwent a complete change. Whether some kindly guardian angel took my hand, I do not know. The feeling of fright immediately vanished to be replaced by sheer exhilaration. Indeed I felt as if I had had a little too much to drink. I thought to myself, 'You've had it chum. The die is cast, and there is nothing you can do about it.'

Major John Howard's *coup-de-main* force was to land right by the bridges, at twenty minutes past midnight on 6 June. At the same time, 22nd Independent Parachute Company, 6th Airborne Division's pathfinders, were to parachute on to three dropping zones (DZs). The pathfinders were to set up beacons to guide in the aircraft dropping the two parachute brigades at fifty minutes past midnight. Brigadier Nigel Poett's 5th Parachute Brigade was to drop on DZ N, about a mile and a half from the two bridges; reinforce Howard's company as quickly as possible; hold the lodgement astride the bridges; and clear landing zones (LZs) to allow gliders carrying anti-tank guns and Divisional HQ to land just before dawn. Brigadier James Hill's 3rd Parachute Brigade was to drop on the other two DZs, K and V. Hill was tasked with destroying a four-gun battery in concrete casemates at Merville, and five bridges over the River Dives. It was hoped that the German counterattack into the eastern flank of the bridgehead would be slowed down by the demolition of these bridges, and assist Major-General Richard Gale's 6th Airborne Division in their task of holding this vital sector. The Division would be reinforced by the glider-borne troops of 6th Airlanding Brigade on the evening of D-Day. Part of the Divisional sector would be taken over by 3rd Infantry Division and Commandos, landing on Sword beach, and advancing inland as quickly as possible.

As the soldiers in the gliders carrying the *coup-de-main* force made out the coast of France far below in the dim moonlight, Edwards in the leading glider:

There came a familiar twang, a jerk, followed by almost total silence. While in tow there had been a continual high-pitched scream of wind and slipstream forcing its way through cracks in the fabric-covered fuselage. Unlike small gliders which can swoop up on air currents, a fully laden Horsa glider released from its tug has one way to go, down.

To clear the stream of towing aircraft, and other bombers on bombardment tasks, the glider pilot put the nose sharply down and descended swiftly from about 6,000 feet to around 1,000, levelled out, descended more slowly, making two sweeping right-handed turns to run in to the landing zone. The senior pilot shouted, 'Link arms'. We held tight and braced for landing. The usual slight bump, a small jerk, and a much heavier thump told us that the glider had made contact with the ground; but only for a moment. It jerked again, left the ground, bumped again, bouncing forward at high speed. For about 40 to 50 yards we bounced in our wooden seats, as the darkness was filled with a stream of sparks caused by the skids scraping the ground; a sound like a giant sheet being ripped apart, a crash, and my body seemed to be moving in several directions. I was perched at an angle, peering into a misty grey haze. From somewhere streams of lights like shooting stars seemed to float in gathering speed towards us.

There was an ominous silence. No one moved. 'We must all be dead,' I thought. To be replaced by the realisation that this was not so, as bodies unstrapped themselves, and the interior of the shattered glider erupted into furious activity.

The door had been right beside me, but now a mass of twisted wood and fabric covered the exit. We smashed our way out. Corporal Bailey and Wally Parr clambered up the canal bank and lobbed grenades through the pillbox slit. My platoon's job was to fight our way across the bridge as quickly as possible. The tall bridge superstructure seemed to tower over us as it shimmered in the moonlight. Major Howard was already standing on the approach to the bridge roaring, 'Come on boys, this is it.' As we reached the bridge, we let fly with rifles, sten guns and grenades. A hidden machine-gun chattered into life, we returned fire and kept going, Lt Brotheridge in the lead. The enemy machine-gun fired another long burst and our platoon commander fell mortally wounded. As we neared the far side the Germans scattered.

Staff Sergeant Geoffrey Barkway, the pilot of the third glider to land:

We cast off. The tug flew on to Caen to bomb the city with light bombs. The hope being that the German radar would not pick up the wooden gliders, and the enemy would think that all the aircraft were bombing Caen. As we turned on to the final leg, Peter, my co-pilot (Staff Sergeant Boyle), and I said, 'There it is', simultaneously. We came into land, and things got a bit hectic, because there was a ridge of earth that hadn't shown up on the air photos. We hit it fairly fast, and slewed into a pond. The front of the cockpit disintegrated, I went out through the front, and sploshed into the water. I struggled out festooned in harness and bits of plywood.

At this stage things went hazy. As I was climbing into the glider to fetch a stretcher for someone, I was shot in the wrist. I fell off the glider into the water. I came round in a house with my arm in a sling, feeling terribly thirsty. I had lost a lot of blood.

Geoffrey Barkway was to lose his right arm as a result of gangrene. The three gliders allocated to the canal bridge had landed within a minute or so of each other with almost perfect precision. A runner arrived from the party at the other bridge to tell Major Howard that they had been successful. By 00.30 D Company had both bridges, intact. Now all they had to do was hold them until reinforcements arrived.

Brigadier Nigel Poett, under whose command D Company operated, had been told by General Gale: 'The seizing of the crossing intact is of the utmost importance to the conduct of future operations.

As the bridges will certainly have been prepared for demolition, the speedy overpowering of the bridge defences should be your first object.'

Poett knew that if the bridge was not taken intact, he had to change the plan immediately. The 7th Parachute Battalion was to seize a crossing further north. So it was imperative that he got down as early as possible. He landed with the pathfinders and the battalion advance parties at 00.20. The main body of the Brigade was due at 00.50. In the event this timing was far too tight. Allowing double the time for the pathfinders to put out beacons and lights would have been about right.

Poett set off with one soldier, collecting another on the way. His problem, when he got close to the bridge, was to avoid being shot by his own side or the enemy. At this stage he had no idea if the assault had been successful. Fortunately, he was recognized at the first bridge, went to the next, and stood waiting for the 7th Battalion. He had seen them drop as he walked towards the bridges.

The two parachute brigades were on their way. The turbulence

The three gliders by the Caen Canal bridge, 6 June 1944. Staff Sergeant Barkway's glider is the centre of the three. (MH2074)

caused by the mass of aircraft, and the westerly wind, resulted in a number of aircraft dropping their sticks of parachute soldiers wide. The muddle was exacerbated by the loss of all beacons for one DZ, and one party of pathfinders intended for DZ K dropping on to DZ N without realizing it, where they set up the beacons and lights giving the DZ K signal. Many parachute soldiers found themselves on the wrong DZ; others west of their correct DZ; some in the flooded valley of the River Dives, where many drowned, or even at sea where their fate was the same. A few landed miles to the west of the lodgement area. Some were killed fighting lonely battles, or were captured. For weeks after D-Day, airborne soldiers trickled in. In the area of the 3rd Parachute Brigade DZs there were deep, water-filled ditches where some men drowned. Despite these losses, all the Division's objectives were taken, and held where ordered. Well-briefed, determined men, under the cover of darkness and using their initiative, achieved their tasks despite scattered drops, losses on landing and chaos.

Poett knew that 21st Panzer Division, which was in the area, would soon counter-attack. Shortly after his arrival, probing attacks began, and he was anxious about the time 7th Battalion were taking to arrive. Everything in war takes far longer than on peacetime exercises, particularly in the dark. Eventually the commanding officer of 7th Battalion set off with only about 200 men at the double, but still did not arrive until 03.00, going straight through to take up their positions. They and the two battalions on the east side had critical tasks, holding off units of 21st Panzer Division. They had very little equipment, and no anti-tank guns, against ever stronger attacks.

At first light, the bombardment from the sea started. The Germans, realizing that an assault on the coast was imminent, left one regiment of 21st Panzer Division to attack the bridges, while the remainder headed for the coast. This relieved some of the pressure on the under-strength, lightly equipped 5th Parachute Brigade. But the position was still critical for several hours.

Nigel Poett:

I was with the CO of the 7th Battalion when we heard the bagpipes of
Lovat's commandos. The people who landed from the sea had a hell of a
tough time – often much tougher than we did.

The arrival of the Air Landing Brigade in the evening on both sides of the Orne was a tremendous sight to Poett's hard-pressed brigade. It also caused part of 21st Panzer Division that had penetrated to the coast to withdraw, for fear of being cut off. In the late evening, 7th Battalion were relieved by units of 3rd British Division advancing from the coast. Meanwhile, Brigadier Hill's 3rd Parachute Brigade had had an even more scattered drop.

The objective of the 9th Parachute Battalion in Brigadier Hill's 3rd Parachute Brigade was the heavily defended Merville Battery, believed to contain four 150mm guns in four emplacements. Each had concrete walls six feet thick, and roofs thirteen feet. It was considered vital that the guns in this battery were destroyed before the seaborne landings began. The Commanding Officer of the 9th Battalion evolved an elaborate plan which relied on a combination of parachute troops, glider-borne troops and a considerable amount of equipment all arriving on time and in the right place. Before the assault started, ninety-nine heavy bombers were to drop 1,000 bombs on the battery. Some in the battalion believed that if the bombing was accurate there would be nothing left for them to do.

Lieutenant Hugh Pond was one of fifty volunteers from A Company who, with eight engineers, were to land inside the Battery in gliders:

The plan involved landing three gliders in the gaps between the casemates. In addition to the arrester parachute, the wings of the gliders would snap off on hitting the casemates stopping the glider more quickly than usual. The Battalion would parachute in ahead of us on a DZ about a mile and a half away. As the gliders crash-landed inside the Battery, the Battalion would be assaulting from the outside. I was twenty years old, had never been in battle before and was tremendously excited at the prospect.

As well as the three *coup-de-main* party gliders, others were to land on the Battalion DZ, with more sappers, explosives, bangalore torpedoes to breach the wire, mine-detectors, and white tape to mark safe lanes.

Private James Bramwell was one of several conscientious objectors who had volunteered to serve in 224 Parachute Field Ambulance in 3rd Parachute Brigade. His section, under Captain Johnson RAMC, was attached to the 9th Parachute Battalion. Such was the detail known about the Merville Battery, and the painstaking, carefully scripted rehearsals, that Bramwell remembers:

Nobody felt anything could possibly go wrong. In retrospect it all seems amazing and totally incredible. My job was to take possession of a small house beside the Battery, with Corporal Jock Cranner, to set up a dressing station.

I could see out of the door of the aircraft; flashes of explosions, and a succession of bright balls of light coming towards us; flak. One shell exploded outside the door, and the pilot took avoiding action. The stick was flung into chaos, grabbing and clutching each other in the darkness. The despatcher tapped Captain Johnson on the shoulder, the green light went on, someone shouted 'Stop'. The light turned red, and green again. Out went the two in front, I followed. I released my kitbag, containing plasma. I could see a white line below, and was convinced this was a road near Varreville, marked on our maps. Just as I thought everything was going to plan, I landed flat on my back in water, like a lake. I stood up, absolutely soaked. As I released my parachute harness, I could see another member of my section, Private Hodge, wading towards me like a wraith through the mist.

After a few yards, I went straight into a six-foot ditch, so did Hodge. The whole place was intersected with these ditches, about 100 yards apart. It was a nightmarish, exhausting wallow, particularly falling into the ditches, because you got no warning.

Finally we stepped onto firm ground, and when, two days later we eventually arrived at Le Mesnil, a cheese farm, we were met by the second-in-command of 224 Parachute Field Ambulance. He was tremendously relieved to see us; two-thirds of the Field Ambulance were missing.

Lieutenant Hugh Pond in one of the three *coup-de-main* gliders bound for the Merville Battery:

We took off at about midnight. I was up front behind the pilots. We had six sappers whose job was to blow the guns. One of my chaps had a flame-thrower. Over the Battery we were hit by light anti-aircraft fire. One shell hit the flame-thrower. The glider and the unfortunate chap were on fire for the last few seconds of the approach. As we swooped in we saw the Battery. We lifted over a wire fence which we thought was outside the Battery, and crash-landed in an orchard about 150 yards away. As we all rushed out, except the poor chap on fire, we heard shooting, which we realised was the Battalion in the Battery.

We heard noises in the opposite direction, and realised they must be Germans coming up a narrow lane. We jumped into the ditch and engaged them. After a while as it was getting light, the firing died down. I heard a shout behind us, and there coming through a minefield was the Battalion Physical Training Instructor. We shouted, 'Go back. It's a minefield.' 'No it's not, it's a dummy, you're to rejoin the Battalion,' he replied. This was our first contact with our Battalion.

The RV (rendezvous) for the 9th Parachute Battalion was a Calvary [a roadside crucifix]. There Pond learned that less than a third of the Battalion had arrived in time to take part in the assault. It was time to move off, because for lack of a radio to transmit the success signal to the cruiser HMS *Arethusa*, she would shortly engage the Battery with her six-inch guns. The assault on the Battery put it out of action for a short time, but not permanently. None of the gliders carrying sappers and explosives had arrived. Of the other two in the *coup-de-main* party, one with a broken tow rope landed in Reading, the other landed miles away from the Battery. None of those loaded with equipment arrived at the Battalion DZ. The Battalion had not been trained to remove the sights from the guns, nor spike them without sapper assistance. Nor were they aware of chambers below the casemates to which the German gunners withdrew. This does not detract from the efforts of those few who did arrive and assault with no support and just small arms. Fortunately the intelligence had been incorrect, the guns were small 100mm Czech field guns of 1914 vintage, unable to wreak the havoc on the beaches feared by the planners. They were eventually withdrawn in August, when the

Germans fell back before the Allies' break-out. Attacks by the RAF, both before and after D-Day, failed to put them out of action.

Brigadier James Hill reached his Brigade Headquarters on the evening of D-Day:

I arrived at my HQ about eleven hours late. I was dropped quarter of a mile from Cabourg into four feet of water. It took four hours to reach dry land. As I had tea bags sewn into my battledress, I was surrounded by cold tea for much of that time. Eventually I reached the Canadian Battalion DZ, to find that they had completed all their tasks. I decided to visit the 9th Battalion, to see what progress they had made. I set off with my party, by now I had collected about 40 chaps. About 20 minutes before H-Hour for the seaborne assault, we were moving along a narrow track, with no ditches. Suddenly, I heard our own aircraft pattern bombing towards us. I shouted 'Down'. I felt myself being hit. When I came round, I propped myself up on my elbows, and in the middle of the track I saw a leg. I thought, 'That's mine'. I had another look and saw it had a brown boot on it. I had a rule that no one was to wear American brown boots. I knew it belonged to Lt Peters, the mortar officer of the 9th Battalion. I was lying on top of him. I had most of my left backside removed, but otherwise I was OK.

Only one other person got up, my Defence Platoon commander. We took the morphia off the dead, and gave it to the wounded. As we moved off, they gave us a cheer and wished us luck. None survived to tell the tale. In Le Plein, I met the 9th Battalion, only 90 strong, after their fight in the Merville Battery, which cost them about 90 casualties; having left England with over 600 men. I was patched up by the 9th Battalion doctor. The 9th Battalion provided me with a lady's bicycle and a pusher. In this manner, I covered the 2 miles to Divisional Headquarters.

On arrival, General Gale told me that my Brigade had achieved all its tasks. The senior doctor said that I had to go to the Main Dressing Station for an operation. I said, 'Not on your nelly.' Having lost my Battalion in North Africa when I was winged, I was not going to lose my Brigade. We did a deal. If he would personally guarantee to return me to my Brigade, I would allow him to operate. When I came round, all strapped up, I was told I was one of the first people to be given penicillin. I had a bottle of the stuff strapped to my side.

Lieutenant-Colonel Alastair Pearson, already decorated with a DSO and two bars, and an MC, after commanding the 1st Parachute Battalion in North Africa, Sicily and Italy, had been evacuated to England with malaria. Now commanding the 8th Battalion:

Our primary role was to destroy three bridges, one at Troarn, and two at Bure. We had to hold Troarn as long as possible. We were then to withdraw to our main position. This we were to hold, there was to be no withdrawal without orders from the Divisional Commander.

We landed at ten minutes to 1 a.m. on 6 June. I had a good DZ, K, about

> 3–4 kilometres from Troarn. The drop was a shambles. Instead of having 600–700 people within half an hour of landing, I had about 100.

Two and a half hours after the drop he still had only eleven officers and 145 soldiers. Most of his Battalion Group had landed on DZs N and V. Of his own battalion the only formed bodies were two platoons. Instead of Major Roseveare's engineer squadron, attached specially for the bridge demolition tasks, there were five sappers under a lance-corporal. Despite these set-backs, thanks to the initiative and determination of Pearson and small groups of officers and soldiers, ail the battalion's tasks were achieved. By 5 p.m., 250 strong, they took up their main defensive position.

Pearson had been shot in the hand by one of his own men on the DZ that morning. The sten bullet remained stuck, just the nose protruding. He tried, unsuccessfully, to extract it using a pair of signaller's pliers.

Although many in the Division arrived late, Major Darling, the second-in-command of the 12th Parachute Battalion started late. As his Stirling began its take-off run at Keevil airfield, it veered sharply to the right and stopped, stuck fast off the runway. Fortunately, Darling had organized spare aircraft and a truck for just this eventuality. He and his stick were soon in another Stirling. They emplaned in any order, and spent a great deal of the flight sorting themselves out, encumbered with kit, in the lurching, vibrating gloom, unable to communicate with each other except by shouting. Darling dictated a letter to his wife from hospital in Bramshott, Surrey, on 9 June:

> We finally 'set sail' at 11.15 on Monday night although I didn't get off until an hour later owing to a false start.
>
> It really was an inspiring sight to see all the aircraft taking off and everyone was in terrific heart. I took precisely 40 minutes to reach France and was dropped about 3 miles wide of the DZ in a very small field which seemed full of poles. I had a fairly heavy landing as there was quite a wind blowing and jerked my left knee a bit. I hadn't the foggiest idea where I was. I almost immediately met another officer, we moved across country through very thick hedges and deep ditches which was very tiring. We moved on judging the direction from some gliders of ours which came in at this time. We then met up with about eight men of the Bn, who were likewise lost and came to a village, where somebody had the brilliant idea of looking to see if there were any signposts, and believe it or not the 'super-efficient' Germans had forgotten to take them down and from then on it was easy to find our way.
>
> Eventually I joined the Bn and found that the majority of the men had come in. During Tuesday the battle developed almost exactly as planned & I think the two outstanding features, first the noise of the supporting barrage, and secondly the really picturesque sight of hundreds of gliders landing that evening. One hardly ever saw a German aeroplane and the RAF were continually very much in evidence.

The next day I was unlucky enough to get wounded in the right arm. Gerald Ritchie who commands a company who had just been wounded by a mortar bomb and his 2ic in command was killed, so I temporarily took over his company.

I was sitting on the road speaking on the wireless when a mortar bomb landed within 2 yards of me, a signaller, who was alongside me was killed outright, and a piece of the bomb went clean through the fleshy part of my forearm. Luckily it hasn't done any real harm. They evacuated me straight away and I've now landed up in a Canadian hospital which is easily the best I have ever been in. But I believe we are being moved again today. As you can see I am not writing this letter as it would be quite illegible.

Please do not worry as I should be fighting fit again very soon.

NEPTUNE – THE GREATEST AMPHIBIOUS OPERATION IN HISTORY

The great day for which we have all been training is at hand. The task allotted to us is a formidable one, and calls for all that is best in every one of us.
And, above all, FIGHT;
FIGHT to help the Army;
FIGHT to help yourselves;
FIGHT to save your ship;
FIGHT to the very end.
A. G. Talbot
Rear-Admiral Force S

Rupert Curtis who commanded 200 Flotilla of the 1st LCI(s) Squadron:
Of the 156,000 troops landed by sea and air on D-Day, some 84,000 were British and Canadian and 72,000 American. Nearly 80 per cent of the maritime support was British and Canadian, and half the vast air support, without which success would have been impossible.

On 20 June 1944, Captain Wight-Boycott, Royal Navy, the Staff Officer Liaison on board HMS *Bulolo*, the headquarters ship for Force G (Commodore Douglas-Pennant, the Naval commander, and Major-General Graham, commanding 50th Infantry Division), described the planned sequence of events for the assault on Gold beach:
The game opens with the heaviest possible bombardment from the air and sea. This bombardment compels the enemy to get their heads down under cover, but it cannot hope finally to silence shore batteries. Only a direct hit on a gun can put it out of action for certain, and this is virtually impossible except by luck. It is therefore necessary to have supporting fire until the very moment that troops land to prevent the enemy getting his head up

again. Naval gunnery is not sufficiently reliable to continue until the last moment, and has to be lifted from the beaches to targets inland at about H−20 minutes. The biggest problem is to fill this awkward and most important interval. This is achieved by rockets fired from converted LCTs, which accompany the first wave, and fire at H−10 and H−3 approximately. At this time the DD tanks, Shermans fitted with compressed-air-operated canvas flotation screens, should be swimming ashore, and should have touched down. These remain on the beaches to deal with strong points as the infantry lands.

The first wave of craft comprises LCTs carrying Assault Vehicles Royal Engineers (AVRE), which are mostly Churchill tanks fitted with flails to detonate mines, carrying bobbins to lay tracks over barbed wire, fascines to fill tank ditches, bridging equipment and petards. Bulldozers are included among these vehicles for clearing beach obstacles. Also in the first wave are LCTs carrying Centaur tanks. These are old tanks, originally intended to act solely as a fort on the beach. In practice they were powered, although they have old and worn out engines. This wave is accompanied by three rocket ships (LCT(R)), several landing craft gun (LCG) with two 4.7-inch guns, and several landing craft flak (LC(F)) fitted with about 8 pom-pom. Hunt class destroyers close the shore as far as they can with the assault wave. The support craft, LCG etc. do not beach.

Seven minutes after the AVRE touch down, is H-Hour; the moment on which the whole assault is timed, when the first wave of infantry arrives in landing craft assault (LCA). These have been lowered by the landing ship infantry (LSI) about seven miles from shore. On a brigade front there are 10 LCA in each wave, roughly three hundred men. The second wave carrying the reserve companies of the two assaulting battalions follows about quarter of an hour later. In the meantime, the LCTs which have delivered their DD tanks are loading up at the LSIs with the reserve battalions, to land anything up to an hour after H-Hour. (The LCAs have all been used to land the assaulting battalions.)

The infantry are followed by self-propelled artillery carried in LCTs. These fire as they close the beaches to give additional support. These touch down at about H plus 60 minutes, and are followed by a continuous stream of LCTs carrying high priority vehicles: mortar and machine-gun carriers, anti-tank guns, scout cars, jeeps and bulldozers.

This completes the first phase of the assault, except for one landing ship tank (LST), carrying 21 DUKWS on the tank deck with 6-pounder anti-tank guns. These are swum off at H plus 60 minutes.

The next arrivals are the reserve brigades carried in landing craft infantry large (LCI(L)). These wait to land until ordered, depending on the state of affairs ashore.

Apart from the fact that the assault on Gold beach did not include commandos landing in LCI(S), Wight-Boycott's description of the planned sequence was followed in the plans for Sword beach, and the

Canadian beach Juno. However, as so often in battle, the sequence did not always go to plan.

As night fell, the vast array of Allied ships turned to head for the ten lanes swept through the German minefields off the Assault Area. Lieutenant-Commander Robert Macnab, the torpedo officer of the cruiser HMS *Glasgow*, attached to the United States Navy Force O, destined for the area off Omaha beach, writing to his parents on 14 June 1944:

> At dusk we went to action stations and remained there for about five days. This entails meals of sandwiches and soup, which palls after a bit; also sleeping on the steel decks with rivets sticking into one – but there wasn't much sleep anyway (two to three hours a night split between quiet moments, but it's enough to keep going on). A tot of rum is issued daily to those who want it (even officers!) and this is as powerful as four normal drinks.
>
> At nightfall we turned to the South'ard and began the approach to the French coast. The padre read Nelson's prayer over the loudspeakers. This passage through the minefields was expected to be a costly one, in spite of the large number of gallant minesweepers who were sweeping us in: in fact it turned out to be quite the opposite. *Glasgow* led our bombardment squadron in, astern of the sweepers – we were prepared to give gunfire support to the minesweepers if they were engaged by shore batteries or enemy forces, but this did not occur. During this anxious period the wind again freshened from the Sou'West, which caused some apprehension – the beaching of landing-craft becomes very dangerous in a high wind and surf.
>
> The sweeping of the approach channels in a two and a half knot cross tide was a complicated business with the laying of numerous buoys and coloured lights – but was achieved, and as the dawn came, several thousand ships lay silently a few miles off the enemy coast, apparently having won complete surprise!

LCAs with Canadian infantry, waiting to run in to the beach.
(MH4506)

HMS *Glasgow*'s D-Day task was bombarding Omaha beach. This is *Glasgow* bombarding Cherbourg later in the campaign; USS *Quincy* in the background.
(A24310)

But all was not quiet ashore during this ponderous approach. The RAF, 'whom God preserve'! had been giving their biggest and best to the beaches and batteries and entire defences. A pyrotechnic display such as this has, I believe, seldom been seen before – it was splendid. One six-inch-gun battery on Pointe du Hoc in particular came in for a terrible time: enormous explosions rent it continuously for about 20 minutes and later it received many broadsides from the US battleship *Texas*. Almost the entire point is now crumbled into the sea and the battery never fired a shot.

Macnab's concern about the effect the weather had on landing craft was to be realized on Omaha beach. Here the assault formations had a long run-in. Only five of the thirty-two amphibious tanks survived the trip. Thirty-two of fifty guns sent to support the infantry sank in DUKWs. Many landing-craft foundered, including those carrying demolition equipment to clear beach obstacles. The attack by the Allied Air Forces, bombing blind on instruments, was less effective than it looked. All of the bombs intended for the Omaha defences fell into the fields behind, as did most of those aimed at the British beaches. Although USS *Texas* fired 250 rounds of 14-inch shells at the Pointe du Hoc, the US Rangers discovered, after a desperate climb up the cliffs under fire, and savage fighting on the top, that the guns were intact some distance in the rear, waiting to be moved into position.

Good navigation to the correct beaches by assault craft with rudimentary navigation aids, and DD tanks with none, was essential. Midget submarines were used to provide beacons. The midget submarine X23 was allocated to Sword beach. Here an error of only 1,000 yards either way would have resulted in chaos for the assaulting soldiers. The

X23 after its long vigil off Sword beach, approaching HMS *Largs*, Rear-Admiral Talbot's flagship.
(PL8979)

task of X23 was to sit 7,000 yards off shore to mark the launching position for the DD tanks, and mark a position 3,000 yards from the beach with a dinghy. After a passage of thirty hours, partly under tow and partly under her own power, submerged in daylight hours, and on the surface to cross a German minefield, X23 arrived at 4 a.m. on 4 June. The signal postponing D-Day was eventually picked up very faintly at 1.00 a.m. on 5 June, only hours before she would have surfaced and showed a light, totally compromising the whole operation. She received confirmation that D-Day would be on 6 June, at 11 p.m. on the 5th. To reduce the interference on her radio, she had switched off the gyro compass. The outcome was a compass with an error of 150 degrees. Nevertheless Lieutenant Lyne, the CO, was able to show a green light, indicating he was within 300 yards of the correct position, which was picked up by the LCTs carrying the DD tanks.

After the tanks were launched, X23 was escorted by motor launch to HMS *Largs*, before being towed home. Sixty-four out of seventy-six hours were spent submerged in the tiny submarine. When on the surface, the rough seas washed her officers off the casing, and continual pumping was necessary to hold back flooding from seas pouring down the hatch. Despite remaining for more than forty-eight hours off the beach, she was not detected. During each of the two days, because of the short midsummer nights, she spent about nineteen hours submerged.

The weather, which had made conditions so hazardous for the crews of the midget submarines, caused great difficulty for the considerable number of craft and ferries that were towed across, there being insufficient places at davits, or deck space, on bigger ships to lift all of them. Many of the tows parted, and craft were swamped. Some were able to complete the journey under their own power. It had been hoped to rest the crews in the towing craft, but in the case of the twelve LCP(L) bound for Sword beach, for example, all kept their crews on board throughout the passage. Continually wallowing, surging forward, and being brought up short with a jerk at the end of towrope was exhausting. Eventually all LCP(L) tows broke. There were numerous breakdowns as engines not designed for such long passages overheated. However, all but one, which sank, arrived, although some were late for the assault. Of a group of nine LCAs(H), heading for Sword beach, only one arrived. Seven foundered, and one broke adrift and was subsequently picked up at sea. LCA(H), the H standing for 'Hedgerow', were craft fitted with spigot mortars, the bombs from which were designed to burst simultaneously along the beach clearing a lane through the minefield.

Among the embarked troops, the weather took its toll. Tom Tateson, in a ship bound for Gold beach:

> Reveille was sounded at 3.15 a.m. and we hastily went for breakfast. This being an American ship, the galley was equipped with multi-course indented trays which I had not encountered previously. In one indentation was porridge and in another minced liver. (We were to see this a second time after we had been at sea in the small assault landing craft for a few hours.) We were also given a rum ration. In spite of the vomit bags and fresh sea air, there was a pervading stench of retched liver and rum in the boats as we approached our encounter with Jerry.

Company Sergeant-Major Bill Brown D Company, 8th Battalion Durham Light Infantry, also in an American ship heading for Gold beach:

> I was so nervous, I hadn't eaten anything for two days so there wasn't anything to come up. The orderly corporal came up as I was leaning over the side. I said, 'Good morning. Where's the parade state?' (the book with

all the company details). He said, 'Here's the bloody parade state,' throwing it over the side. He continued, 'This is our fourth bloody do. I wish I was off this bastard.' We would have gone into the water then and there, anywhere rather than be sick.

Some enjoyed their breakfast. Captain Patterson of 4 Commando, in a ship of Force S:

> Breakfast was at 04.00 hrs, and I only slept a little, rather fitfully. The wind howled, the ship rolled, and the adjutant who was in my cabin was sick in the basin. It was grey dawn when I emerged, and I could just see the shapes of the ships. There was some ack-ack in the distance and the occasional red flare. I went in to breakfast on porridge, bacon and egg, toast and marmalade, which went down very well, though some of the poorer sailors did not make much of it. As I was finishing, there was a distant metallic thump. I went out on deck in time to see a Norwegian Hunt Class destroyer on our port beam roll over with a broken back, and heave her stern and bows out of the sea. It seemed as if no craft took the slightest notice, and like chaff on a stream the swarms of ships drifted on. However, before long, a little tug or trawler was alongside picking up survivors.
>
> The thunder of the big guns now began as the battleships got on to their targets. The coast of France was a low grey strip to the southward, with a cold-looking tossing expanse of sea in between. The anchor went down with a shuddering rattle, as the *Princess Astrid* anchored in her appointed place seven miles out. 'Troops to parade, troops to parade', came over the loud hailer, and we collected for the last time in the mess decks. There seemed to be much less room than usual, as everyone really had everything with him, probably for the first time.

The first sight of battle casualties often came as a shock. As always, accounts of the same event by several witnesses differ. Sapper Alfred Lane, an assault engineer in 263 Field Company, was like the majority, going into action for the first time:

> I saw in the first breaking light of dawn the outline of our escort destroyer close on our starboard side. My sickness and misery was suddenly added to by shock and dismay because of an explosion that lifted the destroyer out of the water amidships. I watched disbelieving as her middle went down, leaving her two ends upturned and floating. I rubbed my eyes as if it was an illusion or hallucination caused by sea sickness. The reality became all too evident when I saw over the side pieces of wreckage floating, some with figures clinging to it. Our ship appeared to me to sail over the drifting wreckage. I was horrified to see some of the wreckage and figures disappearing directly under our ship; and furious that nothing was being done to save the poor devils in the sea. They were obviously doomed to die.

Sub-Lieutenant John Pelly RNVR in the bombarding destroyer HMS

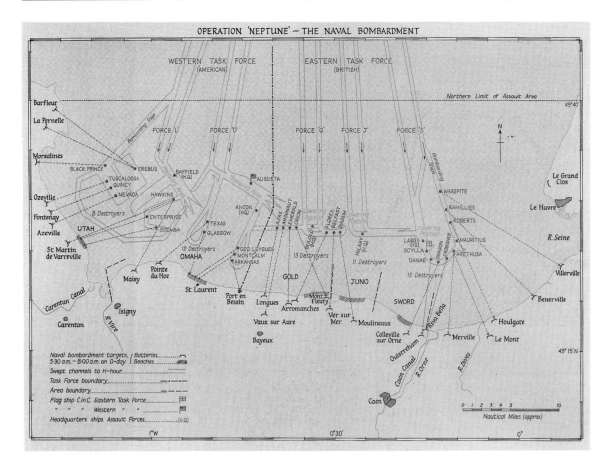

OPERATION 'NEPTUNE' – THE NAVAL BOMBARDMENT

OPERATION
NEPTUNE – THE NAVAL
BOMBARDMENT
**This shows the
principal initial targets
for the bombarding
ships, the ships'
positions on the gun-
line, the ten swept
channels for approach
lanes for bombarding
ships and landing
ships, and the
lowering positions at
which landing craft
were lowered and
troops embarked if not
already in their craft.**
(Negative number
HU63703). From papers of
Rear-Admiral Talbot (p282,
folder AGT2)

Eglinton, who had been at sea in destroyers since 1941, in a letter home written on 24 June:

> Almost immediately the destroyer just to port of us went up – her bows and stern sticking right up and then sinking at once, while at the same time torpedoes were seen approaching from the port side. We went full ahead and avoided them. Fear – before it has just taken the usual form of excitement and an effort to appear calm in speech; but for a few seconds on this occasion, I couldn't get a sound from my mouth. The doctor appeared on the bridge just then and I tried to tell him what was going on and nothing came out. How I envy the man who seems to have no fear and I've met quite a few like that.
>
> All this time we were closing the beaches leading the other destroyers to carry out the initial and inshore bombardment of pillboxes and gun emplacements. The first bombing of the beaches was over and there seemed to be absolute quiet. At six-thirty we opened up and so did the cruisers astern and the battleships behind them – it was a great comfort to know that they were there. Our orders were to destroy anything that might be a gun or mortar site, and we already knew of one or two. We had about two miles of sea front to deal with, including the village of Luc-sur-Mer to the west of Courseilles. Most of the two miles of target area was houses and streets

beyond the beach. The Captain chose his own targets and we were so close we couldn't miss. In fact we all had the time of our lives – pointing out targets that took our fancy – like the green house the Captain thought to be an eyesore.

The monitor HMS *Roberts* was on the eastern flank. Her navigating officer, Lieutenant-Commander Peter Cardale:

> *Roberts* opened fire two hours before the landings took place. Shortly before H-Hour, three E-boats came out from Le Havre and fired torpedoes. One passed close ahead and another close astern of *Roberts*, and as far as I know, no ship was hit. While firing on a concentration of German troops inland from Sword beach, a shell burst in the right 15-inch gun (Sweet Sue) splitting the jacket. We returned to Portsmouth that night to reammunition, but it was decided not to change the gun until Lousy Lou was worn out.

Rear-Admiral A. G. Talbot, Force S, in the Headquarters ship HMS *Largs*:

> As we approached the lowering position, HMS *Warspite*, HMS *Ramillies*, HMS *Roberts* and HMS *Arethusa* were already anchored in their bombarding positions to port of us. Our own aircraft streaked low across the eastern

Admiral Sir Bertram Ramsay (left) **talking to a steel-helmeted Rear-Admiral A. G. Talbot Commanding Force S aboard his flagship the headquarters ship HMS *Largs*, while Air Chief Marshal Sir Arthur Tedder looks on. Tedder, as Eisenhower's deputy, was later to scheme to sack Montgomery. Like all deputy commanders he could comment on plans without bearing responsibility for any decisions.** (A24020)

flank at about this time, and laid a most effective smoke screen to shield the Force from the heavy batteries at Havre. Unfortunately, three German torpedo boats took advantage of this to carry out a torpedo attack and, although engaged by the bombarding squadron, were able to make good their escape in the smoke. Two torpedoes passed between HMS *Warspite* and HMS *Ramillies* and at 05.30 one hit HNorMS *Svenner*.

The shot appeared to have hit *Svenner* immediately under her boiler room. There was a burst of steam amidships and her funnel fell aft as the whole ship seemed to lift out of the water. The ship's company were seen to fall-in on the forecastle and quarterdeck and, as she broke her back and started to sink rapidly, they began to jump into the water.

HMS *St Adrian*, two US coastguard cutters and an empty LCI (L), earmarked for towing duties off the beaches, were ordered to the rescue of the survivors and a large proportion of the ship's company was picked up.

After this *mauvais quart d'heure* things quietened down and when the LSI were all anchored, I took HMS *Largs* to the head of the line and anchored her a few cables south of the lowering position to watch the arrival of the convoys.

At the lowering position, troops who had crossed the channel in the larger ships transferred to craft. Some climbed into craft still hoisted at the davit head. Captain Patterson:

We stepped gingerly over the gap with our heavy loads and began to pack ourselves in. As always the last man couldn't sit down. Soon 'lower away, lower away', sent the LCAs down in turn to bump and wrench on their davits as the swell took them. Quickly the shackles were cast off, and we rode free in that sea.

Others climbed down rope ladders and scrambling nets to craft lurching and crashing against the ships' sides. Sapper Lane:

As assault engineers we were weighed down with heavy personal loads to carry. Even without such cumbersome gear, it would have been difficult getting aboard the assault craft which was now alongside. The craft swung wildly to and from the ship's side, so that men were forced to jump and tumble into the boat as it crashed alongside. It led to the injury of a few and caused ill afforded delay.

Some had to change 'horses' in mid-stream. Private Tateson, a signaller attached to A Company, 7th Battalion the Green Howards, following up behind its sister battalion, 6th Green Howards, the assault battalion of the left-hand assault brigade of 50th Infantry Division:

The landing craft held about thirty men tightly packed, and we were seated so that our heads were below the gunwale. We were ordered to keep our heads down as we approached the coast to avoid enemy fire. However, our landing-craft was disabled by some obstacle and it became impossible to steer. One of the other boats was brought alongside, and although it was already fully loaded with a similar number of men, we had to clamber aboard and abandon our boat. We were now exposed to enemy fire as well as being grossly overloaded.

The cruiser HMS *Belfast* [now moored opposite the Tower of London, and part of the Imperial War Museum] was stationed off Gold beach area; her Captain, Frederick Parham:

> The final approach to our bombarding position was hair-raising; in a narrow swept channel, with a strong cross tide, we were almost constantly under helm, dodging myriads of landing-craft whom we had to overtake in order to open fire on prearranged targets well before the landing-craft went into touchdown.
>
> Just before 09.00 I left the bridge and went into the charthouse. In the charthouse was a loudspeaker connected to the BBC. As I came in on this, perhaps the most momentous day in the annals of the British Empire, a voice said: 'Now girls, are we all ready? Then stretch the arms, stretch the legs.' It was May Brown conducting morning exercises for the ladies.

As the waves of craft approached Sword beach, the guns of three SP artillery regiments carried in LCTs fired on the run-in. On completion, they were to turn away, and land about an hour later. All beach areas, Sword, Juno, Gold, Omaha and Utah, were divided into sectors identified by a letter of the phonetic alphabet of the time. These were sub-divided into coloured sub-sectors. 3rd Infantry Division was to land on Q for Queen Red (left) and White (right). Lieutenant Sidney Rosenbaum in 33rd Field Regiment:

> At 06.55 we opened fire at 11,000 yards, the rounds falling between the beach and 400 hundred yards inland. The rate of fire was three rounds a minute for each of the Division's 72 guns, so that about 4 tons of HE were arriving every minute on our immediate front. At the same time HE-filled rockets were being directed on to the same area from LCTs specially adapted to take them. They made a fearsome sight as they launched their missiles simultaneously.
>
> Amidst the hullabaloo a rending crash on our left flank where there was another LCT signalled the first return of shot from the shore. More enemy fire descended on the forward troops as they neared the beaches. There was a fierce satisfaction in calling out the fire orders, and when we reached the end of the run-in, at H−5, and added 400 yards to the range, before emptying the guns, more than one additional round was shot off for luck. We turned away, having observed the shore, which looked for all the world like an English seaside, and got ready to land.

The information about the enemy defences along the coast was considerable in all sectors, and although there were numerous variations in

Anti-tank obstacles in the streets of St-Aubin-sur-Mer which caused the Canadians considerable trouble. Troops of the Canadian 8th Brigade take cover against snipers. (B5228)

detail along the coast between Arromanches and Ouistreham, the enemy layout facing Brigadier E. E. E. Cass's 8th Infantry Brigade, the assault brigade of 3rd Infantry Division was:

Along the coast there were strong points about every two thousand yards, well garrisoned and strongly defended with all types of weapons, minefields, wire, and in some cases *flammenwerfer* [flamethrowers]. Between them were pillboxes, fortified houses, further minefields and wire, while all exits from the beaches had been blocked. Beach obstacles composed of knife rest ramps, stakes, steel hedgehogs, and concrete tetrahedra, all about six feet high and mined, stretched from the high water mark down the beaches towards the sea for a distance of three hundred yards. In the centre of our two beaches was a strong point named 'COD', on the right flank one in Lion-sur-Mer, and on the left flank one in Ouistreham that included a battery and an anti-tank ditch. In rear of the beaches there were four heavily defended battery positions, several fixed rocket batteries, numerous machine-gun emplacements all covered by minefields and wire. On the left flank a battery of heavy guns commanded the beaches from the opposite side of the Orne. The beaches were smooth and firm except for a strip of soft sand above high water mark, which rose in some places to a height of fifteen feet, but behind the beaches and the houses scattered along them was a belt of marshland, impassable to vehicles, extending back for some five hundred yards.

The plan for 8th Infantry Brigade was to land with two battalions, each supported by a squadron of the 13/18th Royal Hussars in DD tanks. The DD tanks were to touch down at H minus seven and a half minutes, followed by the assault companies of infantry and assault engineers at H-hour. The engineers were to clear the beach obstacles and make exits from the beaches. At H plus 20 minutes the remainder of the assaulting battalions, followed at H plus 30 minutes by two commandos; 41 (Royal Marines) Commando to land on White beach and clear Lion-sur-Mer, and 4 Commando to land on Red beach and clear Ouistreham. At H plus 60 minutes, the reserve battalion, 1st Battalion Suffolk Regiment, was to land on White beach and, supported by a squadron of the 13/18th Royal Hussars, capture the Periers-sur-le-Dan ridge. To land at H plus 75 minutes: the 76th Field Regiment RA; and at H plus 105 minutes the 33rd Field Regiment and the remainder of 1st Special Service Brigade (Brigadier Lovat, consisting of 3, 6 and 45 (Royal Marines) Commando, 4 Commando having already landed).

The landing sequences for the assault brigades on Juno and Gold beaches were broadly similar, although they differed in detail. For example, both 50th Infantry Division (Gold) and 3rd Canadian Infantry Division (Juno), with wider sectors, landed with two assault brigades up. As on Sword beach, commandos on Juno and Gold landed behind the initial waves, some with tasks that took them well beyond the initial beachhead.

Brigadier Cass had returned from the Middle East to take command of 8th Infantry Brigade, and had taken part in landings in Norway, North Africa, Sicily and Italy. In his Headquarter Ship with Captain E. Bush Royal Navy:

> We now steamed up to the front to see what was happening to the DD tanks; the decision to launch them was to be made by the Tank Brigade Commander with his Naval Commander. If too rough the LCT carrying them were to beach in the normal way, but this would mean that the infantry would be without their support as the assault craft touched down. We watched the LCTs close to within 5,000 yards of the shore where the DDs were safely launched. This was a dangerous time as the craft had to stop in order to launch and were sitting targets for some time. We were greatly relieved to see them in the water and making good progress.
>
> We were reminded that we were out in front by a number of water spouts that rose about our ship, flashes from Ouistreham caused us to move out of range. We now had a wonderful view of the assault craft as they closed the beaches in excellent formation despite the heavy seas. The DDs were leading, followed by the LCAs of the infantry and the LCTs of the

LCT(R) firing. (A27942)

engineers, the LCAs of number 4 Commando, the five LCT(R) whose four thousand rockets were all to fall on locality 'COD', the reserve battalion in LCAs, and the Divisional Artillery firing from LCTs also on 'COD'. The beaches could now be seen, and we were able to pick out various landmarks that we had memorised. Above us was a low grey sky, and a stiffish wind whipped the top off the heavy waves and drove the spray across the decks.

Fighter aircraft roamed above us, and punctually at H minus 35 the Divisional Artillery opened fire. The supporting fire now reached its peak and we heard the roar of many aircraft above us as they passed over to saturate the beaches just before H-hour, but we could not see them as they were above the clouds. Soon afterwards we saw an inferno of flame stretching across our front as the bombs rained down, and a mass of debris was flung into the air, while a cloud of smoke and dust rose, in some places bright red, in others black and threatening. It remained for a long time, blinding the enemy Observation Posts on land. A noise like the tearing of calico rent the air and we saw the first three rocket craft discharge their broadsides of 5-inch rockets which could be seen speeding upwards towards the beaches like large packs of grouse going for the next parish with a strong wind under their tails. They were followed soon after by those of the remaining two craft, the whole sight being an impressive finale to the preliminary bombardment, and at any minute now the leading waves would touch down.

In fact on Sword beach the DD tanks, engineers and assault infantry arrived almost together. Twenty-four of the thirty DD tanks of 13/18th Hussars were launched. Two were rammed by LCTs trying to avoid rockets falling short, five were swamped in the surf, and four disabled by enemy fire on landing. The thirteen remaining were joined subsequently by tanks that had been unable to launch at sea. The assaulting waves were faced with formidable obstacles, and only partially silenced guns. Of some fifty major guns in coastal batteries in the Neptune area, attacked from the air, only eighteen were destroyed. Many of the smaller guns and machine-guns were in defilade; their gun ports protected, not visible from seaward, and sited to fire along the beaches from the flank. It was fortunate that sufficient DD tanks landed to support the engineers and infantry.

Among the many assault engineers landing on Queen beach was Sergeant T. R. Kilvert commanding an AVRE in 1 Troop, 77 Assault Squadron:

> Almost in, 400 yards to go when my AVRE had a violent shake, we had been hit. Damage not known, because the LCT had also sustained damage a bit forward and we had to get off at once.
>
> The LCT stopped; again my AVRE was hit. Going down the ramp now and the water was almost up to our cupola. Again we were hit but on our bobbin, it being at a crazy angle. Coming out of the water, hit again, and at

A skilfully sited German 88mm gun, with heavy overhead protection and masked against fire from seaward, but able to fire along the beach taking armoured vehicles in the flank, a perfect defilade position. This gun caused considerable trouble before it was silenced, as did several others along the whole beachhead. Note the Vehicle Exit sign on the left of the picture erected by a beach party after the lane had been cleared by AVRE and infantry.
(A23995)

last dry and following the Troop Leader's AVRE up the sand. Hit a mine, one bogie gone, out following in the leading AVRE's track, we were ordered to put up a windsock [to mark the route]. Struck a second mine, two bogies gone and left track gone. Two of crew jumped out to put up a windsock, one blown up by a mine as he came round the tank, take all arms, and jumped out myself, destroyed slidex and code papers. We were all out now, petrol was pouring out of the AVRE and filling the mine crater.

Captain A. Low, Troop Commander 2 Troop, 77 Assault Squadron:

About 1200 yards out the house known to us all as Sad Sack Villa was spotted, and the LCT commander set course to land ten yards to port of the house. We were ahead of the DD tanks due to touch down before us. All craft were ordered to stop to allow them through. Approximately 1,000 yards off shore the LCT(R) opened up. Rockets collided in mid air, and rained down on craft waiting to go in. One landed immediately under our starboard bow showering the bridge with pieces of casing.

LCT were then ordered to beach at full speed. Our gaps were hidden by dust showered by the barrage on the beach, but at 300 yards the building was again visible a bit to port. Twenty yards from the beach, the craft was attacked by four planes with British markings, two bombs landing very close to our doorway. We climbed on to my tank as the ramp dropped.

Ahead of us was a gun apparently concentrating on the troop on our left. One flail flailed straight for the gun. I followed out with the boase carpet. Another flailed a second path up to the sand dunes, and this I used to push the boase bangalore into a sand dune about six feet high.

I had trouble cutting the rope tackle on the boase bangalore, which had pushed easily into the dunes, as snipers kept up a steady hail of lead whenever I appeared. By this time grenades were being thrown at my tank, so I poked my head out and dealt with the offender, then cut the boase bangalore loose. Driving back from the dune, I saw the bangalore explode. It made a good gap in the dunes, but I could not drop the carpet on it as both flails had gone forward.

The infantry who had landed right behind us were now pushing forward.

Major 'Banger' King commanded the two leading companies of 2nd East Yorks, the left-hand battalion of the whole Allied assault, landing on Sword beach. In a letter to his batman's mother, written a month later:

I cannot express too deeply my admiration for the men I have been commanding. When we landed at H-Hour on D-Day they went straight in over the beaches in spite of a murderous fire & in half an hour had cleared a gap about 200 yards wide in the German defences through which poured the reserve companies – commandos – & it seemed to be about half the British Army. We were the first to land – & there can't be many men in the Allied Armies who got there before your son, as he followed me out the boat & we were the first to touch down on our beach. After making our gap, we swung to the right & mopped up various machine-gun nests & a 50cm gun. Afterwards we went inland and attacked a strongly held German position which we captured with the aid of two other coys – plus 3 cases of champagne which alas was drunk by another coy!

Lieutenant Hugh Bone, the signals officer of 2nd E. Yorks, with Battalion Headquarters and the follow-up companies:

Now was the moment – we clutched our weapons and wireless sets, all carefully waterproofed. A shallow beach we had been told, wet up to our knees or a little over, and then a long stretch of sand and obstacles. Suddenly there was a jarring bump on the left, looking up we saw some of the beach obstacles about two feet above our left gunwale, with a large mine on top of it; just as the photographs had shown us; the mine the same as we had practised disarming. For a few brief moments there was just the music of the guns, whang of occasional bullets overhead, the explosions of mortar bombs, and the background noise of our own fire. The doors opened as we grounded; the Colonel was out. The boat swung, as one by one we followed him. Several fell and got soaked. I stopped for a few seconds to help my men with their heavy wireless sets to ensure they kept them dry. I began to recognise men of the assault companies. Some were dead, others struggling to crawl out of the water, the tide was rising very rapidly. We could not help them, our job was to push on. I saw one of my signals corporals with a wound in his leg, and I took his codes with me, promising to send a man back for his set before he was evacuated.

Just off the beach, among some ruined buildings, we began to collect the HQ. The other boat party was mostly missing, also three-quarters of my sets. The Colonel was getting a grip on the battle, and I was sent back to the beach to collect the rest of us. I did not feel afraid, but rather elated and full of beans. There were some horrible sights there, and not a few men calling out for help. I had no time or duty there, the beach medical people would gradually get round to them all. Under the sides of a tank that had been hit, I saw a bunch of my people. I bawled at them to get up and start moving, since they were doing no good there, and could safely get along to HQ. I felt a little callous when I found nearly all of them had been hit, and some were dead. But sorting them out, I made up half a wireless team, and went in search of more.

Further on were the Adjutant and the Padre with their party, also taking cover. I took them back with me. By persuading a couple of blokes with shrapnel in their legs and feet they were good for a few more hours yet, I got my wireless lifted, and we returned to HQ, which was just moving off further inland. Later I discovered that numerous others had been killed on the beach landing at the same time as myself. The move inland was not much fun. Although we had cleared the beach defences, Jerry was mortaring us pretty badly from positions in his rear. Besides we had to cross a marsh, in places up to our armpits in muddy water and slime. The mortars had our range. As I helped my wireless people through the deep parts (why are all Yorkshire signallers only 5 foot 2 inches?), the bombs were bursting only 50 yards behind us.

Even after the beaches had been gapped the assault engineers could not rest on their laurels. All the AVREs of 77 Assault Squadron were grouped together to support 41 (Royal Marines) Commando and A Company of the South Lancashires to attack Lion-sur-Mer, which did not fall for two days. In bitter fighting the sappers suffered more casualties. For their work that day, 77 and 79 Assault Squadrons were awarded two DSOs, four MCs, two DCMs, and three MMs.

While the assault engineers and infantry were clearing an initial foothold, more craft were approaching the beach. Captain Patterson of 4 Commando in an LCA due to touch down thirty minutes after the leading wave:

> We were rolling heavily in a big south-westerly swell which broke continually over us, drenching us and chilling us to the marrow. My hands grew numb and dead, and my teeth were chattering with cold and fright. My batman looked awful, but he gave me a big grin through his green. It was H-Hour, 07.00, and the first infantry were going in. We passed round the rum, and those who were not too seasick took a good swig. The sea was well dotted with 'bags vomit', and I could see the boys on the LCIs rushing to the rail.
>
> The chaps in the other boats were passing round the rum. I could hear snatches of song through the hellish din. Hutch Burt's boat went in singing 'Jerusalem'. We didn't sing in ours. My mouth was as dry as a bone, I was shaking all over, and I doubt if I could have produced a note. The shore was still obscured by smoke, but I began to make out the fountains of shell bursts, and the rattle of small-arms fire cut through the roar and scream of heavy shells. Something was hit on our starboard bow, and a huge cloud of black smoke went up with orange flame flickering against the murk of battle. It was now 07.30 and with 400 yards to go we were a little late. We began to struggle with our rucksacks, an almost impossible feat. I gave it up until we grounded.
>
> Bullets began to rattle on the side of the craft and splinters whined overhead. 'Ready on the ramp,' we cowered down. The explosions were very near now, and one threw spray over us. 'Going in to land.' We touched, bumped, slewed round. 'Ramp down,' the boat began to empty. At the stern, my men and I were the last to leave. I heaved on my rucksack and seized a stretcher. No one seemed ready to take the other one, so I picked it up too, staggered to the bows, cautiously down the ramp, and flopped into the water. It came up about midthigh. I struggled desperately for the shore. There was a thick fog of smoke all over the beach. The tide was flooding. There were many bodies in the water. One was hanging on the wire round one of the tripod obstacles. As I got nearer the shore, I saw wounded among the dead, pinned down by the weight of their equipment. The first I came to was little Sapper Mullen, submerged to the chin and helpless. I got my scissors out, with numb hands which felt weak and useless, I began to cut away his rucksack and equipment. Hindmarch

Commandos on an LCI(S) during the run-in to Sword beach. (Film still MH33547)

appeared beside me worked on the other side. He was a bit rattled, but soon steadied when I spoke to him and told him what to do.

As I was bending over, I felt a smack across my bottom as if someone had hit me with a big stick. It was a shell splinter I found out later, but it hit nothing important; I just swore and carried on. We dragged Mullen to the water's edge at last, and he was able to shuffle himself up the beach, so we let him carry on. I looked round to take stock. The Commando were up at the wire, and clearly having trouble getting through. As there was no point in standing about, Hindmarch and I went back to the wounded in the water. I noticed how fast the tide was rising, and the wounded men began to shout and scream as they saw they must soon drown. We worked desperately. I don't know how many we pulled clear, not more than two or three.

I saw Donald Glass at the water's edge, badly hit in the back. I went to him and started to cut away his equipment. As I was doing so, I was conscious of a machine-gun enfilading us from the left front. In a minute I was knocked over by a smack in the right knee, and fell on Donald, who protested violently. I tried my leg, and found it still worked though not very well. I got Hindmarch to open a stretcher and put Donald on it. I looked round for help, but the only other standing figure anywhere was my batman, who was working on his own with drowning wounded in the water. He smiled, and waved to me. I tried my leg again, and took one end of the stretcher. Hindmarch is a big strong fellow, between us we began to carry Donald up towards the wire. At the finish I was beat, and just lay and gasped. We took the stretcher from Donald, we knew we would be needing it later, and left him in a hollow in the sand. The troops had by now got through the wire, and recognising where I was, I stumbled after them, across the minefield, to the demolished buildings, our assembly area, which the air photograph had showed so clearly.

The vulnerable LCIs landing the commandos took heavy casualties from gunfire and mines. LCI(S) 509 was mined about 600 yards off Queen Red beach. She was severely damaged and making water fast. The captain ordered abandon ship. Another craft came alongside, although damaged in its own touchdown. As the transfer of troops and wounded was under way, the enemy gunners ashore took advantage of a sitting target. Private Kenneth Holmes, back in 3 Commando, after recovering from wounds suffered in Italy, was in number 509:

> D-Day was to be my eighth landing with number 3 Commando, but I was most unhappy about it for it was to be my first in daylight and the first time we were not to be first in. We were in the second flight and due to land after the hornet's nest had been disturbed. When ordered below for the run-in, I was sitting in the forward space on the port side. The next thing I remember is coming to with my head just above the water which had flooded the compartment. The craft had a terrible list and the space was littered with bodies and flotsam. The water was cold and bloodstained.
>
> I saw a hatchway some feet away. I struggled to my feet, but found it almost impossible, for I was still wearing my special combat waistcoat, which was packed with ammunition, explosive charges and two 3-inch mortar shells, which every man had to carry. As I tried to get to my feet, I must have impacted what transpired to be a bad fracture of both tibula and fibula above my left ankle. As I struggled to unstrap my waistcoat, a crew member looked down through the hatchway I had seen, and lowered a rope which I tied round my waist. With another crew member, he pulled me to the deck.
>
> We were told we had been hit badly, were sinking, but another craft was alongside. I was strapped into a stretcher, made of split cane and canvas, like a mummy, from shoulders to ankles, with my arms inside. I was carried to another LCI(S) lurching alongside. My end had come, or so I thought, when I landed on the other craft, for I seemed just to roll across the deck. I was carried, laid beside the bridge, and told not to worry as we were returning immediately to Blighty. I heard an almighty crash, and was told that the engine room had been hit and the craft was being abandoned.
>
> The second transfer was to a floating tank. I was laid across the turret in my wrapper, with the tank commander holding me in position. [By this time the damaged craft had in fact beached.] On the beach I was laid in the tracks of a tank or similar vehicle, where I lay petrified for most of the day thinking that other tanks would grind me into the beach. The medics eventually found me.

Holmes was evacuated to England. Out of the 63 men from 3 Commando, in the LCI, 54 were found dead in an after-battle survey.

Royal Marines Commandos disembarking from an LCI(S) of 202 Flotilla on 6 June 1944; one man takes a header. The gangplanks were pushed out over rollers. Landing from these vulnerable craft, many of which were damaged or sunk on D-Day, could be wet and unpleasant. Although the bows were grounded, the swell lifted the stern so that the gangplanks see-sawed. (B5219)

Lieutenant Alex Sudborough, nineteen years old, of 45 (Royal Marines) Commando in LCI(S) 518:

> As we hit the beach, I went forrard to see if the brows had been shot over their rollers. The party of seamen – four or six – were a mass of duffel-coats, steel helmets, teeth, jaws, brains and blood. There was a sweet sickly smell, stronger than all the cordite, grease, and oil normally present in almost any small craft in action. I saw a rope trailing into the sea. Shouting 'Follow me', I swung myself over the side into what I expected to be three or four feet of water. In my panic, I had not ensured that the rope was made fast inboard; the loose end snaked across the deck as I, gripping the rope, neatly dropped like a plummet into a six-foot shell hole which the tide had covered. I was well and truly stuck in the sands of Normandy with eighteen inches of water over my head.
>
>   Help was quickly forthcoming. An RAMC medical orderly waded into the water and dragged me ashore to the cheers of those on board the craft who had the sense to make their exit in a more dignified way. Wading to the water's edge, I could not help noticing the number of battle-dressed bodies,

all face down, gently floating on the tide line surrounded by a pinkish tinge.
The sound of the Adjutant's hunting horn made me gather my wits,
impressing on me the need to make for the Commando RV.

On the extreme right of the British beachhead, 47 (Royal Marines)
Commando had been ordered to capture Port-en-Bessin, some six miles
west of Arromanches; a daunting task for lightly equipped Commandos,
whose maximum fighting strength was under 450 all ranks. It was
important to secure Port-en-Bessin early as the junction point between
the American and British sectors, and because it had been selected as the
terminal for Pluto. The port was very strongly defended, dominated by
three hills. After studying the problem, the Commando decided to land
on Jig Green beach, after it had been secured and cleared by 231 Brigade
of 50th Division, and move through German-held country to attack the
port from the rear.

The Commando embarked in fourteen LCAs from two LSIs, and the
run-in was uneventful until about 2,000 yards from the beach. Major
Paddy Donnell, then second-in-command:

It became obvious that Jig Green beach was deserted except for four Support
tanks under heavy fire. At about this time a 75mm battery on the high
ground above Le Hamel opened accurate fire on the LCAs. The CO ordered
a turn to port and all craft in some disorder, started running east, parallel to
the beach. At least one craft was hit and sunk, and it soon became a case of
every craft for itself. The beach was crowded with craft and all types of
vehicles and equipment, mostly wrecked or swamped. Each craft picked its
own landing place. Very few had a dry landing; most grounding off shore,
in some cases on obstacles in water so deep that the only way ashore was
to dump equipment and swim. One craft at least ran onto a mine, and
had its bows blown off. Of the fourteen craft, only two returned to the
LSI.

   The landing was a shambles. The Commando was spread over a frontage
of some 1,500 yards. As planned the Commando moved west, in groups of
boat-loads, along the road running parallel to the beach towards the RV, the
church in Le Hamel. It soon became obvious that Le Hamel was still in
enemy hands, and 231 Brigade was heavily involved clearing the town.

Donnell made contact with the commander of 231 Brigade who suggested they swing south to avoid Le Hamel, before returning to the
original route. By now it was possible to take stock.

The CO, four officers and 73 other ranks were missing, practically all the
bangalores and 3-inch mortar bombs had been sunk. X and B Troops were
reasonably dry and equipped, A Troop were complete, but had lost most of
their weapons, Q and Y Troop had each lost a craftload. There was only one
Vickers and one 3-inch mortar out of four of each, and the latter was
without a sight. Commando HQ was almost complete, but all the wireless
sets were doubtful starters.

Royal Marine Corporal Tandy's LCA had its steering wheel and telegraphs carried away by the hook on the wire just after being lowered by the parent ship. He steered the craft seven miles into the beach and seven miles back again with his foot as shown in this reconstruction. (A24146)

The Commando set off under the second-in-command. As they were moving round Le Hamel, the CO appeared, riding on an ammunition sledge behind an SP gun. That night after overcoming or bypassing pockets of enemy, the Commando established a firm base on Point 72, part of the high ground about two miles south of Port-en-Bessin. Many of the commandos were now armed with German weapons, and there was no shortage of ammunition for these.

Le Hamel proved a hard nut to crack. Major Warren, commanding C Company, 1st Hampshires assaulting Jig sector opposite Le Hamel:

I didn't sleep much on the night before we landed. I was rather
apprehensive. I hadn't got back into the rhythm of war; once you do, you
sleep very easily, you're very tired.

The AVREs on the beach all seemed to have been knocked out. We did not find the gaps we expected. The beach was raked with enfiladed fire, and there was an anti-tank gun in a concrete and steel emplacement in Le Hamel. The Germans did not show much sign of giving up. I realised we would have to gap our way through ourselves, using bangalores which we had with us. Casualties began to pile up. While gapping our way off the beach, I saw the CO limping badly. He had been hit by mortar fragments as he left his LCA. He told me to take command of the Battalion. A Company who should have landed close to Le Hamel, climbed the sea wall, and silenced the position, had almost ceased to exist as a company. We incorporated all the people we could find into C Company.

I decided we must deal with the Le Hamel position. Having gapped our way off the beach, we met a petard-equipped AVRE. I told the commander that I wanted his support in attacking Le Hamel. He fired his petard at the position, an old, reinforced sanatorium, and we assaulted and silenced it. This was a great relief to all concerned. In the fire plan, Le Hamel east was to receive the bombs of 200 Flying Fortresses. We found out later that the bombs had all fallen 700–800 yards inland. Even the effect of 2,000 rockets from the LCT(R) did not seem to have any great impact on the very strong German defences.

Major Goode, a company commander in the 2nd Glosters:

I have a clear recollection of one embrasure out of which a German officer had tried to climb. It had descended on him, squashing his top half, leaving his legs with a well-polished pair of boots protruding.

Trooper Austin Baker, in his C Squadron ARV, also landed on Gold beach opposite La Rivière, behind most of his Regiment, 4/7th Royal Dragoon Guards which landed in the first wave. His RV was the village of Ver-sur-Mer.

Captain Collins' scout car was first down the ramp and it was immediately knocked out by a shell. Collins was unhurt, but Steeles his driver, was wounded. All the rest of the vehicles, including the ARV, landed safely.

A number of DD tanks were still on the beach, but I couldn't see whose they were. Dabby, our commander, seemed to know where he was going fairly well, and in quite a short time we were off the beach, going up a track with a procession of other vehicles. There were grassy banks on either side, and notices bearing skulls and crossbones and the words 'Achtung Minen'. Before long we were in Ver-sur-Mer. We went straight through the village and out the other end. Quite suddenly, I realised that all the other vehicles had disappeared and we were quite alone, charging up a quiet country lane by ourselves. I knew this was wrong, because I had seen the orchard where we were to rendezvous on the map, and knew it was on the edge of the village. I told Dabby this, and had a bit of an argument – the first of many that I had with various commanders over similar things – before I managed to convince him. We turned round in a field about half a mile up the lane.

A DUKW loaded with ammunition swims off the ramp of an LST, en route to the beach.
(B5016)

On the way back to the village we met Muddy Waters with the leading troop of B Squadron, advancing up the road with their infantry. They had no idea anybody had gone ahead of them. In Ver we found Captain Collins waving us into an orchard opposite the original RV which was mined. Everybody seemed to have arrived safely. One C Squadron crew was there. Their tank had been swamped on landing, they had lost all their kit, and been soaked to the skin. They said it had been too rough for a DD landing and the tanks had done a deep wade instead, so all the months of DD training had been wasted.

Captain Collins announced his intention of travelling on the ARV, until he could get another vehicle of his own. I was rather pleased as he was a decent sort of chap, and less likely to get us lost than Dabby.

As A Company, 7th Green Howards, moved inland to Ver-sur-Mer, Private Tateson was carrying one of the radio sets:

Without warning, a salvo of gunfire landed right in the middle of the troops to our immediate left, followed by a second shortly afterwards. From messages being passed on the wireless, I learned that no one knew who was responsible, except that it was coming from behind us. When a third salvo descended with the most enormous crack, my signals training deserted me, and I sent the unauthorised message, 'Stop this fucking barrage'. By a complete coincidence, but to the flattery of my ego, the firing ceased. We later learned that it came from the Navy off shore, who did not realise we had advanced so far. Unfortunately, C Company had casualties as a result of this mistake.

Some badly damaged craft withdrawing from the beaches were rescued by ships on the bombardment line. Sub Lieutenant Pelly of HMS *Eglinton*:

I'll never forget the chaos and awfulness of landing craft returning out of control, full to almost sinking with a red mixture of blood, water and oil fuel, with legs and heads sticking out. One or two came alongside. We hauled the wounded out, mostly Canadians and Marines, and placed them in their awful suffering along the upper deck, doing what little we could. The wardroom was turned into a ward, so was the entire forehead mess deck – bottles of plasma tied up and hanging over nearly every man – the doctor and his assistants of stewards and stokers doing wonders.

Sergeant James Bellows, the battle-experienced Signals Platoon Sergeant of 1st Hampshires, was landed late. He was travelling in an LCT with part of Battalion Headquarters, three armoured engineer vehicles and two reconnaissance vehicles. It was, and is, normal practice to split battalion headquarters into more than one craft. The CO with his tactical headquarters lands early, while main headquarters, usually under the adjutant, lands some minutes later.

One of the crocodiles was first off, and went straight down. All you could see was the schnorkel and the top of the turret, so the water must have been about ten feet deep. One recce vehicle was next, and turned right. It went straight out to sea. We never saw it again. The next recce vehicle turned left. It got ashore safely. The armoured bulldozer went straight down. One wheel on the trailer caught the chain on the ramp, tipping the trailer over into the water. Men fell off, the trailer floated away. One of my signallers, bomb-happy since Italy, huddled under his gas cape shaking like a jelly. The naval officer said he was returning to England for repairs, nothing would persuade him to change his mind.

I hailed a nearby LCA, and he came to the ramp. We loaded our stores, including the Brigade rear link set on its trolley. I left the bomb-happy signaller behind. The LCA pulled in to within six feet of the beach, the ramp went down, and a sailor said we are among mines. I told them they would be all right. But they pulled off.

An LCT was approaching, with her ramp already down, and we hailed her. We transferred. Despite the obstacles, up the beach he goes. Down goes the ramp. At last we've made it. On arrival, I found I had the whole of the Battalion communications on my shoulders. The Signal Officer was bomb-happy and useless. It was not his fault. It's one of the worst wounds there is.

The landings of the follow-up brigades were in some cases not under fire, but did not pass without incident. The 8th Battalion the Durham Light Infantry had been issued with anti-gas trousers. These were an attempt to keep the soldiers' legs dry. The Brigadier had ordered these to be worn, after a landing exercise involving a long march inland in wet trousers, when both battalions of the DLI had developed sore, raw crutches. Of waterproof material, with an attached foot, they came up about chest high, and tied with tapes over the wearer's battle order. No one in the Battalion had seen them before. CSM Brown:

> After a couple of tries, the ship got within 200 yards of the beach, and stuck fast. A young American sailor swam ashore with a rope and some of the beach party hung on to it. We stepped in. The water was out of our depth for the first 100 yards. By hooking on to that rope, we got every man ashore. If it hadn't been for the rope we wouldn't have done it, wearing gas trousers, and some of us carrying bikes. When we got to the beach the gas trousers were full of water, like balloons. There we were standing like idiots trying to undo the tapes which had shrunk tight. If there had been any opposition on the beach the battalion would have been wiped out.

Men of 1st Battalion the Royal Norfolk Regiment, in 185 Brigade, a follow-up brigade in British 3rd Infantry Division, wading in from an LCI(L) 6 June 1944. (B5092)

[Unknown to Brown, after seeing the first party land, the senior company commander had ordered the remainder of C and D Companies to remove their gas trousers.]

I had to get off the beach as soon as possible, to the battalion 'hide' [sic] where we would all meet up. I asked one of the beach group if he had a knife; he produced a big jacknife with which he cut the trousers. In the 'hide' we had a self-inflicted wound in D Company. I heard a rifle shot. An old fellow of forty, a bundle of nerves, had shot himself in the hand.

I said, 'You've shot yourself, you bastard.'

He said, 'I'm sorry sergeant-major, I cannot go on.'

I replied, 'It's all right, leave your bundook [rifle] there. Get yourself back – you've been hit in the hand.'

I wasn't going to court martial him.

The bicycles had been useful to get to the 'hide' before the Battalion arrived. But it was pretty daft, when the Battalion moved off to try to bike alongside at a marching pace. So sometime on that first day, when we were stopped and out of sight of the Company Commander, I asked a passing tank to run over our bikes.

Major Peter Martin supporting 151 Infantry Brigade landing as follow-up on Gold beach, had been told:

'Your day will not end when 151 Brigade reaches its objectives. Your company will come under command 8th Armoured Brigade, for a lightning dash forward to Villers-Bocage, an important communications centre, on high ground twenty miles inland. There you will form a firm base and pivot for future action.'

We landed on time, walked up to our assembly area behind Ver-sur-Mer and met our transport. Everything was going to plan. There was a little sniping, and the odd mortar bomb. I could hear 231 Brigade battling it out in the Arromanches area. We sat around in the assembly area until about 14.00. Two mobile columns from 6 and 9 DLI pushed forward to the line of the road Caen–Bayeux, without any opposition. Long before nightfall the Brigade had reached its D-Day objectives. I was supposed, at this stage, to join the 8th Armoured Brigade column, consisting of the Sherwood Rangers and 24th Lancers in Shermans, 147 Field Regiment Royal Artillery, 1st Battalion the Dorsets in trucks, and an anti-tank battery of the Northumberland Hussars. We were due to RV just north of St Leger. As all was quiet I went to the RV, and from there to the Bayeux–Caen road.

I said to my jeep driver, 'Shall we just potter down to Bayeux, and liberate it?' He thought this was a good idea. I thought it must be in our hands by now. In the outskirts a Frenchman whistled at us, and pointed down the road 'Boche, Boche'. We did a quick turn, and were driving back the way we had come when we were machine-gunned by an American fighter. We dived for the ditch, but one of the tyres was holed. We returned to Brigade HQ after quickest wheel change outside a Grand Prix meeting.

Here we were told that the move of the armoured column would not take

place, as 1st Dorsets were still heavily engaged on the beaches, as were 8th Armoured Brigade. So after all our apprehension about murder on the beaches, it had been a real 'doddle'; the quietest day of the war as far as 2nd Cheshires were concerned.

Others had been having a busier time. Number 4 Commando had been tasked by Brigadier Cass of 8th Infantry Brigade with destroying a battery in Ouistreham, and capturing the town. Captain Patterson joined them in the assembly area by the beach:

> I found the unit assembling in some confusion among the buildings. Someone gave me a swig of rum, which did me good. Lance-Corporal Cunningham put a dressing on my leg. It turned out to be a lucky wound through the muscles and tendons behind the knee joint, which had missed the popliteal artery very narrowly. The little bit of shell in my buttock made me very stiff, but it was not worth bothering about. Soon we moved off through the minefield and wire to the main east–west road leading straight into Ouistreham. The road was under heavy mortar fire, and I came on six of our men lying dead only about 100 yards along the road at the corner of a

Number 4 Commando engaged in house-to-house fighting in the streets of Ouistreham, supported by Sherman DD tanks. This is a still from a film shot by Sergeant George Laws of the Army Film and Photographic Unit. (MH2012)

copse. We hurried on at the end of the column. I was very lame, but a Marine carried my rucksack and gave me an arm. The gaps between the houses were my trouble, it was unwise to linger there.

About 200 yards further on, we passed two more of our chaps, one dead, the other almost gone with his head smashed. I pushed his helmet over his face and went on. A mortar bomb had severely wounded another of our men in the shoulder. I nearly gave up on him, as his shoulder was practically severed and blood was gushing from it. With some trouble we got the bleeding under control with finger pressure in the neck, and holding on to this point, we put him on a stretcher, carrying him to where the assaulting troops had left their rucksacks about 300 yards further on.

Here I set up my RAP on a patch of grass between some villas and under some pine trees. The attack on the battery and the casino was soon well under way. I was very preoccupied with my badly wounded man. I packed the wound as best I could, before giving him a pint of plasma, which brought his pulse round, although I thought it was going to be too late. By this time casualties were pouring in, and I was hard at it until late afternoon.

The battle died down at about 11.00 hours, and the troops began to reassemble for the move to the Orne bridges. The Troop leaders reported the numbers missing. We had suffered heavily, about 150 all ranks killed or wounded. The French doctor was among the dead, killed by a burst of fire from the Casino as he was tying up someone.

I remained in Ouistreham for the rest of D-Day. I drove around the town in a jeep collecting the wounded, becoming increasingly cautious when it became clear that the only troops in town were the Germans.

Eventually the Germans became very frisky, shooting from the direction of the Casino, the lock gates and the battery area. I went to the beachhead with a plea for troops to clear them. Soon a column of AVREs came down the road, and following my directions, discouraged the Germans, most of whom surrendered, except for about fifty in the Casino area. These were rounded up in the morning. As soon as it was dark, the Boche began air attacks on the beach. I dozed rather fitfully in a shell hole on the edge of the road, deriving slight comfort from the fact that the drivers of the tanks rumbling past my head had not yet learnt the continental rule of the road, and still drove on the left. I was so exhausted, my wounds were so stiff and sore, that I preferred to stay in my little shell hole, with tracks grinding within a few feet of my head, than attempt moving to somewhere off the road.

By nightfall the Allies had gained a foothold on the Continent of Europe. Surprise had been achieved, the troops had fought with spirit and determination. Losses had been lower than had been expected, although that was little consolation to the wounded and the relatives of the dead. All assaulting divisions were ashore, but not all D-Day objectives had been achieved.

There have been a number of reasons advanced for the failure to

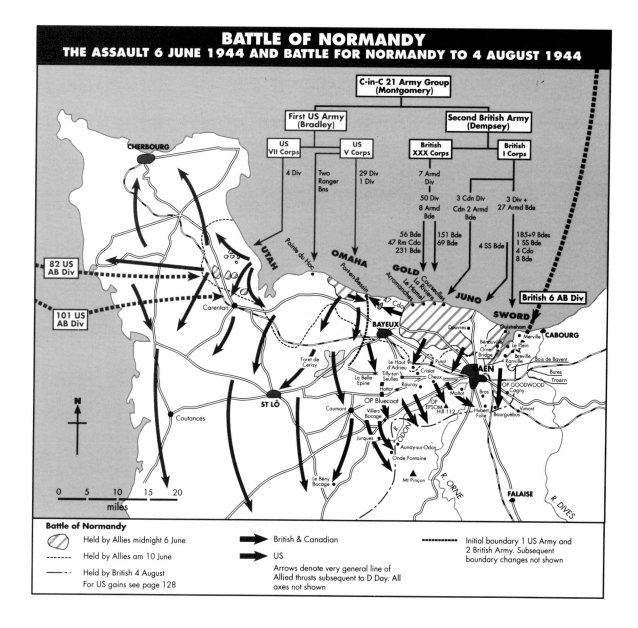

BATTLE OF NORMANDY
THE ASSAULT 6 JUNE 1944 AND BATTLE FOR NORMANDY TO 4 AUGUST 1944

C-in-C 21 Army Group (Montgomery)

First US Army (Bradley)

Second British Army (Dempsey)

US VII Corps

US V Corps

British XXX Corps

British I Corps

4 Div

Two Ranger Bns

29 Div
1 Div

7 Armd Div

50 Div
8 Armd Bde

3 Cdn Div
Cdn 2 Armd Bde

3 Div +
27 Armd Bde

56 Bde
47 Rm Cdo
231 Bde

151 Bde
69 Bde

4 SS Bde

185+9 Bdes
1 SS Bde
4 Cdo
8 Bde

CHERBOURG

82 US AB Div

101 US AB Div

British 6 AB Div

UTAH

Pointe du Hoc

OMAHA

Port-en-Bessin

Arromanches

Le Hamel

La Rivière

Courseulles

GOLD

JUNO

SWORD

47 Cdo

BAYEUX

Carentan

Douvres

Ouistreham

Merville

CABOURG

Bénouville
Orne Bridge

Le Plein
Ranville

Bréville

Bois de Bavent

Foret de Cerisy

Le Haut d'Adrieu

Tilly-sur-Seulles

Cristot

Putot

Cheux

Rauray

Bures

Troarn

La Belle Epine

Hottot

CAEN

OP GOODWOOD
Cagny

ST LÔ

Coutances

OP Bluecoat

Caumont

Villers Bocage

OP EPSOM
Hill 112

Maltot

Bras

Hubert Folie

Vimont

Bourguébus

Jurques

Aunay-sur-Odon

R. ODON

Onde Fontaine

Mt Pinçon

R. ORNE

FALAISE

R. DIVES

Le Bény Bocage

N

0   5   10   15   20
miles

Battle of Normandy

Held by Allies midnight 6 June

Held by Allies am 10 June

Held by British 4 August
For US gains see page 128

British & Canadian

US

Arrows denote very general line of Allied thrusts subsequent to D Day. All axes not shown

Initial boundary 1 US Army and 2 British Army. Subsequent boundary changes not shown

take Caen in particular. Because of the strong winds piling the sea up on to the beach, it was only thirty feet wide at high tide, instead of thirty yards. The congestion, both on the beach and on narrow roads bordered with uncleared minefields, delayed the Staffordshire Yeomanry from marrying up with the 185 Infantry Brigade whose objective was Caen. Without armour the Brigade had no hope of advancing all the way to Caen, although an attempt was made. Cass's 8th Infantry Brigade have been criticized for being too slow to clear two German strong points which blocked the way, but these could have been bypassed by 185 Brigade, as they were by Lovat's 1st Special Service Brigade.

Despite the disappointment over the failure to take, or at least mask, Caen, the link-up with 6th Airborne Division was achieved, and the left flank was secure. This is more than can be said about the situation on

The highly respected and much loved Major-General T. G. Rennie who commanded 3rd Infantry Division, an assault division, on D-Day, and was wounded shortly after. Montgomery brought him back from convalescence to command the battle-weary 51st Highland Division, which he restored to its former efficiency. He is wearing the Highland Division Flash in this picture. His Division was an assault division for the Rhine crossing, where he was killed. (BU1518)

Omaha beach. Here a desperate struggle had secured a precarious toehold. At times the outcome had swung in the balance. Inspired leadership by individuals, the fighting qualities of the United States 1st Infantry Division (The Big Red One), and fire support from destroyers closing the beach saved the day at Omaha.

There were still gaps between the Second British Army, V US Corps and VII US Corps. There were still pockets of enemy resistance within all beachhead areas to be mopped up. There was still a dangerous salient at Douvres between the Canadians and I British Corps.

Fortunately the German reaction had been slow and unco-ordinated. Only 21st Panzer Division had counter-attacked that day, and the Douvres salient was a result of their work. There were reports that 12th SS Panzer Division was moving west from the area of Lisieux and Evreux.

Montgomery ordered First US Army (Bradley) to complete the capture of its D-Day objectives, secure Carentan and Isigny in order to link up its beachheads, then to thrust across the base of the Cotentin peninsula to isolate Cherbourg as a prelude to its reduction. Second British Army was to continue the battle to secure Caen, link up with the Americans at Port-en-Bessin, and expand the bridgehead across the Bayeux–Caen road.

Sapper Lane, whose Squadron was to build two Bailey bridges across the Orne and the Caen Canal, had arrived at the two bridges seized by the 52nd Light Infantry, with a small group of Royal Engineers

before Lovat. He was ordered to take up a defensive position with his bren in a German slit trench near the Canal Bridge. As night fell:

> I was not particularly cheered by the company of corpses close to me. The most gruesome of the three was a German who had his brains blown out through a jagged hole in his helmet. I was a cold, frightened, confused, terribly tired and hungry, not very brave young soldier. Before being swallowed up by the night, I reflected on the long, long day called D-Day, and consoled myself with the thought that if D plus 1 was perhaps a tenth as bad, I should only have to survive a mere ten possibilities of being killed.

Corporal Ferris had landed by glider earlier that evening at Ranville, with the rest of his Battalion, 1st Royal Ulster Rifles. He was sent on patrol from his defensive position by the Orne Canal to investigate

> a farm cottage close to us. We crawled most of the way and charged from close in. Someone on my left fired a burst of Sten, resulting in a loud metallic impact. I heard a voice just above a whisper, 'that sentry had a suit of armour on.' Then a louder voice, 'Suit of armour my foot, you just shot a bleeding dustbin.' The cottage was empty, we just flopped down and laughed like hell.

Men of the United States 1st Infantry Division (The Big Red One) from drowned craft clinging to obstacles off Omaha beach. The casualties were so high on this beach it became known as 'Bloody Omaha'. Taken by the famous war photographer Robert Capa. (AP25724)

CHAPTER THREE

'... A good and firm lodgement ...'

EXPANDING THE BRIDGEHEAD

Vickers medium machine-guns of 2nd Cheshires in the area of Tilly-sur-Seulles in mid July 1944. The number one is ready to fire the gun. The dial sight on the gun shows that it has been engaging an indirect target, i.e. out of sight, or is registering Defensive Fire tasks. The steam rising from the far gun's condenser can is an indication that it has just fired. With Mark 8Z ammunition, the Vickers had a maximum range of 4,500 yards. The nearest man, the number two, holds a liner (box) of belted ammunition ready to reload. A Thermos flask stands under his right elbow. (B6940)

With the morning came the task of linking up and expanding the bridgehead. The Allies had to clear enough elbow room to enable them to develop their full power, using follow-up formations as these poured ashore. The story of the next two and a half months is of relentless pressure to maintain the initiative and gain ground in preparation for the breakout. From the outset, Montgomery intended that the British on the left would, with a series of offensives, draw in the German armour. This would allow the Americans on the right to clear the Cotentin peninsula, capture Cherbourg, and then burst out to the south in an armoured torrent. By engaging the German Army south and west of the River Seine, Montgomery sought their destruction. Hitler, by forcing his generals to accept battle on his adversaries' terms, ensured that Montgomery's aim would be realized. It was to be the greatest and most decisive battle in the Second World War in the West. Montgomery's soldiers were to find the fighting tough. But their commander's path was also set about with enemies of a different kind; a coterie, mainly of Eisenhower's staff at Supreme Headquarters Allied Expeditionary Force (SHAEF), who, failing to comprehend the strategy underpinning Montgomery's plans, constantly carped and attempted to undermine him.

As German divisions moved to rope off the Allies, and throw them back into the sea, the fighting intensified.

There was little sleep for those off the Normandy beachhead that first night, and for nights afterwards. Lieutenant James Holladay commanded a troop equipped with 40mm Bofors and 20mm Oerlikon anti-aircraft guns. They travelled to Normandy in the merchant ship *Empire Bunting*. On arrival, the ship was to be sunk as part of the Gooseberry for the Canadian Juno beach, off Courseulles. His troop was to remain on board as part of the anti-aircraft defence of the beachhead. All the Gooseberry ships were fitted with charges below the waterline. With holes blown in the hull, and sea-cocks opened, they would settle on the bottom, decks awash; only superstructure and gun mountings clear. As *Empire Bunting* approached, he wrote in his diary:

> *7 June (D+1):* Directed to our waiting position and anchor. No sign of fighting on beaches four miles off, but can hear infantry and tanks talking on the wireless.

> *8 June (D+2):* As soon as fighter cover disappears – at midnight – the fun begins. Enemy a/c (aircraft) over beaches and terrific Bofors barrage goes up. Red chains of floating lights covering the sky for miles like a Brock's benefit. We open on a FW and an ME, & score a hit on the FW. It finally crashes. Day shows two or three LCTs sunk, one with broken ends sticking out of the water quarter of a mile away. One destroyer badly hit – funnel gone. We are untouched. We move closer in to shore and RN officer begins to plant the Gooseberry. An assault landing craft mysteriously blows up a few hundred yards from us and disappears with all hands. At 23.00 the merchant crew is taken off in Yankee tug; we stay on and they blow us all

**Gooseberry
blockships sunk off
one of the two
American beaches
soon after D-Day.**
(EA41376)

up [sic]. Ship settles smoothly, but main deck almost entirely awash. Life is to be very uncomfortable. Sleep in crowded wireless cabin. Another terrific barrage, and we put up a noisesome smoke screen, which chokes TSM Phillips.

9 June (D+3): Another early morning sneak raid by FWs. Our Gooseberry begins to function and landing craft huddle round us for shelter. What a target! Our exact position one and a half miles off Courseulles and Bernières.

10 June (D+4): Heavy air raids in morning for 3 hours continuously. Town on coast set on fire and Jerry bombed us in the light of it. Bombs within yards of us all round. Manned Oerlikon myself. Two planes down – we claim a share in one. Flak absolutely incredible. Horrid explosions all night.

Ashore, there was little time for rest, even for those in D-Day assault units. Corporal G. E. Hughes of 1st Hampshires, part of the right-hand Brigade in the British Second Army:

7 Wed: Still going. Dug in at 02.00 hrs. Away again at 05.30. NO FOOD. Writing few notes before we go into another village. CO out of action,

The completed British Mulberry off Arromanches, showing from left to right: the floating piers and pier-heads running into the beach; anchored ships and craft; the breakwater consisting of a line of sunken concrete Phoenixes and Gooseberries (sunken blockships). Each Mulberry was the size of Dover harbour. (MH2405)

adjutant killed, platoon sergeant lost. I do platoon sergeant. More later.

8 Thur: 07.30 fire coming from village. Village cleared. Prisoners taken. Night quite good but German snipers lurking in wood. Had 2 hours sleep, second rest since the 6th.

9 Fri: 06.00 hrs, went on wood clearing. Germans had flown. Only one killed for our morning s work. We are now about 8–10 miles inland. 7th Armoured Div ahead. PROMOTED TO SGT.

10 Sat: T-God I have come so far, we have lost some good men. Our brigade was only one to gain full objectives on D-Day. The French people gave us a good welcome, had wine. Our casualties high. The landing was terrible. Had a near miss. Passed through Bayeux last night. Dive bombers about also snipers. MONTY AND DIV COMMANDER CONGRATULATES BATT.

South of Port-en-Bessin, 47 (RM) Commando attempted to contact the
American artillery whose support figured so prominently in the plan for
the capture of the port; to no avail. Eventually communication was
established with 231 Brigade and ships off shore, including HMS
Emerald. The attack started at 16.00, supported by naval and air bombardment, smoke from one of 231 Brigade's field batteries, and the one
Vickers and one mortar without a sight. The fighting in the town was
confused and bitter. Having secured one feature dominating the town,
the eastern feature was captured at the second attempt by about midnight. The Troop Commander, Captain Cousins, having found a route
through the wire, was killed leading the attack. The next day the
Commando was relieved; of the 431 who had embarked in the LCAs on
D-Day, 276 remained. The accumulation of set-backs the Commando

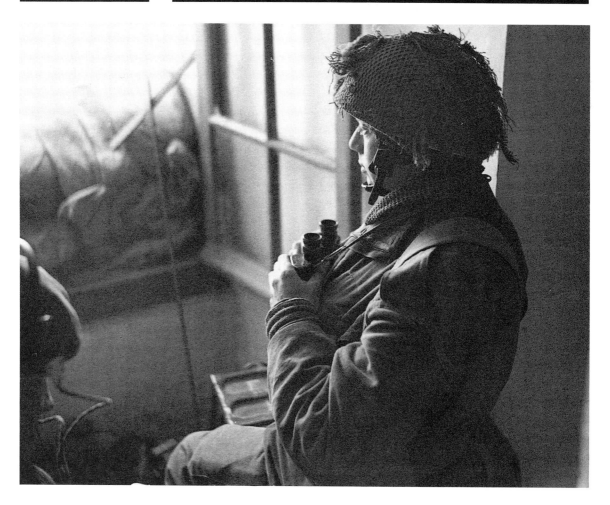

Captain F. Vere Hodge MC, Royal Artillery, a Naval Gunfire Forward Observer with 6th Airborne Division. He had fought in Sicily and Italy with 1st Airborne Division. (B5866)

had encountered, such as losing weapons and equipment on landing, might have tempted less well-trained and led units to withdraw from the contest, on the grounds that it was all too difficult. General Montgomery visited to congratulate them, before they moved on to join 4th Special Service Brigade, under command of 6th Airborne Division which was holding the left flank of 2nd British Army, east of the Orne. As more German formations arrived, the pressure on this vulnerable flank increased. Brigadier James Hill's 3rd Parachute Brigade, faced by 346 Infantry Division, experienced

> five days of the hardest fighting I had seen in the war. A narrow road ran along a ridge. We had to hold this ridge at all costs. If the Germans had secured it, the bridgehead at Ranville would have been untenable. Involved in the fighting were the 9th Parachute Battalion, 1st Canadian Parachute Battalion and 5th Battalion Black Watch. Imagine what it was like for a 9th Battalion soldier. They had never seen a shot fired in anger until 48 hours before. Their average age was 20. They had suffered an appalling night drop on D-Day. They had stormed the Merville Battery, and attacked Le Plein. They arrived on the ridge at midnight on 7th June, 90 strong, having set off

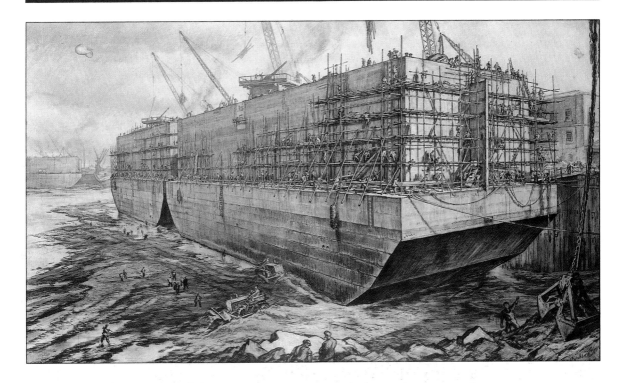

Building a caisson for Mulberry Harbour by Muirhead Bone

The figures of the construction workers give an indication of the size of these concrete caissons which formed the outer breakwater for each of the two Mulberries. (LD4333)

A glider pilot at the controls by Leslie Cole.

This depicts the view from behind the pilot, looking through the cockpit at the tug aircraft. The Deputy Chief of the Air Staff wrote on the subject of flying the large military gliders: 'It is equivalent to force-landing the largest aircraft without engine aid . . . there is no higher test of pilot skill.' (LD2644)

A stick of paratroopers jumping at Ringway 1945 by William Dring.

Ringway was the training centre for British parachute soldiers. Some of the stick have already gone. The man about the exit is in the classic 'stand in the door' position, one hand on the door frame, the other grasping the top of his kitbag strapped to his leg. The strap connecting the parachute to the static line can be seen running from the top of the left-hand man's parachute pack. The despatcher, at that time usually the navigator, can be seen peering over the shoulder of the man in the door. If this had been an operational jump, steel helmets would be covered with camouflage netting. (LD5471)

Off the Normandy Beaches by Stephen Bone.

The view from a warship of landing-craft and landing ships closing the beaches, with barrage balloons overhead. (LD4381)

The landings in Normandy, Arromanches, D-Day plus 20, 26th June 1944 by Barnett Freedman. (LD5816)

A tank of C Squadron 4/7th Royal Dragon Guards at La Folliot Farm, 20th June 1944 by Edward Raymond Payne.

The scene depicts a typical squadron leaguer in daylight. The tanks are Shermans. The crews are maintaining their tanks, cleaning guns, re-ammunitioning, and brewing up. In the foreground is a petrol cooker, and what looks like an army issue thermos flask. Trooper Austin Baker, who appears in the text, was in C Squadron. (LD5454)

A shower-bath at the Rest Centre, Luc-sur-Mer, Normandy, June 1944 by Thomas Hennell. (LD4267)

Two destroyed bridges with 'Churchill Bridge' alongside, Caen 1944 by Thomas Hennell.

The bridges were destroyed by the Germans retreating across the Orne. (LD4448)

First light stand-to. When all the world seems to hold its breath – and listen and wait by E. Shepherd from his sketchbook on north-west Europe 1944.

This depicts a Vickers machine-gun crew. (LD5203)

German anti-personnel mines were sown lavishly along road verges, in ditches, and anywhere infantry were likely to walk, causing many casualties throughout the campaign. Two members of an RAF beach party examine a Schumine which, being made of wood, except for the detonator, was difficult to find with a mine-detector. (CL293)

from England with over 600 officers and soldiers. They were minus most of their equipment, and not exactly fresh.

In the first eight days of the battle of Normandy, my Brigade, which started around 2,000 strong, lost about 50 officers and 1,000 other ranks. We had trained to fight in the type of country in which we found ourselves. We were fit, well trained, young and well disciplined. We had few cases of battle shock. It is easy for me to talk like this. If you were in an ordinary infantry battalion, and you lost a lot of chaps in an attack, knowing you had to go on the next day pushing on. You are sent 60 to 90 people, as reinforcements, who know nothing about your battalion. They are shoved into the line and expected to fight the next day. It does not work.

The debate over the wisdom of Montgomery's decision to employ three battle-experienced divisions, the 50th, the 51st Highland and 7th Armoured in Normandy, continues to this day. There is little doubt that many of the troops in these divisions were weary after years of fighting in the Desert, Sicily and Italy. At least two of the divisions, 51st and 7th Armoured, seem to have been ill prepared to adapt their tactics to the very different terrain in Normandy. They were slow and unwilling to take risks. However, it would be grossly unfair to lay the blame for the slow rate of progress of the British Second Army on D-Day, and until the break out, at the door of these two divisions. There were many other factors.

Junior leadership in some units was patchy. Among the reasons for this was the drain on the finite number of potential leaders among those of military age in the British population to provide aircrew. Commandos and airborne units also creamed off the most adventurous spirits. Many of the private soldiers in these units, were at least NCO material by normal infantry division standards. Lack of good junior leaders could lead to a high rate of casualties in company and battalion commanders. The 50th Infantry Division was not plagued by the problems encountered by its fellow veteran divisions. But, in his excellent book, *Decision in Normandy*, the American author Carlo d'Este includes an extract from a very experienced New Zealand officer attached to 50th Division, written towards the end of the campaign in Normandy:

> The high percentage of officer casualties is due to the necessity of them being ALWAYS in front to direct advances in the difficult country. Since D-Day the [50th] Div has lost 2 Brigadiers and 12 Commanding Officers . . . and a great number of Coy Cmdrs and Senior NCOs.

The standard set by the platoon commander was crucial. Most but not all were up to the mark. A sergeant of 8th DLI had a platoon commander who had been a school teacher. He had little time for him. Returning from a standing patrol, the officer ignored his sergeant's advice, and taking a wrong turning, ran into an ambush. In the ensuing mayhem, the patrol abandoned its radio. That night, the sergeant was ordered to take out a reconnaissance patrol to recover the radio, covered by a fighting patrol led by this platoon commander. At a pre-arranged point the two patrols, having left together according to plan, split and took different routes. Thanks to bad navigation by the platoon commander, the two patrols clashed. In the bout of what today we call 'friendly fire', one of the sergeant's men, a lance-corporal, was hit. As the sergeant pulled the pin from a grenade, the officer jumped through the hedge:

> I got up from where I had been lying, and said, 'I've got a 36 grenade here, I've thrown the pin away, and I've got a good mind to put it down your battle-dress blouse front.' At that I threw it away. When I saw that my Lance-Corporal was dead, I lost my temper, and told the platoon commander that the first time he got in front of me, I would shoot him. I was sent for by the CO, who asked what had happened. Next morning the officer had been posted. Many of the officers were straight from OCTU, and wouldn't be told. Our CO used to tell them to take advice from their platoon sergeants. Our company commander was experienced and very good. He made decisions quickly and was always right. We had two company commanders the whole Battalion trusted and would have always followed.

Morale, the incidence of battle fatigue and general fighting effectiveness of units were factors of the quality of leadership and training. Confidence, or lack of it, in equipment was also an important ingredient in determining whether or not troops would press on or hesitate. The majority of British and American armoured units were equipped with Shermans. Trooper Austin Baker:

> The tank's top speed varied with the kind of engine fitted, and could be as low as 20 m.p.h. or as high as 30. It weighed 30 tons. Some Shermans were fitted in British factories with 17-pounder anti-tank guns, replacing the 75mm. There was very little room in the turrets of these tanks, known as 'Fireflies', because the guns were so much larger than the 75mm, and co-drivers had to be dispensed with to make room for the ammunition.
>
> The Sherman was no match for most German tanks. The 75mm could not penetrate the heavy ones at all, while the German 88mm, or long 75mm, could not fail to knock out a Sherman at almost any range – certainly 2,000 yards. The 17-pounder was capable of knocking out a Tiger or a Panther at a moderate range, and was comparable to the German guns, but the Sherman was still at a disadvantage because of its much inferior armour.
>
> Anti-tank shot does not depend on an explosion to penetrate a tank's armour. An ordinary HE shell would not affect a Sherman, unless it was very large – a 6-inch shell for instance. The armour-piercing projectile effectiveness depends largely on its velocity. The damage inside a tank is caused by the projectile tearing through, and by flying fragments of armour spraying around inside, where the crew are so huddled together that it is unlikely that all will escape. A petrol-engined Sherman would almost always catch fire because of the vapour inside. The tremendous impact of the projectile on armour would generate tremendous heat, producing something very like an explosion.

One can only express boundless admiration for the British, Canadian and American tank crews' persistence in taking part in the contest, knowing the discrepancy between their tanks and those of the enemy. Although less vulnerable, the Cromwells and Churchills with which some British units were equipped were outgunned by the German tanks. Baker, describing one of the many brewed-up tanks he saw:

> A brewed-up tank is always a grim sight – the outside is usually a dull, dirty rust colour, and the inside is a blackened shambles. There is a queer indescribable smell. The bottom of Jonah's tank had been blown right out, and we could peer inside from underneath. There was no trace of anybody in the turret, but some stuff in the driving seat that must have been Walker. There was a body on the ground by the left-hand track. Somebody had thrown a groundsheet over it, but we lifted it off. It was probably Brigham Young, but it was impossible to recognise him – he was burnt quite black all over, and only parts of his anklets remained of his clothes. Nobody ever found any sign of Wally.

The lack of sufficient armoured personnel carriers (APC) for the infantry accompanying tanks was a grave disadvantage. In Normandy the Canadians converted priests to APCs (known as unfrocked priests), by removing the 105mm artillery piece. By the end of 1944, Kangaroos, based on a Sherman chassis, were produced. In the closing months of the war, the Americans produced the M39 APC. All were open at the top, and the troops inside vulnerable to air-burst shells, as were half-tracks and carriers. Infantry sometimes rode the tanks, or followed in trucks. Whatever their mode of transport, once battle was joined, they dismounted, and reverted to the means of mobility of foot soldiers since antiquity, that of the boot. On the move they were totally unprotected. APCs would have provided protection against artillery, mortar splinters and small arms in the attack, and during the often precarious time reorganizing on the objective. In the closest bocage country, APCs might well have been a liability. But elsewhere they would have speeded up the tempo, by enabling the infantry to keep up. Too often tanks outstripped the infantry, to be engaged by well-concealed anti-tank guns and panzerfaust (a hand-held anti-tank rocket launcher), which should have been winkled out by infantry with tanks and artillery working as a team. Trooper Baker:

> It was the Regiment's first set-piece attack with infantry, and it was planned, just as in the text books, to have tanks (B Squadron) leading, followed by infantry, followed by more tanks (C Squadron). This arrangement proved to be a dismal failure. The Jerries lay low until the tanks had passed, and opened up on the infantry with Spandaus. Then they set on the cut-off tanks.

Given the experience gained by the British in armoured warfare over the previous five years, the failure to provide APCs was a major oversight.

There was another important factor in the slow rate of advance by British, and American, troops at times. Despite the years of bloodletting in Russia, the Germans, without the air power and other benefits enjoyed by the Allies, fought with ferocity and skill. The static coastal defence formations, filled with large numbers of the medically down-graded, and Russians, Ukrainians and others encountered on landing, were a totally different proposition from the panzer grenadier, panzer and parachute divisions; whether SS or Wehrmacht they were led by shrewd, battle-experienced officers and NCOs. In modern parlance the Germans were outstanding at the tactical level, sometimes good at the operational level; only their strategy was flawed.

General Freddie Graham, then a Captain and Intelligence Officer of 2nd Battalion the Argyll and Sutherland Highlanders in 15th Scottish Division:

> I believe they were unquestionably the best army in the world. They fought with great skill. Their use of ground was remarkable. Their ability to plug gaps by junior commanders taking the initiative, without waiting for orders

German infantry, including a man carrying a panzerfaust, move into an ambush position in Normandy. (Captured German film FLM2404)

Panzerfaust in position, and an American tank appears in the gap in the hedge. (Captured German film FLM2405)

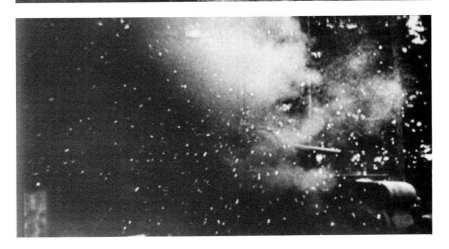

A hit. (Captured German film FLM2400)

from on high was far superior to ours. Much later, when the German army had been defeated in France, pulled back over the Seine and chased into Holland and Belgium, they were able to produce a cohesive defence against us by bringing in remnants of batteries, regiments and battalions. They formed battle groups on an *ad hoc* basis to produce a swift and resolute defence. If the German Army had not been bled white in the East, and continued to be engaged by the Russians, I do not know how we would have defeated them.

Lieutenant-Colonel Alastair Pearson, commanding 8th Parachute Battalion, respected, but was not in the least overawed by, his adversaries, describing his aggressive tactics against 21st Panzer Division, and others, in the Bois de Bavent:

Practically everyone was out on patrol every night to give the impression that we were very strong, which we were not, and to keep the enemy off balance. It is easy to knock the German off his stride. He is a great book man, very well organised, but if you disorganise him he finds it hard to reorganise. You have got to keep hitting him, not necessarily cause many casualties, just keep at them.

Others, like Sydney Jary, not in airborne or commando units, would agree with this and would add that the Germans disliked fighting at night. But in the end, the difference between success and failure often hung upon the quality of training and leadership, from CO down to corporal.

By now, the Americans had cut the Cotentin peninsula, and were advancing on Cherbourg. On the left flank of Second British Army, by 13 June, very little headway had been made in developing the bridgehead beyond that established by 6th Airborne and 3rd Infantry Division D-Day and D plus 1. In the centre, the Canadians threw back the attempts to break through to the sea by 12th SS Panzer Division (Hitler Jugend) in a day of bitter fighting. On the British right, 50th Division advanced through Bayeux, abandoned by the Germans on D-Day, and pressed on to Tilly-sur-Seulles. The Villers-Bocage operation between 11 and 14 June, by the recently arrived 7th Armoured Division, supported by 50th Division, did not achieve the objectives set by Montgomery. Although 7th Armoured reached the town of Villers-Bocage, they were eventually ejected by 2nd Panzer Division and forced back about five miles.

Meanwhile 50th Division could make very little progress beyond La Belle Epine and Tilly-sur-Seulles. 7th Armoured Division were ordered to hold, while 50th Division and 49th Division, which had landed on 13 June, were to strike towards Tilly and Hottot. By 19 June, after heavy fighting, Tilly was captured.

Tom Tateson, of 7th Green Howards:

The bocage in which the 50th Division was now fighting was entirely

Infantry soldiers of The Royal Scots Fusiliers, either of 15th Scottish Division or 49th West Riding Division, in long grass in a Normandy orchard wait for the artillery barrage to lift before advancing. (B5950)

different from anything they had encountered before. There are many woods and orchards. It is granite country, and over the centuries the peasants had built the outcropping chunks of granite into the fences and hedges. The undergrowth has grown up through the rocks, so that every hedge is a natural fortified obstacle. The fields are small, and the roads are often sunk well below the level of the fields. The houses and farms are built of granite, and each is a ready-made fortress.

On 7 June, Major Peter Martin waited for news of the armoured column to dash to seize Villers-Bocage:

Not until 23.30 on 7 June did orders arrive to assemble the armoured column at first light on 8 June; to advance to Villers-Bocage. I am quite certain after my experience on 6 June, that if an armoured column had set off on the afternoon of D-Day, there would have been absolutely nothing to stop it. But having wasted 36 hours, it was much too much to expect an easy drive to Villers-Bocage.

We assembled, but no move was made until 10.00 hours. As we advanced, we found that the whole complex of hamlets that make up the village of Audrieu was held and 1st Dorsets was committed to fighting through as a battalion. So we didn't get very far that day.

All that night, 1st Dorsets battled away in Audrieu, and as there was nothing for my company to do, I went to sleep. Shortly after midnight, I was ordered to report to the Brigadier. He told me that a squadron of Sherwood Rangers, by following a circuitous route, had reached Point 103, a dominating feature south of Le Haut d'Audrieu, the southernmost hamlet. My company and the Northumberland Hussars anti-tank battery were to move across country to join the Sherwood Foresters, who had sent a troop of tanks back to lead us up. We had a nightmare journey through enemy territory. By 02.30 we were up on Point 103.

At first light German tanks approached from the south, engaged the forward tanks of the Sherwood Rangers, knocking out some. The remainder withdrew to the reverse slope of Point 103, leaving my two platoons completely isolated.

The enemy tanks stood off about 120 yards away, hull down, and shelled our bank with high explosive. These burst in the trees above the platoon positions, raining shrapnel down on the gun positions, causing casualties. On several occasions, when the Tigers cruised too far forward, with turrets open, our machine-gunners fired at them to make them close down. The situation was precarious, because if the enemy put in a determined attack from the south, he would be right on top of us before encountering our tanks or anti-tank guns. So we were very cheered when soon after midday, recce parties from the 1st Dorsets arrived to say that Audrieu was being cleared, and the Battalion would soon come to join us. They also said the 8th DLI was to come under command of 8th Armoured Brigade, and was to capture St Pierre. At about that time, one of my platoons came up on the wireless and asked for help with evacuating a seriously wounded corporal. The only way was by jeep over an open field being shelled like fury. I thought I'd better drive the jeep myself. I told my driver to get out. To my disappointment, instead of saying, 'No, sir. I will go,' he said, 'Right, sir', and got out.

I drove the jeep to a gap in the hedge of the field where the shells were bursting. I remember saying, 'Oh God, please stop the shells. If you stop them, I'll be good for always.' They stopped. I got the corporal out. Many times during the war one promised one would be a better person if one was allowed to survive. The promises did not last all that long.

The Reverend Leslie Skinner, with the Sherwood Rangers:
Thursday 8 June: In action for first time as a Regiment [since returning from the Middle East]. Attack on Point 103.
Late evening Lt Verner brought in, sniper wound to left chest – serious. Doctor dressed wound and I helped evacuate Verner to ADS riding on rear door and bumper all way, holding bottle giving blood drip – nearly five miles of rough going.
Friday 9 June: News of death Captain Douglas on forward slopes Point 103. CO refused permission for me to go forward to recover body – enemy dug in with tank support. News death Lt Peter Pepler on same slopes as Douglas. Clearing area forward of Pt 103 effective but costly. By midnight, our tanks pulling back, refuel etc, leaving one Squadron in open leaguer to hold the hill. Bed by 03.00 after a few sharp words with CO about not being allowed forward to recover bodies of Douglas and Pepler.

For the next two days the battle for St Pierre and Point 103 swayed back and forth. 8th DLI hung tenaciously onto the outskirts of St Pierre, having been forced to withdraw partly. The Reverend Skinner:

> Major Mike Laycock (Acting CO since D-Day) held final conference with DLIs in farm prior to action. Captain McCraith, who had distinguished himself in N. Africa both with the Regt and with Long Range Desert Group, arrived from beach with the Regt'l Recce Troop of Honey Tanks, spoke to me in orchard asking where CO was. He hurried to farmhouse. Moments later conference ended and group emerged and paused briefly beside nearby Command Tank (Robin Hood) outside farmhouse door. An accurate mortar stonk on tank and around. Mike Laycock (CO), George Jones (Adjt), Lawrence Head (Intelligence Officer) all killed outright. Sgt Towers, Patrick McCraith and a DLI officer all wounded.

As the battle to hold Point 103 progressed Major Martin found, as often happens, that just as things seem to be at their worst, the situation changes dramatically for the better:

> At dusk, enemy tanks closed in on Point 103. Shermans were blazing everywhere. Going to the Brigadier's tank, I was hailed by the CO of 24th Lancers, sitting on the ground, with his arm in a sling. He handed me a rifle, saying, 'Put a round in the breech, at least I'll take one of them with me.' I thought, 'Good God, it's as bad as that is it?' Shortly after, all firing ceased. It was the final attempt by the enemy, before pulling out and leaving St Pierre.

That day, Bucknall's XXX Corps had launched 7th Armoured Division on a new thrust to Villers-Bocage.

The battle fought by 7th Armoured Division against 2nd Panzer Division lasted two days. After confused and often close-range tank battles, the leading brigade, 22nd Armoured, was forced to withdraw. The fighting in and around Villers-Bocage had cost 4th County of London Yeomanry (CLY), their Commanding Officer, most of Regimental Headquarters, and a complete squadron. Infantry losses had also been high. Rocket-firing Typhoons, the divisional and corps artillery and heavy bombers pounded the German counter-attacks. Major Aird, having taken command of 4th CLY:

> The slaughter was intense, widespread and gratifying. The artillery laid down a concentration in the direction of Villers, and after dark the Lancasters came in to bomb.

The heavy bombing reduced Villers-Bocage to rubble, and 2nd Panzer Division temporarily withdrew to lick their wounds. But because 50th Division could make little headway, 7th Armoured were out on limb, hence the need for withdrawal. 49th and 50th Divisions were ordered to capture Hottot and Tilly. Although from battalion level upwards the

Cristot village after the advance to Tilly-sur-Seulles, 17 June 1944. (B5652)

different phases of the campaign could usually be seen clearly, for an infantry platoon battles just merged into each other, with the odd day in between. Sergeant Hughes's diary:

12 Mon: This day indescribable. Mortar fire and wood fighting. Many casualties. T God I survived another day.

13 Tue: Just had my first meal since Monday morning. Up all night, everyone in a terrible state.

14 Wed: Counter-attacked by Jerry from woods. Mortar fire. 13 of my platoon killed or missing after heavy fighting yesterday, CSM also wounded, also Joe OC killed. I am one mass of scratches.

15 Thur: Advanced under creeping barrage for ? 3 miles, drove Jerry back. It is hell here, 3 Tiger tanks came up to lines during night. ? 2 out of action, the sobbing sisters [mortar bombs known as moaning minnies] keep on coming over.

16 Fri: We are resting in woods front line 3 miles away.

17 Sat: Still resting prelude to another attack. Took patrol out over battle area to locate dead. Found some wine and cherries.

Memo: Monday night's news said assault troops were having well-earned rest, little did they know we have been fighting for our lives since landing.

18 Sun: Day of Hell. Counter attack.

19 Mon: Day of Hell. Counter attack.

20 Tues: Day of Hell. Advanced, counter-attacked.

21 Wed: Quiet day. We have been fighting near Tilly? Bayonet charge, shelled all day.

22 Thur: Out on patrol, got within 35 yards of Tiger before spotting it. Got back safe T God. Shelled to blazes. Feeling tired out.

23 Fri: No sleep last night. Exchange of fire, out on patrol all day. Went on OP for 4 hrs. Stand to all night. Casualties.

24 Sat: Up to now all right. 14.00 hrs, just had a good dinner, chicken. Had to go back to CCS, malaria.

Memo: We all expect to have a leave soon, how true I don't know. Just about had enough after 19 days.

Malaria, which occurred in a number who had fought in Sicily, at least allowed Hughes a rest until early July. Tom Tateson:

On 16 June we began to advance along the road leading out of Berniers-Bocage. Almost immediately the Battalion encountered strong opposition. A Company, to which I was attached, was behind C Company. An 88 was firing directly down the road. The two leading companies came under heavy mortar and machine-gun fire. Their commanders Majors Bowley and Boyle were killed. On my wireless, I heard the signaller with Major Bowley desperately pleading for the Medical Officer to come to the Major's aid as he was dying. Major Bowley was a gentle-mannered, civilised person, and it affected me to hear, so poignantly his actual dying. Major Boyle was also a popular officer, but of an entirely opposite personality – extrovert, dashing and courageous to the point of foolhardiness, a bit of a showman. The sudden loss of these two officers had a depressing effect on us all, particularly on those who had served with the Battalion all through the Western Desert and Sicily campaigns.

On the morning of the 18th, morale was pretty low all round. The heavy casualties of the previous two days had a depressing effect on everyone. While fear seems to be forgotten when everything is happening, the dread moment comes when, after a few hours rest, the word is given we are to make another attack. The stomach sinks, and a leaden feeling spreads through the body. By this time the Battalion had lost fifteen officers and over two hundred NCOs and soldiers.

At the end of that day the Battalion, having advanced, was heavily counter-attacked, and Tateson along with several others was taken prisoner. Casualties included the commanding officer, six officers, and 123 NCOs and soldiers killed, wounded or captured. Only one of the four company commanders with whom the Battalion had landed on D-Day survived.

The psychological effect of being taken prisoner is an almost complete numbing of the senses. We were lined up by men with Schmeiser automatics, and it went through my head that they might shoot us out of hand.

The next morning we were woken by shouts of '*Raus*', and demands for 'clocks'. I slipped my watch off, wrapped it round my ankle under my sock, and was re-tying by boot laces when a guard hit me across the face, demanding 'clock'. I responded, 'Nix clock', and he passed on to gather his harvest elsewhere.

50th Division was to fight in the bocage in the neighbourhood of Hottot, Belle Epine and Tilly, until the end of July. Major Peter Martin:

The battles had a purpose, although we did not know it at the time and became rather disillusioned. It's about the only time during the whole war [which for Martin had started in France in 1939], when I was ever less than happy with the high command. Little did we know the greaty Monty plan to keep constant pressure in that area, to open the way for the Americans. Because I was part of the Brigadier's Tactical HQ, and went with him wherever he visited, I saw more of the Brigade than many more senior officers. I could see the effect of casualties on battalions. By the end of June, 50 Div had lost, killed, wounded and missing, over 300 officers and 3,000 soldiers. Reinforcements came up every night to plug the holes before the next day's attack. The individual soldiers were as super as they always had been, the courage was still there, but the skills were going, and it showed. If our own artillery or mortar fire failed to dislodge the enemy, our infantry seemed to become at a loss about what to do, instead of using fire and movement to get forward, they stopped. Untrained or semi-skilled 3-inch mortarmen would fire their mortars from underneath trees; killing themselves with their own bombs exploding in the branches above.

I began to see worrying signs in my own company. Because there were four brigades in the Division, and only three machine-gun companies, we never got a rest. My soldiers had been with me right through the Desert, the invasion of Sicily and now Normandy. Battle fatigue was beginning to show in one or two cases. A superb corporal suddenly broke into tears and had to be sent back. His reserves of courage had run out; he had been at it too long.

Morale remained remarkably high despite this awful time in Normandy; to which was added the terrible stench of dead animals, and the bad weather in June so that you couldn't ever get dry.

It was not only 50 Div that was affected by battle fatigue, but the two other desert divs, 51st and 7th Armoured. Of the desert divs, only 50 Div 'kept its name'. Horrocks said so. By now other divisions were pouring ashore, 15th Scottish in particular impressed us as a really good division.

On 19 July, four weeks late, our remaining transport arrived, and a lot of welcome reinforcements. The evening a new officer arrived, we were in a farmhouse; the first time we had been under a roof, and we were stonked by enemy artillery. The new officer broke down completely and had to be sent back. He'd never seen a shot fired in the whole war. I suppose in the First World War he would have been taken out and shot. We felt sorry for him, not angry. I expect he went and did a good, if less demanding, job elsewhere for the rest of the war.

A 4.2-inch heavy mortar being fired from a Normandy orchard. (B5577)

The delay in the arrival of Major Martin's transport, and in much else of greater urgency for all the Allied Armies in Normandy was caused by the great gale in mid June. Lieutenant James Holladay on his Gooseberry:

19 June (D+13) Monday TWO WEEKS: Our decks are completely engulfed

The gale lashes one of the floating piers off Arromanches. (B6062)

and the waves are terrific. All the small craft rush to our shelter, but lengthen their hawsers & lie discreetly off when they see how we are shifting. Our stern is brushing up against the bows of 308 and plates on both ships are buckled. Wind still blowing gale force in evening, as tide rises, storm grows in ferocity and lashes over boat deck, tearing up the decking and flying bridge. Steel hawser holding us to next ship parts. Water comes lashing up round bridge.

20 June (D+14) Storm continues if anything worse than before. Only one rope holding us now. Flying bridge completely smashed. Half the planking of the boat deck gone. Detachment on gun deck cut off on duty for 6 hours. Tide comes in very high indeed and enters my cabin, fo'c'sle and wireless cabin. Men in fo'c'sle get on forepeak where they are doused in waves and spray, huddling miserably together clinging to the rail to avoid being swept away. Wireless operators climb on top of wireless cabin & are half drowned and buffeted there. We get on top of bridge. Power of sea simply terrific – slowly smashing the boat to pieces. Wireless ops can't be rescued & spend a bloody night soaked to skin and in considerable danger of being swept away.

21 June (D+15) Air raid during the night, but we are cut off from our gun! Tide goes down at about 3.30 a.m. Find wireless ops soaked through and all sleeping in one bed at back of cabin. Rest of cabin completely wrecked, including wireless sets.

22 June (D+16) Weather breaks at last: calm sea and sunshine in evening.

Captain Harold Hickling RN, who took over as Naval Officer in command at Arromanches on 23 June:

At the height of the storm, Admiral Sir Philip Vian, Commanding the Eastern Task Force, signalled, 'the Gooseberries have saved the day'. Even at Mulberry B [the British Mulberry], it was possible to land 800 tons of much needed ammunition.

Despite the shelters provided, some 800 ships and craft were driven ashore on the Normandy beaches, although a large proportion of these were repaired and salvaged before the next spring tides.

The storm wrecked Mulberry A [US Mulberry] completely. As Cherbourg was likely to fall quite shortly, it was decided not to proceed with the American harbour, although for several months this Gooseberry reinforced by Phoenix continued to give excellent service.

The last troops of the German garrison of Cherbourg surrendered to the Americans on 27 June. Because of mining and demolition, the port was not open for unloading alongside wharves until late August. However, the whole of Bradley's 1st US Army could now devote its full attention to attacking south. Meanwhile, 2nd British Army's main effort was concentrated to the west of Caen: Operation Epsom. On 25 June, 49th Division and 8th Armoured Brigade of XXX Corps was to start the ball rolling by occupying a commanding feature in the area of Rauray.

Durham Light Infantry anti-tank gunners of 70th Infantry Brigade, 49th Infantry Division with their 6-pounder and carrier by the Panther tank they knocked out in the area of Rauray-Fontenay. (B6045)

Trooper Austin Baker, having moved from the C Squadron ARV to a tank:

> We heard that we were to put in an attack at first light the following morning. The Regiment was to be under command of the 49th (West Riding) Division. Our attack was part of a big plan. C Squadron with 1st Tyneside Scottish was to lead the attack. As usual in the bocage, visibility was limited to one field. The field sloped downhill away from us, but beyond the far gap the ground rose again. The leading Troop bowled off merrily down the field, with Lilly leading, followed by the remainder of the Squadron. None of the tanks fired, but the infantry charged towards the wood, blazing away. Nobody fired back, and I was beginning to think that this was going to be a quiet affair. I was very much mistaken. Second Lieutenant Thompson, on our right, came over the air with a message that made my stomach turn over. His tank had pushed through a hedge and had been knocked out by a Jerry tank just across the field. None of the crew had been hurt, and amazingly had stayed in and knocked out Jerry before bailing out. Thompson was speaking over his Troop sergeant's wireless. I guessed there would be other Jerry tanks about and there were.

The whole of Baker's squadron was trapped in the field, with Tigers and Panthers all around.

> The infantry were pinned down by Spandau fire, and there was a fair amount of mortaring, but Knocker Bell (the Squadron Leader), was prowling around on foot, with a pair of field glasses round his neck. I admired his nerve. A tank on the other side of the field brewed up. It was Sergeant Andy Rogers's tank, from 1st Troop. We watched as the

ammunition inside began to explode, flames and black smoke poured up. Eric Santer and Cowper baled out safely, but Sid Francis was killed, and Andy, having been carried away delirious with one leg sliced off, died shortly after.

Suddenly Sergeant Harris, presumably on Knocker's orders, started a little offensive action. He was having trouble with his wireless on his tank, so he changed places with Freddie (in my tank) for a few hectic minutes. Bill fired, I slammed in another round. This was the first time either of us had fired a shot at the enemy. We loosed off eleven rounds, dropping them in line all along the hedge, at a range of two hundred yards. I was loading as fast as I could, but not fast enough for Harris, who shouted for more speed. 'Now give them a belt of Browning,' he said. I think he was enjoying himself. He was an impressive looking bloke with a bristling waxed moustache, and a mad gleam in his eye. We sprayed the hedge from end to end with Browning.

'Driver forward,' said Harris, and we moved back behind cover. I have no idea why we were not knocked out.

By late afternoon, the infantry had a lot of casualties from mortars and Spandaus. We had lost six tanks, with nothing to show for it. A message came over the air to Knocker from the CO that the Brigadier was anxious to organise a Tiger hunt. We were to withdraw immediately and take part. The last thing we wanted by then was to be involved in a Tiger hunt, but were all in favour of a withdrawal. The trouble was Jerry covered the only way back out of the field.

Eventually, after two attempts, a smoke screen was laid on by the supporting artillery and the squadron made a dash for it.

There was quite a steep bank up to the next field. Going up, Tom stalled, so we slipped backwards and stopped right in the gap. For a moment that seemed like an hour, I felt that every 88mm gunner in the German Army had his sights dead on our turret, but if they had, they didn't fire. Tom started up, we were up the bank, through the gap, and away across the field.

About a mile away, we stopped to refuel and bomb-up, from fuel and ammunition dumped in piles. Unfortunately it was on top of a ridge. An AP shot whistled over, and we hurried into a valley beyond. Even there shells started coming over, close enough to make everybody crawl under the nearest tank. I got under one, so many people came after me, I was nearly pushed out at the other end. The Tiger hunt was called off, to everyone's intense relief. Eventually we went back to our previous harbour, where all was quiet.

On 25 June the Sherwood Rangers, in the same Brigade, were supporting infantry in an attack. Leslie Skinner:

04.30 attack moves down hill behind barrage, 100 yards at time. Half way down hill to valley a heavy ground mist thickens as we go and in minutes visibility down to a few feet. Infantry lose visual contact with each other and with tanks. Only contacts by radio. All at standstill. Then infantry sections moved a little further forward and dig in fast. Boche opens up with everything they have got – MG, mortars, 88mms – the lot.

Infantry in slit trenches lower down have a tough time. I scrounged a couple of pints of rum from MO's half-track – borrowed half a dozen water bottles and filled them with 50–50 rum and water and set off to see what I could do. Met Ronnie Hutton on his Dingo talking to Infantry Officer – Coy Commander. Without interrupting conversation reached up and put one of bottles into Ronnie's hand. When he got the taste his face was a picture. Both he and Inf Officer took a hefty swig.

Went further down the hill finding several infantry pockets and one or two tanks. Between them they empty the cans [canteens – bottles] and are glad to have done so.

In burst German MG fire, I dived into slit trench on top of young soldier who was somewhat scared at my arrival. It was his first show and he was all alone. Others were dug in nearby but in the mist quite invisible. I assured him the MG fire was way up in the air. He swore at me and to prove his point picked up a ration box lid and held it above ground. Burst MG fire cut it in two. It shook me. Didn't know which of us was more frightened. When firing stopped I move out. He, poor devil, had to stay.

As mist slowly lifted attack moving again. Casualty collecting began again, taking them as found, infantry and tank alike. About 11.30 hours bringing in R Scots soldier on stretcher as approached RAP a mortar shell burst about 20 yards away. Shrapnel got me across forehead and knocked me out.

Came round to find Hylda (nickname for Medical Officer) dressing my head. Lots of blood but soon conscious. Hylda later informed me a piece of shrapnel about size and shape pen nib penetrated my skull, and cap badge, much damaged, probably saved my life.

On 26 June, Lieutenant-General O'Connor's VII Corps in the main part of Operation Epsom, drove forward a corridor across the River Odon. O'Connor, after his crushing defeat of the Italians in the Western Desert in 1941, had been taken prisoner, and subsequently escaped when Italy surrendered. He had three fine divisions, 11th Armoured, 15th Scottish and 43rd Wessex. O'Connor's Corps advanced with 15th Scottish Division leading. The weather was bad, with heavy rain and low cloud. Captain Freddie Graham, Intelligence Officer, 2nd Argylls, standing in for the Adjutant, who was away sick:

The aim was to capture bridges across the River Odon to the west of Caen. We in 227 Highland Brigade were to follow behind the other two brigades in the Division, and subsequently push through to capture the bridges. The Division formed up in fields the night before. The bridgehead was not very deep then, and there wasn't a field that did not have some unit in it. We shared a field with a gun line. We did not get much sleep that night.

Infantry advancing through corn. (Film still FLM2381)

The plan for the leading brigades did not go as predicted. We spent a dreary day moving forward behind them. Our inexperience showed. We couldn't tell the difference between incoming and outgoing fire. The cry would go up, 'Sniper'. The soldiers would go to ground and fire at the trees. I don't believe there were any snipers at all. But if you get a large body of soldiers firing skywards, other people a mile or so away will receive these bullets and will fire back. My memory of the first two days is of almost continuous fusillades between our people, who thought the Germans were firing at them, and some other British unit perhaps a mile away. It wasted time and ammunition. There were no casualties. It was a mark of inexperience. There was a tendency throughout the war for infantry to go to ground, not when under effective enemy fire, but just when under fire.

After a soaking wet night in a field, we were ordered to pass through the other two brigades, through Cheux, and press on to the bridges. Cheux, quite a big town, had been well bombed and shelled, and was in a fine old state. All the landmarks had been demolished. If you bomb a town, your chances of doing much damage to the enemy are small, but you create a barrier for your own advance.

10th Highland Light Infantry (HLI) and 2nd Argylls groped our way forward, still tending to shoot at each other. 2nd Argylls found a track which by sheer luck, we discovered later, led down the boundary between two enemy formations. We advanced through Coleville, over the road to Caen at Tourville and, in a wonderful dash by C Company and the Carrier Platoon, took the bridge over the Odon, for the loss of three dead and eleven wounded. Half an hour later up came 11th Armoured Division. We cheered and said, 'Next stop Paris'.

What happened? A panzer grenadier battalion dug in on Hill 112. The advance got that far and no further. The whole offensive petered out

Soldiers of 2nd Argylls, 15th Scottish Division, moving up near Hill 112. (B7427)

because armour could not get past 112 and the remainder of the SS Panzer Divisions.

Lieutenant Steel Brownlie, a troop leader in the 2nd Fife and Forfar Yeomanry, 11th Armoured Division, was in action for the first time at Cheux, as the first day ended:

> In the dark it was a matter of finding the Squadron harbour, blundering about by the light of flaming wrecks and getting mixed up with other units. It took an hour or so, and then there was the business of reorganising the Troop, taking on fuel, ammunition and rations from the Echelon trucks, reporting mechanical defects and seeing them dealt with by the fitters, attending an O Group to receive orders for the next day, folding and marking maps, ensuring that a member of the crew was cooking and another arranging the bedding, sometimes fitting in a wash, or a visit to a hedge outside the harbour, with a shovel and a supply of Army Form Blank, which was issued on a scale of two-and-a-half sheets per man per day. What time would it be after all that lot? It might be one, two or three in the morning, and orders were to be ready to move at dawn.
>
> That night after our first action, I don't think anyone slept. The petrol and ammo took three hours to reach us, the enemy were only a few hundred yards away, and everybody was shattered by the day's events. Long afterwards you thought about Cheux as just about the worst, and anything else seemed an improvement.
>
> At dawn we moved to the east of the village, where the infantry had made good progress during the night. Churchill tanks were to take the woods south-east of Cheux, when we would pass through and take the ground beyond. There was great confusion, and four Panthers came into the village, scattering the infantry, getting to within 200 yards of us before

being knocked out. I saw the commander of one of them blown out of his turret, twenty feet into the air, in the middle of a huge smoke ring.

The Churchill attack got nowhere, and we took over. We advanced in the prescribed manner, Troop Sergeant leading, and Firefly in rear. My Troop Sergeant topped the ridge safely, and was going flat out down the slope, when I saw a Panther emerging from the woods to his left, firing at him. On top of the ridge, I was ranging on the Panther, trying to warn my Troop Sergeant on the air, when everything went wrong. A shell jammed in my breech, and all my electrics went dead: no radio, intercom, engine, power traverse. Immobile on the skyline, all I could do was fire MG manually at the Panther. Its gun traversed towards me, my .300 bullets bouncing off it. Suddenly it turned and disappeared into the wood. The Troop Sergeant was not so lucky. He had gone on alone, and unsupported, and was brewed up. Three of his crew were killed, he and one other were burned and never rejoined.

The Squadron passed on. Jumping down, the first thing I saw was a complete leg in a boot and gaiter, and a bit of battledress trouser with quite a good crease in it. Nearby was a tank, not fully burnt out, and a corporal crouching underneath. He and I got his tank moving, and arranged for it to tow mine back off the ridge. While the towrope was being shackled, I crawled around looking for a sergeant, whom I had seen struggling out of his burning tank, with both legs blown off. I found no trace of him.

The corporal towed us back to near the village, where we set to work trying to repair the fault, which turned out to be a damaged master switch. We were heavily mortared, and at one point dived under the tank for shelter. We were astonished to see Padre Oswald Welsh walking towards us in the open. My driver Jock McKinnon poked out his head and shouted: 'For fuck's sake, Padre, come in oot o' there.' Oswald replied: 'Now, McKinnon, watch your language.' And pointing to his dog-collar: 'I'm a non-combatant,' he walked on.

My tank was repaired by the fitters, and I moved to a more sheltered spot. I was told to wait till the Squadron returned to refuel. On their return, I reassembled what remained of my troop, and was told to lead the way up to the railway by Grainville. We crossed it unopposed 300 yards from the village. I sat in the shelter of smoke from a burning house, and watched the Recce Troop go into the village to see if it was clear. It wasn't. They lost a tank, but no men, to a Panther sitting in or beside the church. As they belted back past us, having done their job, the Colonel came on the air asking for their exact position. The troop leader replied: 'Position be buggered, wait out.'

The Churchills appeared again, and with infantry went into Grainville, while we supported by fire. They met strong opposition and were repulsed. Dozens of wounded were dragged back to where we were sitting, and some lay in the shelter of my tank until Jeeps took them back. One infantryman, both legs blown off, lay with his head pillowed on a groundsheet, puffing at a cigarette. I doubt if he made it.

Lieutenant Blower, 5th Coldstream Guards, Guards Armoured Division, asleep at Carpiquet. (HU63950)

Some were hopeless cases when they arrived at regimental aid posts. Private James Bramwell with the 9th Parachute Battalion:

> A chap was brought in with the top of his head blown off, brains spilling out in to the stretcher. The MO took one look at him. I said, 'Is there anything we can do?' He shrugged. So I gave him a lethal shot of morphine. When the MO came back, I told him. He said, 'It's OK, you did quite right. If he'd lived, he'd have been a vegetable for the rest of his days.' I am sure there were others like this. But we did not talk about it.

On the left of 15th Scottish Division, 43rd Wessex Division, after bitter fighting in woods on both banks of the river, also established a brigade across the Odon. As there were now nearly eight panzer divisions on the 2nd British Army front between Caumont and Caen, VIIIth Corps was ordered to stabilize just south-east of the Odon, and withdraw from Hill 112. There was little let-up even for the D-Day assault battalions. Major 'Banger' King, writing to his batman's mother on 6 July 1944:

> This is a short note to let you know that your son is keeping fit & well, although very tired like all of us. I keep an eye on him & try & keep him out of trouble if I can. Many of his comrades have not been so fortunate & perhaps this may depress him a little, but we shall get relieved in due course and then a week or so behind the line will set him right. We have been fighting the toughest troops in the German army – Panzers – and a few days ago they beat it. They had had enough. But it has been a long and bitter fight. We have been in the line since D-Day. The war seems to be going pretty well according to plan as far as I can see – & if it continues to do so we shall be home for Xmas if not sooner. I think myself the Huns will suddenly crack.

Listening to the news on the wireless, officers of 5th Coldstream Guards in the rest area at Bayeux. (HU63954)

On 1 July, 1st, 2nd, 9th, 10th and 12th SS Panzer Divisions made what turned out to be their last, and strongest, concerted attempt to break through 2nd British Army. It was beaten off. Montgomery's intentions were for the Americans to break out to the south and then swing east to Le Mans and Alençon. In order to assist this, he wanted to prevent the transfer of German reserves to the American sector. This could best be done by mounting operations by 2nd British Army between the Odon and the Orne. At the same time, 2nd Army had to be ready to thrust south from positions east of the Orne: to start when the Americans had gathered momentum and had turned east. While preparations were in hand for the major attack east of the Orne, the main part of the city of Caen was captured on 9 July, leaving the Germans occupying the suburbs on the east bank of the Orne. The fall of Caen was the outcome of attacks by 3rd Canadian and 3rd British Divisions, both D-Day assault divisions, and 59th British Division. An attack on Verson by 43rd Division protected the left flank of the Canadians.

The attack on Caen had been preceded by a massive strike by Bomber Command, after which Air Marshal Harris is alleged to have said, 'I and my batman will now capture Caen.' Although this may be

apocryphal, his scorn for the slow progress by the British Army seems to have filtered down to his crews. Flight Lieutenant Ronald Williams, a Lancaster navigator with 57 Squadron, writing to his parents on 8 July:

> We were off last night on the 1,000 bomber do, to try and coax the British Army forward. The suggestion is we go and bomb behind *our* lines today to try and push them forward that way.

Although Williams exaggerated the number of bombers taking part, it was impressive enough to watch 467 Lancasters and Halifaxes dropping 2,560 tons of bombs on the city. Major Bill Renison had recently arrived as the second-in-command of 2nd East Yorks:

> On the evening of 8 July, the final assault on Caen opened with the heaviest bomber attack I had ever seen. As we were only about four miles from the target and plumb on the line of their fly-in, we had a grandstand view. It was magnificent to see the majestic approach of wave after wave of big bombers, flying quite low in very tight formation at an almost pin-point target. As far as the eye could see they stretched out towards the sea and the sinking sun. As the raid progressed, a cloud of dust rose high into the air and blotted out almost everything, drifting slowly towards us and up the valley of the Orne. By the end of the raid the troops were standing on the end (sic) of their slit trenches clapping and cheering; the effect on morale was electric.

The original intention had been to bomb at first light on 8 July, immediately followed by the ground assault. Unfortunately, because of an unfavourable weather forecast for the morning of the 8th, the air bombardment was brought forward to the evening of the 7th. By the time

Machine-gunners of 8th Battalion the Middlesex Regiment take cover from mortar fire as their division, 43rd Wessex, advances to take Verson, as part of VIII Corps in the battle for Caen, July 1944. (B6852)

this was known, it was too late to change the army plan. Thus the Germans were given the night to recover. This, plus desperately slow progress imposed by streets choked for hundreds of yards by rubble, gave the Germans time to blow every bridge across the Orne.

Immediately following the fall of Caen, six infantry divisions inched their way forward in a series of bloody battles in the detested bocage, heading for objectives such as Hottot and Hill 112. Although 8th Middlesex, the machine-gun battalion in 43rd Division, had been in Normandy only since 24 June, Epsom and the fighting at Verson had started to take their toll. Lieutenant-Colonel Mervyn Crawford, at forty-two quite old to be a battalion CO, in his diary:

> Geoff (OC Company) very worried about one of his platoon commanders, who was not standing up to the strain. I had an interview with him but it was very trying, he was in an awful state in tears, most difficult experience as I felt very sorry for the poor fellow. However decided he was no good to risk the lives of his platoon with any longer, so although I told him to stick it, I promised Geoff I would get a relief up to him before nightfall.

German propaganda leaflet dropped into Normandy logement area. (From Department of Printed Books, negative numbers HU63701 and 63702)

YOU HAVE BEEN TRAPPED!

YOU HAVE LANDED on the Continent to face the armed might of Germany — but not for the benefit of Britain !

Your country will gain ABSOLUTELY NOTHING from this struggle, no matter how well you may fight.

THE BOLSHEVISTS ALONE WILL PROFIT by your sacrifices. You have been trapped into risking your life for but one purpose — the Bolshevization of Europe !

Consider these points, and ask yourself:

WHY SHOULD YOU FIGHT FOR STALIN?

INVASION — WHY?

Have you any clear idea of the purpose of the attempted invasion of Western Europe?

One thing is certain — the Allied casualties are and will continue to be enormous, although the amount of territory captured will be small.

The only strategic effect that the invasion could have would be to lessen the resistance of the Germans in the East.

If this plan succeeded, Bolshevism would triumph over Europe — and

TRIUMPH OVER BRITAIN AS WELL!

E114 / 3.44

At about this time the Germans were dropping leaflets on the British telling them about the V-1 attacks on England in an attempt to lower morale.

Later 43rd Division, as part of the pressure being exerted on the Germans west of Caen, was tasked with taking Maltot in the Orne valley. Sergeant Walter Caines, Signal Platoon sergeant 4th Dorsets at Battalion Headquarters, was therefore well placed to know what his Battalion tasks were:

> The Brigadier ordered the Battalion to reinforce the Hampshires in their task of capturing Maltot. The Battalion formed up with two companies up and two in reserve. The Companies entered the village supported by tanks protecting the flanks, only to be met with terrific opposition. Tanks were

knocked out from all directions. Tigers were concealed in orchards, and machine-guns fired from all angles. Neither we nor the Hampshires stood an earthly chance of securing the village. Most of our tracked vehicles were knocked out by 88s. Our anti-tank gunners did not have time to place their guns in position. The main body of tactical headquarters were moving towards the village crossing a cornfield on the outskirts. Jerry must have observed, and allowing us to come close, engaged with a Spandau. No one dared raise his head above the corn. At about 19.00 hours, orders were given to withdraw to the original start line, dig in and hold. Remnants of the companies came back, but A Company complete had been killed, wounded or captured. After several anxious hours, the Battalion collected and established a defensive position along several hundred yards of front. Some men were without rifles or ammunition, and many had lost their complete equipment. Those without gathered from the wounded and dead, so by nightfall almost every man possessed some sort of fighting iron.

The Signal Officer told me that the Carrier with the bulk of the Signals equipment had been destroyed by a shell. So there were no

German Nebelwerfer firing. (Captured German film FLM2399)

communications facilities in the Battalion. Most of the wireless sets carried by the company signallers had been knocked out, or left behind in Maltot as ordered [sic].

As dawn broke, most of us were as cold as stone and dog tired. It has been a terrible twenty-four hours, seeing men fall, and hearing the wounded cry and moan as they were evacuated. However, somehow I felt that the worst had happened, and all had learned a good lesson; having passed through this terrible ordeal, we had gained in experience.

Captain Paul Cash, a young artillery forward observation officer, was instrumental in saving the reverse at Maltot from being catastrophic. He was awarded a Military Cross, but killed by a stray shell bursting above

A self-propelled gun (Priest), camouflaged while the crew dig in in a field of vegetables outside Caen. (B5766)

his slit trench some days later. His battery commander wrote to his widow:

> I can tell you something of the action on July 10th in which Paul was slightly wounded. During an attack by the 7th Hampshires on the village of Maltot on the Orne, we got into a very sticky place. Paul was in a tank, but had to abandon this when things became too hot. My scout car was knocked out by an 88mm. Atkins was wounded and had to be left when the infantry withdrew. Thus Paul, Blinks and I found ourselves with only two wireless sets. We were stuck in a ditch on the outskirts of the village with Colonel Raye and the remnants of his battalion HQ and one company. The Boche was counter-attacking from three sides. We therefore put down shell fire as close as we dared. Paul and I did this between us – he observing, and I on the wireless – until I was wounded in the hand and in the leg, and later in the arm. By this time things were very serious, and none of us expected to get out alive. The Boche was sweeping our position with machine-gun fire, and shot up both our carriers and wireless sets with 88s. Paul got the blast from one of these shells in his mouth which was badly swollen, but otherwise all right.
>
> Another battalion arrived to relieve us in the nick of time. We collected our party to withdraw as we could do nothing further without communications. At this time Blinks went up to a tank to show the commander where an 88 was shooting from. The 88 fired at that moment and blew up the tank and poor old Blinks.
>
> Paul and I found our way to Brigade HQ, and then to the dressing station, from which Paul returned to take command of the battery, while I was evacuated.

Mortar fire was often the most dangerous, particularly when the bombs burst in trees, showering splinters directly down. Colonel Tony

Nursing sisters bed down in a slit trench as a precaution against night bombing. (B5816)

Wingfield, who had won a DSO and MC in the desert, and was now deputy commander of 34th Tank Brigade, which operated in support of infantry divisions:

> I joined the tactical HQ of the 44th Infantry Brigade and watched the start of the attack. It had only been launched a few minutes when I heard the characteristic sound of a *nebelwerfer* firing. This was a multi-barrelled mortar which, when being fired, sounded like the winding-up of a grandfather clock. Within a few seconds there was a hailstorm of mortar bombs descending on Brigade HQ. I dived into a slit trench which I had been told was reserved for visitors. A few seconds later someone dived on top of me, and I found myself lying on my back with that someone's head resting on my private parts. More mortar bombs arrived and the earth shook all round us. I prayed the German mortarmen would not 'hole out in one on my green'.
>
> My unknown companion said: 'Isn't it strange that you and I are lying here in this extraordinary position, not knowing each other, and likely to be blown into the next world at any minute.' I agreed. Then, after a few more minutes of conversation on that theme, the mortar fire ceased, and we scrambled out into the moonlight. My unknown companion, who was a subaltern, took one look at my red tabs, cried 'Oh God', and fled into the night.

Although to some of the weary infantry and tank crews fighting in the detested bocage, which greatly favoured the defenders, there must at times have seemed to be no end to the blood and sacrifice, their dogged persistence overcame the Germans and paved the way for victory. The Americans were gathering momentum, and 2nd British Army was about to launch a huge punch east of the Orne.

CHAPTER FOUR

'. . . It is not always easy to keep up the pressure . . .'

THE BATTLES FOR THE BREAKOUT AND THE PURSUIT TO BELGIUM AND HOLLAND

'Our route lay through the Falaise pocket, and we went along roads where Jerry columns had been caught by Typhoons. There were miles of wrecked and burnt vehicles, tanks, trucks, horse-drawn carts, limbers and wagons. There was a horrible stink of dead horses and men.'
TROOPER AUSTIN BAKER,
C Squadron, 4/7th Royal Dragoon Guards

An RAF officer looks at an appropriate sign in the Falaise pocket, August 1944. (CH887)

In early July criticism of Montgomery's failure to break out began to be voiced, both in Eisenhower's Supreme Headquarters Allied Expeditionary Force (SHAEF) and in the United States. Eisenhower, lacking battle experience, and remote from the scene of operations, expressed his concern in a letter to Montgomery. In his turn, Montgomery was more understanding of Bradley's wish to delay the American offensive by ten days. He was well aware of the close country that Bradley must fight through, and the need to build up his supplies, as well as secure a good position from which to start his push. Thinking in the terms of the 'door and hinge' analogy of his strategy, Montgomery decided to mount a major operation east of Caen on 18 July to pull the enemy armour on to the British 'hinge', thereby allowing Bradley to mount his break-out operation (Cobra) at the western end of the bridgehead on the 20th.

Goodwood, which involved the three armoured divisions of O'Connor's VIII Corps (7th, 11th and Guards) has been the subject of great controversy ever since. Not only did the plan involve launching the

Cromwell tanks waiting to move off for the start of Operation Goodwood, 18 July 1944. B7649 and B7650)

divisions, one after the other, through a very narrow gap in the 1 Corps minefields, but even its aim has been in doubt. Certainly there was no clear understanding of Montgomery's intentions in Eisenhower's headquarters. In his notes to Dempsey, Montgomery makes it perfectly plain that his initial aim was 'to destroy the enemy' in a limited advance to the area of Vimont and what became known as the Bourguébus Ridge. Meanwhile the Canadians were to break out of Caen so that they came up on O'Connor's right flank. The VIII Corps armoured cars were to exploit towards Falaise 'to find the form' and then 'to crack about as the situation demands'. However Eisenhower certainly believed that Montgomery intended a much more ambitious aim. Lieutenant Brownlie of the Fife and Forfar Yeomanry, in 11th Armoured Division, did not, and does not, believe that Goodwood was intended to be a diversion for Cobra: 'We were certainly given the impression that it was to be "Falaise and beyond".'

Putting aside hindsight and the natural cynicism of the fighting soldier about statements from on high, it would be perfectly natural for

all but those at the top level to be given the impression that Goodwood was the main thrust. Troops are unlikely to give their all for a diversion, and to be convincing, the offensive had to bear all the hallmarks of a break-out. The operation would certainly lack conviction if prisoners told the Germans that it was only a diversion to assist the Americans.

Rommel undoubtedly took the impending attack seriously. It was impossible to conceal the British preparations. The Germans overlooked the southern part of the Orne bridgehead from Colombelles, on the outskirts of Caen. The movement of 700 tanks from west to east could clearly be heard, and the erection of additional bridges and other sapper preparations could have only one meaning. The German defences were ten miles deep. Three infantry divisions, and the best part of three panzer divisions, formed a series of layers through which the attackers would have to pass.

Although the ground was open and, unlike the bocage, looked ideal for armour, it was also very adaptable to defence in the hands of good soldiers, and the Germans were just that. The rolling cornfields sloped down from the Orne bridgehead, to the embankment carrying the railway from Caen to the east. And downhill again to a second railway line running south-east from Caen to Vimont. South after this line, the ground began to rise to the Bourguébus ridge, where the third railway line, embanked like the others, ran south to Falaise. The open plain was liberally strewn with small villages. These gave cover for anti-tank guns, and were close enough to each other to provide the textbook requirement for good anti-tank gunnery, mutual support: armour attacking one gun will be vulnerable, particularly from a flank, to fire from a neighbouring gun. The Germans were amply supplied with anti-tank guns, including plenty of 88s. The exit from the bridgehead ran into a corridor four miles long, and only 1,500 yards wide. It would only be possible to widen this when the advance reached the village of Cagny.

The VIII Corps plan was for 11th Armoured Division to lead down the corridor, followed in succession by Guards Armoured and 7th Armoured. Once through the corridor, 11th Armoured would head south-west for Bourguébus, 7th due south, and Guards Armoured south-east. To advance with three armoured divisions nose-to-tail down so narrow a corridor was certainly unique and in defiance of all the conventions of armoured warfare. One fatal result was that the supporting arms of the leading division became hopelessly entangled with the advanced elements of the second, and a traffic jam, which spelled disaster to the whole operation, ensued. One consequence of this was the inability of the medium guns that should have supported 11th Armoured Division to deploy forward, so that the leading brigade soon moved out of range of its artillery support. An air bombardment by Bomber Command was to precede the ground advance. But, because there were not enough aircraft to attack all targets, the enemy guns on the Bourguébus ridge were not included in this bombardment.

A Royal Tank Regiment tank crew wait for the order to advance.
(B9538)

Although the Tactical Air Forces offered to bomb these later in the day, their assistance was refused, because it was thought that the armour would be on the ridge by that time. 3rd Royal Tanks were to lead the advance through the corridor, followed by the 2nd Fife and Forfar Yeomanry. Lieutenant Brownlie:

> At 5.30 a.m. the clear blue sky was filled by a stream of bombers, which plastered the country ahead. Many of us stood up and cheered. The Regiment assembled behind the Start Line, having gone through the lanes in the minefields [British], cleared by 51st Highland Division the previous day. The 1500-gun crawling barrage began, and the mass of tanks moved forward behind it. To us it was a solid grey wall of shell-bursts. We drove on in formation for about a mile. We had never before driven in formation for more than a couple of hundred yards, except on exercises. Was it all over bar the shouting?

Major-General Pip Roberts, the GOC of 11th Armoured Division, had been ordered by O'Connor to release 159 Lorried Infantry Brigade to attack two villages on the right flank of the advance, leaving him without any infantry to support the armoured brigade except the 8th Battalion the Rifle Brigade, 29th Armoured Brigade's own motor battalion, mounted in armoured half-tracks. The tank crews were keenly aware of this weakness in the plan. Trooper John Thorpe, hull gunner and co-driver of a Sherman of the Fife and Forfar Yeomanry:

> We tanks are on our own, no infantry, being shelled we settle down (you can only be scared up to a point, but you have to win through, it's like getting your second wind when you're running). Objective we are told is

Burning tanks during Operation Goodwood.
(Film still FLM2411)

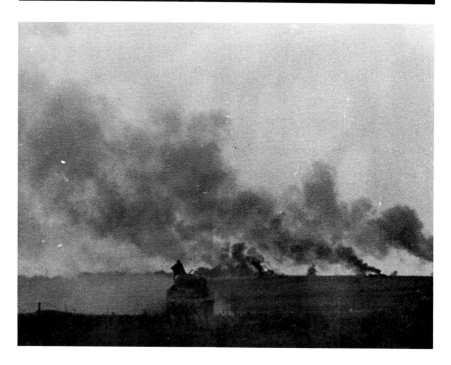

Falaise, don't stop for anything, charge down their anti-tank guns, run over their trails (some hope!). Climb over one railway embankment, and chase down to another, over the second, tanks are spread out over about 100 yards, but all heading the same way. We are some way behind the leading ones, which are still in view, when very severe armour-piercing fire comes from a coppice on our left front. Several tanks go on fire. My orders are to fire into this coppice, while our 75mm is shooting in some AP and HE. My Browning stops, and I find the canvas bag for the empty cartridge cases is jammed full, blocking the gun. I pull off the bag, and feed in belt after belt, my barrel warps, and the tracer is leaving the gun in a cone of fire. I try to change the barrel, but it is too hot – no matter – keep on firing, my feet are buried in a thick carpet of empties all over the floor. In front, brew-up after brew-up, some tank crews are on fire and rolling about on the ground trying to put out the flames in their clothes. Soon what with burning tanks, burning corn, and mortar smoke, visibility is short. Now all the tanks in front are burning fiercely, and 20 yards away, I see a tank boy climbing out of a turret spurting flames. He does not make it. After putting one leg up to step out, he falls back inside. Ammunition explodes in the burning tanks. In the still air, huge smoke rings rise out of their turrets. Cliff orders Robby to Reverse, 'right stick', guns still firing, 'left stick, right stick', and we back to the railway embankment, up over, and down the other side, into a hull-down position. But the embankment is too steep, and we back all the way down. We seem to have lost the whole of our Regiment.

Sergeant David Jones, 8th Rifle Brigade, the infantry battalion in the same brigade, in half-tracks:

When we got closer to the main force about midday, progress didn't seem so smooth, and by the afternoon, we were digging in hard. The slopes in front were littered with brewed-up Shermans; initial confidence had given way to doubt. We had the job of clearing two 88 positions. The Germans were well dug in; their positions had that familiar but indefinable smell.

Steel Brownlie:

The regimental leaguer [that night], initially consisted of precisely nine tanks out of the sixty or so that had started in the morning. Gradually others came in, but the losses had been very heavy. Nobody said very much, except things like; 'You know so-and-so's had it.' The surviving reserve crews brought up spare tanks, and the whole night was spent replenishing, re-organising, repairing, and getting set for the next day. Once more, sleep did not figure on the programme.

John Thorpe:

We lived to see another day, but I will always remember those pathetic blackened and burnt tank crews who crawled back towards us through the burning corn. We could give them no succour, we were still engaged, and it was against standing orders to assist any disabled tank or crew during a battle. The sickening thing was, we gave them a burst of machine-gun fire, before we realized they were our own blokes creeping towards us in the corn.

By nightfall, VIII Corps was short of the Bourguébus ridge. The 11th Armoured Division had lost 126 tanks, Guards Armoured sixty, and 7th Armoured six. 7th Armoured had been slow to advance, possibly reflecting the view of their commander, Major-General Erskine, that the operation was a misuse of armour. The traffic jam certainly impeded the division's advance. The German armour and anti-tank guns, in well-prepared positions, and forewarned of the impending attack, had taken a terrible toll, particularly 88s sited at Cagny, which caused 11th Armoured and the Guards so much trouble, and mobile anti-tank guns mounted on Hotchkiss chassis.

For the next two days, VIII Corps mounted a series of attacks on the villages on the northern slope of the Bourgébus Ridge. With 3rd Royal Tanks, now reorganized and largely re-equipped, H and F Companies of 8th Rifle Brigade, attacked Bras. Sergeant Jones:

We set off in the afternoon to carry out an attack on the hamlet of Bras, about two miles away. For this my platoon mustered 9 men. I decided to try my hand at firing the Bren from the hip as we advanced and found it reassuring, almost exhilarating. This was spoilt by realizing, as we approached the rubble of Bras, that the moving figure I was firing at was a woman in black, who, with the reluctance of people to leave their homes, was now caught up in our advance. Happily I missed. This successful attack, with the support of tanks and carriers, produced a good haul of

A German 88mm gun in the anti-tank role. Originally designed as an anti-aircraft gun, it was also used as an anti-tank gun from early in the War, and fitted in tanks from 1942. Its high velocity and flat trajectory made it a greatly feared weapon.
(B8847)

prisoners, and visible success for our trials. We left Bras, and with our remaining vehicles stayed on higher ground for some hours, suffering further mortar casualties. Our platoon commander who had been with us for a matter of days was slightly wounded; and when I led the platoon away, I was accompanied by six others. Our serviceable half-tracks were loaded with kit from knocked-out vehicles, we piled in and retired into harbour late that night. At least we could look back on the success in Bras, but in general we retired battered and confused. From our position at the base of the pyramid, we felt that we had taken part in a great effort that hadn't come off.

It says much for the spirit and training of this magnificent division that, despite the heavy battering taken by the armoured regiments involved in the initial attack, the two worst hit were now back in the battle and fighting with their usual elan. The Fife and Forfar Yeomanry attacked Hubert Folie that afternoon. Brownlie:

There was not much opposition in Hubert Folie, and we lost only one tank. As we withdrew, I saw an arm waving in a patch of scrub; a wounded

Heavy rain fell at the end of Operation Goodwood, turning the ground to mud.
(Film still FLM2413)

German private. We hoisted him on to the tank, and I fed him with grapes we had picked up, until finding a dressing station where he was dropped off.

On 20 July, the armoured divisions were withdrawn. As they reached their leaguers, the skies opened and the rain poured down, turning the ground to mud. Unfortunately Montgomery's optimistic reports, including a press conference, about the results of Goodwood on the afternoon of the first day, were seized upon by his enemies in SHAEF to castigate the operation itself, and him as a commander. Whatever Montgomery's real intentions, critics of Goodwood ignore the tangible gain made by VIII Corps. The cramped Orne bridgehead had been expanded by some thirty square miles, and the Canadians had taken the rest of Caen. Artillery could be moved forward, and with the Orne bridges within Caen repaired, there was now, for the first time since D-Day, enough elbow room for the British and Canadians, particularly 1st Canadian Army, to develop their full power when the time came for the break-out. The 1st Canadian Army, under Lieutenant-General Crerar, became operational three days after Goodwood was closed down, with IInd Canadian and Ist British Corps under command.

On 25 July, five days late, the Americans launched Operation Cobra. By 4 August American spearheads, at least out of the bocage, had reached Mortain and were driving into Brittany. The British Operation Bluecoat (a strong thrust by 2nd British Army south from Caumont to ease the pressure on the Americans' left flank) started on 30 July. On 4 August VIII Corps was alongside the Americans just north of Vire, and

German prisoners captured in Coutances by American troops, 29 July 1944. KY31758)

XXX Corps was heading for Mont Pinçon. That day, Major Peter Martin of 2nd Cheshires:

> Learned that Villers-Bocage had been captured, two months after we were supposed to have captured the place on D plus one. For the first time since D-Day, the whole company was relieved and went into a rest area, where we stayed for a couple of days. The following day, I was ordered to attend a briefing by XXX Corps commander. I had no idea who this was. Who should we find but General Horrocks. The lift to morale at seeing Horrocks again was terrific. He congratulated us all on what 50 Div had done. Now he said there was one more obstacle, Mount Pinçon, and then we could start motoring. There was a feeling of great exhilaration, that at last we were to get out of this terrible bocage. But before this, was the mammoth obstacle of Mont Pinçon, the highest feature in Normandy.

Trooper William Hewison of 1st Royal Tanks in 7th Armoured Division pulled back through the shattered city of Caen, to take part in XXX Corps part of Bluecoat.

> I've never seen such devastation in my existence – or otherwise. Practically the whole city a mass of rubble – slivers of walls and lone chimneys and unbelievable standing parts of buildings.
>
> Had griff talk from CO last night – told us what we are doing here. Through us drawing practically all the Boche armour south of Caen, the Yanks had hardly any opposition in their push. Jerry retreating orderly, with pivot at Caumont. We (30 Corps) and 8 Corps to dislodge this pivot and make his retreat quicker. 43 Div and 50 Div already in, progressing slowly – we (7th), waiting until there is some sort of breakthrough.

A French boy eating an apple he has just picked up from the road in the wreckage of Caen. (Film still FLM2380)

An American Sherman tank passes an 88mm. The sandbags on the glacis plate of the tank are an attempt to add protection against the powerful German anti-tank guns. (EA33681)

An aerial photograph of armour advancing in the bocage, with its pattern of small fields. The high banks were a considerable obstacle to armour. As a tank climbed over, it exposed its belly to waiting gunners and tanks. The problem was overcome by fitting short lengths of railway track to the front of some tanks, like horns on a buffalo. The tank would then charge the bank, gouging out a gap. (KY31764)

Few Americans would agree with Hewison's CO's assessment of the quality of the opposition they encountered in the hard fighting since 28 July. But their break-out, and ability to maintain momentum owed much to Bluecoat, and hard fighting by 2nd British Army. While Bradley's 12th US Army Group pushed south, and then began to swing north-east, the British VIII and XXX Corps flogged forward. Every village, every field, every orchard had to be cleared. The Germans fought cunningly. Anti-tank guns and machine-guns bypassed, remained and fired into the flanks of armour and infantry. After holding a hamlet for a day of bitter fighting, the enemy would withdraw to a fresh position.

Major 'Banger' King, 2nd East Yorkshires, writing to his batman who had been wounded:

> On the day you got hit we stopped rather a packet further on and I didn't know that you had been hit until about an hour afterwards. I sent back a message for the ambulance jeep to come up the road where you were but the Jerries came back across it after we had cleared it and the jeep couldn't get through. I had a lot of wounded blokes at coy HQ, including Mr Brown (who unfortunately died afterwards) and couldn't get them back. Several of the stretcher-bearers were hit. About the same time Jerry put in a counter-attack and some of our bomb-happy crowd beat it. We were pretty disorganised and cut off from the rest of the battalion, so I decided to push on to a farm where we could form a firm base until the rest of the battalion

turned up. Actually they couldn't get through, but we were reasonably secure and about six o'clock Lance-Corporal Robinson (who was the only man alive who knew where you were) & I set off back to the cornfield to look for you. We could find no trace of you although we went *right back to the spot where you had been hit* so I thought either the stretcher-bearers had got through to you or you had been pinched by the Jerries. Captain Swinburn got a nice Blighty one and so did Mr Mercer. We are having a so-called rest. There are now nine D-Day wallahs left, including CSM Webb and self, but several wounded men have come back. I was very pleased to see them, as the stuff we have been getting lately was pretty bad as you know.

Please give my regards to your Mother, and let me know how you are getting on. I think the ruddy war will be over by the time you are boarded fit but if not try to get back to us. I took some French money out of your wallet equivalent to 35 shillings as I feared that otherwise some base wallah might pinch it. I enclose a cheque for same plus something to have a drink with me when you get out of Hospital.

For the infantry it was, in the words of A. P. Herbert, quoted in Crawford's diary:

> *New men, new weapons, bear the brunt*
> *New slogans guild the ancient game*
> *The infantry are still in front*
> *And mud and dust are much the same*
>
> *Hail humble footman, poised to fly*
> *Across the West or any Wall*
> *Proud, plodding, peerless PBI*
> *The foulest, finest job of all*

Sergeant Walter Caines, signal sergeant of 4th Dorsets:

1 August: The weather was blistering hot. The Colonel, now Lieut-Col G. Tilly, called his O group and issued orders. This was to be the first breakthrough in Normandy worth speaking of. The 4th Dorsets were to lead 130 Brigade, and were to be supported by tanks. It was anticipated that the battalion would cover some twenty miles before encountering the enemy (which proved to be wrong).

2 August: The advance started somewhere in the region of 00.15 hours and carried on heading south towards the village of Jurques. It was a terrible night, troops were lifted on tanks, and were continually dropping off to sleep. No one knew when the first pocket of resistance would be met, or whether we would be ambushed. I was as usual riding a motor cycle behind the second company. I don't know how I kept my eyes open.

After a brisk little battle, Jurques was cleared.

Just as the Battalion was passing through Jurques, I was notified that the signals scout car had been blown up on a mine. The adjutant and a corporal

Infantry takes cover from mortar fire on the move up to Ondefontaine. (B8589)

had been killed. The Signal officer had escaped, but was badly burnt on the face and hands. As we left the battered town, Jerry opened up with all he had, self-propelled guns and Spandaus. We were certainly in it again, and myself realising that I was now responsible for the Battalion communications. After heavy fighting we succeeded in capturing La Bigne, some two miles south of Jurques. All night long men dug and reinforced positions, while signallers were kept working on the endless task of getting a line through.

4 August: Orders were given to attack Ondefontaine. At 13.30 hours the attack started. By about 15.30 hours we were back in our original positions, badly shaken. Casualties had been heavy. Many wounded still lay out in the cornfield. Some managed to crawl back, others lay out until dark, or died of their wounds where they fell. Before the attack, all the lines had been reeled in, and now had to be relaid. We were short of signallers: one had been killed, and several wounded. Those that were left were tired and badly shaken up. I was feeling in no stout-hearted mood, but something had to be done. So Lance-Corporal Harris and myself set out to relay all the lines to forward companies. We were reeling out up a sunken road when suddenly shells whistled over. All was quiet for a moment, followed by a hell of a stonk. We dashed for cover behind a bank. One shell burst on the bank above Harris, shrapnel dented his crash helmet. Another crashed down knocking us silly. After some minutes of intense shelling, we pulled ourselves together, and returned, as Harris was a bit knocked up with shock. Taking Private Gapper, I started off to where we had left off. By the trenches of D Company, there were many corpses. Some of them looked as though they were asleep, but they were as dead as door nails. The night

Infantry waiting to advance in a narrow Normandy lane. The stretcher-bearers, the carrier and radios indicate that this is possibly a company headquarters or even part of a battalion headquarters.
(HU63662)

before Jerry had shelled the whole night as the boys were digging in. Some of the dead had shovels in their hands. Just as we set off again, a shot rang out, crack, crack, the dust kicked up around us. I shouted 'Come on, Gapper, let's beat it out of here.' I believe we could have won the 880 yards race. I think I lived about ten years in about ten seconds. The last two hundred yards, I told Gapper to go on to Tactical Headquarters, while I checked the line back. More shells came over, crash, crash, more and more. I lay flat in a ditch. This time I really did feel scared, probably because I had been without sleep for so long. Somehow I felt I should say a prayer, so lying on the ground, clasping my hands together, I prayed. It was terrifying. The stonk seemed as if it would not stop. After a while it was quiet, and having caught a glimpse of some boys of the Carrier Platoon, I decided to join them in their trench. To have dashed back to my trench at Tactical Headquarters would be stupid, as another rain of shells would shortly follow. I dived head first into their trench as another stonk came down. What a shambles, I had to laugh. When it was quiet, I rejoined the boys at Tactical Headquarters, to be told that the line had gone again. A few bloody words were said. But this time Corporal Hales went out. I heard nothing more of them until the early hours of the morning, when they reported 'through'. After a cold meal, I sat chatting on the edge of my dug-out with the Brigade Signal Officer who had paid us a visit, and promised fresh supply of cable in the morning.

5 August: Orders to pack up and advance to Ondefontaine again. At 14.00 hours, companies again left their trenches, and advanced up the winding roadway through a wood towards this village, but resistance was so stiff that the Colonel had no alternative to postponing the advance, and hold a

Shermans of 43rd Wessex Division near La Bigne moving up towards Ondefontaine. The banks and thick hedgerows of the bocage impeded vision and mobility. The prow on the front of the leading tank shows that it is a DD. (B8588)

position 300 yards from the village, where companies dug in. Because the set to Brigade Headquarters was not working, I was sent back to the Brigadier at about 22.00 hours with a message from the Colonel asking for instructions. I had to push my motor cycle down the road for a couple of hundred yards before starting up as quietly as possible. At one point I had to haul my machine over a tree blown to pieces across the road by a shell. Carrying on down the winding, narrow road, I had to be careful not to run over the dead from yesterday's failed attack completely littering the road in one place. Eventually I found Brigade Headquarters. It was about 01.00 hours when I saw the Brigadier who gave me a note instructing the Battalion to assault Ondefontaine at first light. The Colonel stressed the matter of fire control during the attack, and ordered bayonets to be used before bullets. The village was taken with hardly a shot being fired. Most of the enemy had pulled out, leaving many bodies behind. What opposition remained was quickly overcome.

On 8 August, Lieutenant-Colonel Gerald Tilly, CO of the 4th Dorsets, wrote to his wife telling her that he had been confirmed in command:

I am afraid I have not the foggiest idea what my pay is but I am pretty certain I get 10/– a day extra, knock off 5/– a day income tax, and at any rate that gives me £8 a month more. I will continue to send you another fiver a month as long as I have this exalted rank!

Lovely weather again as we are at long last in reserve for two days. Wash

Exhausted British Infantry. The censor has blanked out their shoulder titles and formation flashes to avoid the unit being identified. (HU63661)

and brush up. Had a hell of a meal last night – chicken, peas, potatoes, cabbage & whisky, & now for a spot of sleep – badly needed. A few dirty big bangs going on are liable to keep one awake. I have said to hell with a slit trench tonight & I am sleeping in a slightly shattered farm house.

In a letter written a few days later:

The Battalion has done very well & from the point of view of bouquets it is Roses, Roses, all the way. From the point of view of fighting it is chiefly Thorns.

Almost every day that his Regiment (Sherwood Rangers Yeomanry) was in battle, the Reverend Leslie Skinner had the distressing job of recovering bodies from tanks, in order to identify and bury them:

Friday 4 August: On foot located brewed-up tanks – Watson and Heslewood died of wounds at Dorsets RAP. Only ash and burnt metal in Birkett's tank. Dorsets MO says other members of crew consumed by fire having been KIA. Searched ash and found remains pelvic bones. At other tank three still bodies inside – partly burned and firmly welded together. Managed with difficult to identify Lt Campbell. Unable to remove bodies after long struggle – nasty business – sick. C Sqdn still wanting me for 2 burials; but after three unsuccessful attempts to reach them had to give up. Heavy fire each time I tried.

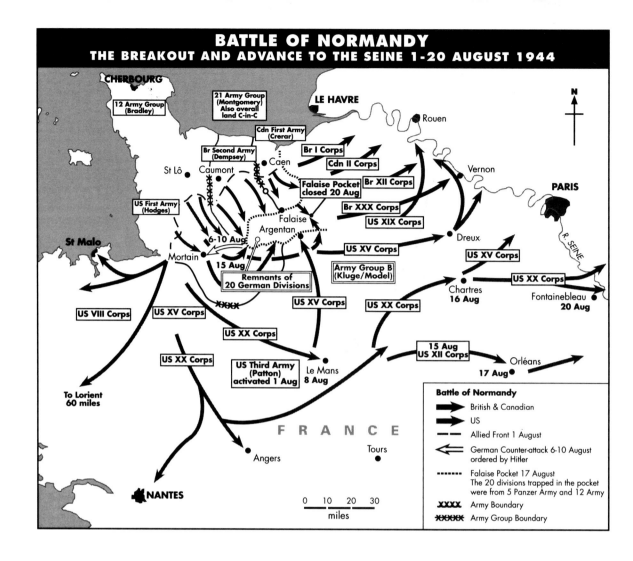

CHERBOURG

12 Army Group (Bradley)

21 Army Group (Montgomery) Also overall land C-in-C

LE HAVRE

Rouen

Cdn First Army (Crerar)

Br Second Army (Dempsey)

St Lô   Caumont   Caen

Br I Corps

Cdn II Corps

Falaise Pocket closed 20 Aug

Br XII Corps

Vernon

PARIS

US First Army (Hodges)

Br XXX Corps

US XIX Corps

Falaise

Argentan

St Malo

6-10 Aug

US XV Corps

Dreux

R. SEINE

15 Aug

Mortain

Remnants of 20 German Divisions

Army Group B (Kluge/Model)

US XV Corps

US XX Corps

US VIII Corps   US XV Corps

US XV Corps   US XX Corps

Chartres 16 Aug

Fontainebleau 20 Aug

US XX Corps

US XX Corps

US Third Army (Patton) activated 1 Aug

Le Mans 8 Aug

15 Aug US XII Corps

Orléans 17 Aug

F R A N C E

Tours

To Lorient 60 miles

Angers

Battle of Normandy

→ British & Canadian

→ US

– – – Allied Front 1 August

← German Counter-attack 6-10 August ordered by Hitler

····· Falaise Pocket 17 August The 20 divisions trapped in the pocket were from 5 Panzer Army and 12 Army

XXXX Army Boundary

XXXXX Army Group Boundary

NANTES

0   10   20   30
miles

Eventually Mont Pinçon fell to 129 Brigade of 43rd Division after two days of hard fighting. With the seizure of Mont Pinçon, the British and Canadian advance began to gain momentum, but slowly at first. Although defeat for the Germans in Normandy was around the corner, there was no let-up in the manner in which they fought. Hitler refused to allow a tactical withdrawal to the Seine. He ordered von Kluge, Rundstedt's successor as C.-in-C. West, to stand fast and counter-attack. By now Rommel was in hospital in Germany, after his staff car had been attacked by a Typhoon. He never returned to the battle, being forced to commit suicide some three months later in the aftermath of the failed attempt on Hitler's life.

One of the greatest handicaps suffered by German commanders was Hitler's constant interference in the conduct of every battle, and his refusal to give even the Commanders-in-Chief any freedom of action. Alarmed by the possible consequences of the American advance, Hitler ordered von Kluge to muster five panzer divisions (2nd, 1st SS, 2nd SS, 116 and 10th SS) together with 84th and 363rd Infantry Divisions and

A camera-gun shot of Typhoons firing rockets at a level crossing in France. (FLM2406)

An RAF pilot whose Typhoon has just crash-landed in a Normandy cornfield. The wing in the background belongs to a glider which had landed on D-Day or D plus one. (FLM2408)

On the left, Field Marshal Gerd von Rundstedt, German C.-in-C. West until superseded by von Kluge on 1 July 1944, for telling Field Marshal Keitel, Chief of the Wehrmacht Supreme Command, 'Make peace, you fools'. Hitler reinstated von Rundstedt as C.-in-C. West in September that year. (Captured German film FLM2374)

launch a counter-attack against the American left flank at Mortain, with the intention of reaching Avranches and cutting Bradley's forces in half. Sepp Dietrich, once Hitler's chauffeur, now the SS General commanding Vth Panzer Corps, spent an hour protesting to von Kluge that sending this force west would make holding Falaise impossible; massing armour would invite retaliation from the air; the Americans were already so strong south of Falaise that such an attack would only wedge the Germans tighter in the jaws of a trap, not destroy it. Von Kluge had only one reply; 'Es ist ein Führer Befehl' ('They are the Führer's orders').

Thanks to Ultra, the code-name for information gleaned from radio intercept, Bradley was forewarned. The brunt of the assault was borne by 30th US Infantry Division supported by two others. But alerted by intelligence, although they did not know it at the time, the Tactical Air Forces played a major part in the defeat of the panzer divisions. Sergeant Pilot Golley:

> The biggest deal was 7 August, there was quite a lot of mist about. Our wing leader flew off on a recce towards the Cherbourg peninsula. On his way there, he spotted a small hole in the cloud, and diving through, saw hundreds of tanks. He pulled up, and down again, really low this time. It was a whole panzer division at least. The wing leader radioed back, and every Typhoon squadron in Normandy was scrambled to attack this concentration of armour just outside Mortain. As the mist cleared, at about 11.45, we made our first attack. Twenty squadrons of Typhoons under Air Vice-Marshal Harry Broadhurst kept up a cycle of attacks from midday to about 16.00 hours under a blazing sun. It only took about 10 minutes to return to the strip, refuel, re-arm, and off again. The German gunners never

Air Vice-Marshal Harry Broadhurst, Commander 83 Group RAF, about to take off in his Spitfire from a strip in France. Broadhurst fought in the Battle of Britain, which gave him a credibility with his pilots, lacking in some senior officers whose most recent battle experience dated back to the First World War. He initiated the 'cab rank' system of on call close air support for the army when commanding the Desert Air Force. With his American opposite number, General 'Pete' Queseda, he was one of the few senior Allied airmen who was wholeheartedly committed to close air support for ground operations. (CL105)

had a chance to re-ammunition, but they kept fighting as long as they could. They were a great adversary.

On the same day, 1st Canadian Army, with 51st Highland Division under command, began its advance south to Falaise. By 17 August with the bulk of 7th German Army still west of the Orne, on Hitler's orders, the sack was closing round them, with the neck at Falaise and Argentan. As the sack was squeezed, particularly by the Canadians at Falaise, and on the western end where VIII and XXX Corps were still fighting in the fields and hedgerows, the texture of the battle was unchanged. But the advance was slowly beginning to gather momentum; Skinner:

Thursday 17 August: Up and on the move early at first light. Progress fast. Passing an orchard on hillside saw a tree of ripening apples as distinct from ever present cider apples. Dashed up hillside to get some. When I got there, two heavily armed German soldiers got up out of a slit trench and surrendered. Wot a lark.

On to all objectives by lunchtime. C Squadron [Sherwood Rangers Yeomanry] on other axis had rough time. Wounded evacuated along infantry stream. 8 men killed, 5 still in tanks. Went back to start line then forward along C Squadron axis. Buried the 3 dead and tried to reach remaining dead in tanks still too hot and burning. Place absolute shambles. Infantry dead and some Germans lying around. Horrible mess. Fearful job picking up bits and pieces and re-assembling for identification and putting men in blankets for burial. No infantry to help. Squadron Leader offered to lend me some men to help. Refused. Less men who live and fight in tanks have to do with this side of things the better. They know it happens, but to

An officer of the
Queens Royal
Regiment and an RAF
forward air controller
(with scarf round neck)
call down an air strike.
(CL568)

Helmets mark the
graves of crews of
wrecked German
tanks belonging to 2nd
SS Panzer Division
(Das Reich), caught by
Typhoons. Members of
this Division
massacred 640 French
civilians in the town of
Oradour-sur-Glane in
Central France en
route to the Normandy
battlefront in June
1944. (CL632)

force it on their attention is not good. My job. This was more than normally sick-making. Really ill – vomiting.

On return to C Squadron found tension vastly relieved by a Trooper who had gone up hillside with spade to relieve himself and having squatted down found himself facing a German soldier complete with hand grenades and automatic rifle who was staring at him from a bush about four feet away. Both leapt to their feet – the German to surrender. The sight of the heroic trooper clutching his trousers with one hand, brandishing his spade with the other, and marching his still-armed prisoner down the hill to captivity was quite a sight.

Late in the evening caught up with Regt'l HQ to find them leaguering up for the night in farm yard and paddock. Several Boche dead lying around. Very tired and fed up I started to tie them up for burial. Before I had finished the Brigadier turned up. He stopped to speak to me as I finished the burials and was being sick in the ditch.

But the end of the battle of Normandy was in sight. Trooper Baker:

Every one in the Regiment [4/7 Dragoon Guards] had to go over by lorry to hear a lecture by General Horrocks, who had just taken over command of XXX Corps. He was very good, and made us feel quite cheerful. He told us about the Falaise pocket – how the German Army was practically encircled and how the RAF were beating up fleeing columns on the roads. He was so up to the minute on his information, that just as he was telling us about a big new raid on the pocket, we saw the Lancasters passing overhead. He said that very soon we should be breaking out of the bridgehead and swanning off across France. That seemed absolutely incredible to us. We all

A Spitfire taxis to dispersal on an RAF airstrip in France alongside a French farmer reaping. (CL614)

RAF fighter pilots in France, summer 1944. Flying Officer Max Lloyd has his hair cut by Leading Aircraftsman William Heasman. (CL550)

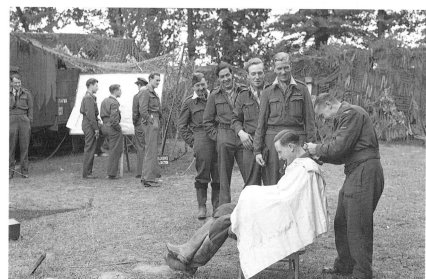

The daughter of a French farmer receives dental treatment from Flight Lieutenant B. D. Clark. (CL623)

Returning French civilians look at their wrecked home during the battle of Normandy. During the German occupation the rich farming countryside of Normandy had suffered little. Damage caused by the fighting was extensive. (B7692)

thought we should have to fight for every field all the way to Germany.

But Horrocks was right. We didn't know it, but the battle of Normandy was over for us. In a few days we should be starting on the next phase – 'The Great Swan'.

Major Martin wrote to his mother on 15 August:

At long last a day's rest. The War is much more amusing now we are on the move. I think I said in one of my earlier letters that once we got started things would happen with a rush. The weather incidentally is 'sans reproche', and we're getting pretty brown. My address is now BLA (British Liberation Army), a change from BWEF. The story is that it was changed when the troops thought it meant 'Burma When Europe's Finished'. [Unlikely, but fruitless, since BLA became 'Burma Looms Ahead'.]

Talking about liberation, that word is becoming, in our jargon, synonymous with total ruin and destruction. If you ask a chap what Villers-Bocage is like now, he will tell you it's been well and truly liberated. You can have no idea what some of these places look like. I have seen newly returned refugees staring at the rubble for hours on end, wondering if this gutted, brick-strewn ground was really their home. However in this cider apple orchard where I am writing, you would never have known there was a war on, except for the distant rumble as bombers pound the Falaise gap.

**Wreckage on one of
the roads in the Falaise
pocket.** (CL909WB)

**Wreckage on one of
the roads in the Falaise
pocket.** (CL909WB)

Captain Peter Balfour, squadron second-in-command of Left Flank, 3rd Mechanized Battalion Scots Guards, in 6th Guards Tank Brigade, writing to his parents on 19 August:

> When I wrote my last letter, we were involved in a whole series of scrappy and rather messy battles. At the time they seemed rather badly laid on and, as they were extremely tiring and caused a constant drain of casualties, we got a bit fed up, hence the slightly peevish tone of my last letter. But now as the 'Master Plan' unfolds, we realise how necessary they were and how they fitted into the bigger picture. It has been a most brilliantly managed campaign. I don't say it is over yet, but I don't think we shall fight in the bocage again at any rate.
>
> Anne writes to me that she supposes that there is some hope for Sydney, as he is only reported missing. I am afraid there is no hope of his turning up

German prisoners taken in the Falaise pocket. (B9670)

as the only reason he was reported missing is that the tank he was in was in such a mess that nobody could be identified.

On 20 August, the Falaise Pocket was closed; meanwhile the drive for the Seine had begun. By 24 August, the French and Americans had entered Paris. The battle for Normandy had cost the Germans 1,500 tanks, 3,500 guns and 20,000 vehicles. More than 40 German divisions had been destroyed, for the loss of 450,000 men. Only two German armies in the West retained any cohesion: the 15th Army in the Pas de Calais, and 19th Army in the south of France. The latter pulling back up the Rhône valley in front of the Americans after their invasion between Toulon and Cannes, on 15 August. Although huge numbers of Germans were taken prisoner, many of the better and more determined troops,

Infantry advancing into Falaise pass a scout car. (HU63660)

and their tough commanders got away across the Seine; for example, 2nd SS Panzer Corps, who were to cause so much trouble at Arnhem and Nijmegen less than a month after one of the greatest disasters to befall the German Army. This and other formations were to demonstrate the remarkable capacity for regeneration which characterized the German Army of the Second World War, no less than in the First.

The Allies had suffered 209,672 casualties, including 36,976 dead. In addition, around 28,000 Allied aircrew were lost in operations over France before D-Day, and in the subsequent battle. The Allied casualty rate surprises those who imagine that fighting the Germans in this War would be easier than in the Great War. The daily casualty rate of 2,723 suffered by the Allied Armies, over the seventy-seven days of the Battle for Normandy, was greater by 502 than the daily rate inflicted on the British Army, including the Royal Flying Corps, at the Third Battle of Ypres. If the associated aircrew, and ships and landing-craft crews are included, the figure is even higher.

Led by Horrocks's XXX Corps, with Guards and 11th Armoured Divisions in the van, the British dash to cross the Seine and on into Belgium and Holland was now on. Despite the horrors of Falaise and the total lack of air support, the Germans soon began to put up a stout resistance; at first in easily defeated small groups, but gradually as the advance neared Germany and the Siegfried Line, in a hastily co-ordinated but surprisingly effective defensive system.

Trooper Baker:

> For eight days we simply motored across France without firing a shot, or having a shot fired at us. It was amazing. The whole of XXX Corps was moving with XII Corps on the left, and the American XIX Corps on the right. Nobody knew where we were going from one day to the next. Gill (Commanding Officer), would call commander's conferences and say, 'The form is, there is no form', and we'd be off into the blue. Sometimes we would be in the lead, and sometimes following other Regiments, it made no difference. Often the advance would be led by the Regimental Harbourer, known as the 'Herald Angel', in a scout car. We had a new harbour every night.
>
> Our route lay through part of the Falaise Pocket, and we went along roads where Jerry columns had been caught by Typhoons. There were miles of wrecked and burnt vehicles, tanks, trucks, horse-drawn carts, limbers and wagons. There was a horrible stink of dead horses and men. In one place we came to an orchard where an SP had evidently had all its ammunition set off by a rocket. The blast had caught a Jerry 'jeep' about a hundred yards up the road, burning it and the driver to a frazzle.

Not everybody found the advance without incident. Trooper William Hewison of 1st RTR:

> *22 August*: Stopped in St-Martin-de-Lieu all afternoon where we had a sticky job clearing the houses. Not many RBs [Rifle Brigade] around for that job, and Jerry had a bazooka going which got Jerry German's tank, killing Corporal Mayberry, and also Sgt Bennett's. Late at night Queens and RBs supported us in clearing the houses. We halted near the truck that 5 Troop brewed [up] – HE clean on windscreen. Poor blighters inside absolutely torn up. I didn't have the guts to loot the bodies – too gruesome, but Ted Watkins and Vick hadn't any scruples, and got quite a haul. From the officer they got 1300 francs, a gold watch, camera and binoculars. Another watch was got and odd objects, and loot the Huns had taken. We buried them by the roadside and stuck their paybooks on the crosses.

Although, as in all wars there were cases of serious looting, most soldiers took things from damaged and deserted houses to make life more comfortable: knives, forks, a kettle, a small silk table-cloth as a scarf, perhaps a few bottles of calvados. Although strictly looting, pilfering would be a better description, and perfectly understandable given the circumstances. Even so, many soldiers had moral qualms and shared the view expressed by one nineteen-year-old:

An Allied psychological operations leaflet in the form of a newspaper dropped on the Germans after the closure of the Falaise pocket. The headline reads:

The Second Battle of France The Destruction of the German West Front

Underneath the left hand picture:

Everything is ripped up

The column on the right headed, I Lived Through It, **consists of accounts by captured German NCOs.**

Nummer 44

Luftpost

Extrablatt

Die zweite Schlacht um Frankreich

"ALLES IST ZERFETZT . . ."
So beschreibt der britische Kriegsberichter Alan Moorehead diese Szene völliger Vernichtung, die deutsches Kriegsgerät nur noch als Müllhaufen übriglässt.

Der Zerfall der deutschen Westfront

Die deutsche Front im Westen ist zusammengebrochen. Die 7. deutsche Armee, die einzige deutsche Elite-Armee im Westen, hat auf den Schlachtfeldern der Normandie und an der Seine ihr Grab gefunden. Mit ihr wurden alle Panzer-Verbände im Westen entweder vernichtet oder so schwer zusammengeschlagen, dass sie auf lange Zeit nicht mehr einsatzfähig sind, und das heisst: für die Dauer dieses Krieges sind sie damit ausgeschieden.

Allein an Gefangenen haben die deutschen Truppen in Frankreich in den ersten elf Wochen seit Beginn der Invasion mehr als 300 000 Mann verloren. 92 000 deutsche Soldaten wurden allein in den zwei Wochen vom 10. bis 25. August gefangengenommen.

Die deutsche Luftwaffe hat in den ersten 70 Tagen nach der alliierten Landung 2990 Flug-

zeuge verloren. Im gleichen Zeitraum wurden 1200 deutsche Panzer vernichtet.

Die deutsche 19. Armee, die Südfrankreich verteidigen sollte, befindet sich in voller Auflösung. Sie hat als Armee aufgehört zu existieren.

Die zweite Schlacht in Frankreich hat mit dem vollen Sieg der alliierten Waffen, mit der Vernichtung der deutschen Panzerkräfte im Westen, mit der Zerschlagung der deutschen Elite-Armeen geendet. Damit ist der Krieg endgültig entschieden. Es mag hier und da noch zu Kampfhandlungen kommen, zu Rückzugsgefechten, zu Verzögerungsaktionen. Aber die zweite Schlacht um Frankreich ist zu Ende. Die Schlacht um Deutschland in Deutschland beginnt.

Wie kam es zu der Katastrophe?

Drei Gründe sind es, die den katastrophalen Zerfall der deutschen Westfront in der Hauptsache verursacht haben:

1. Während der ganzen Dauer der Kämpfe hat sich die deutsche Führung als unterlegen erwiesen. Immer wieder hat sie sich geirrt, hat die Bewegungen des Gegners falsch eingeschätzt, hat die feindlichen Kräfte unter- und die eigenen überschätzt, hat nicht für einen einzigen Augenblick die Initiative zurückgewinnen können, die sie mit dem Augenblick der alliierten Landung verloren hatte, hat sich von der Hitler-Mentalität anstecken lassen und daher versucht, zu halten, was nach den Gesetzen der Strategie nicht zu halten war — bis es zu spät war, bis die Katastrophe unausbleiblich geworden war.

2. Die alliierte Überlegenheit in der Luft und der hoffnungslose Mangel an Maschinen in der deutschen Luftwaffe

machte eine deutsche Luftaufklärung unmöglich. Das war der Grund, warum es den Alliierten immer wieder gelang, das strategisch so wichtige Moment der Überraschung zur Anwendung zu bringen.

3. Auf dem Schlachtfeld selbst war die alliierte Überlegenheit an Material schlechthin überwältigend. Die alliierten Armeen sind heute die höchstmotorisierten Truppen der Welt. Um nur eine Vergleichszahl zu nennen: eine britische Infanterie-Division verfügt über 3 300 Kraftfahrzeuge, eine deutsche nur über 800.

Es gibt keine Wälle und keine "Linien" mehr, die imstande wären, gegen die gewaltige Zerfall der alliierten Panzer, Flugzeuge, Bomben und Granaten standzuhalten.

BOMBEN LEISTEN GANZE ARBEIT
Eine der Fluchtstrassen nach einem Angriff alliierter Jagdbomber.

"Ich war dabei"
Deutsche Soldaten berichten

Wie der deutsche Soldat selbst die zweite Schlacht um Frankreich gesehen und erlebt hat, das schildern die folgenden kurzen Berichte. Es sind Auszüge aus Erlebnisberichten, die deutsche Soldaten nach ihrer Gefangennahme über den Londoner Rundfunk gegeben haben.

"Wir sind einfach von der ungeheuren Materialüberlegenheit des Gegners erdrückt worden", erklärt ein Obergrenadier aus einem Panzergrenadier-Regiment. "Als unser Regiment von der Loire an die Normandie-Front abging, da hatten wir im ganzen Panzerregiment keinen einzigen Schützenpanzerwagen. Wir mussten französische Personenwagen beschlagnahmen, und mit diesen schnell zusammengeflickten Fahrzeugen fuhr unser stolzes Panzerregiment zum Einsatz. Auf dem Marsch hatten wir keinen Fliegerschutz. Schon schwerangeschlagen kamen wir ins Kampfgebiet. Eingesetzt wurden wir als gewöhnliche Infanterie. Das Ergebnis: Von meiner Kompanie sind noch ganze sechs Mann übrig."

Ein Obergefreiter aus München unterstreicht in seinem Bericht vor allem das Gefühl der Wehrlosigkeit des deutschen Soldaten gegenüber der Materialfülle des Gegners. Er sagt: "Die alliierten Geschütze zerfetzten Stellung auf Stellung. Flugzeuge lenkten ungestört das Feuer mit einer unheimlichen Präzision. Wir rechneten jeden Augenblick mit dem Auftreten deutscher Jäger. Ja, der ganze Himmel war schwarz von Flugzeugen, aber es waren Marauders, Taifuns, Liberators, Festungen, Mustangs, Wehrlos auf die Erde gepresst, lagen wir in unseren Stellungen."

Ein Unteroffizier aus einer thüringischen Kampfgruppe, der bei Cherbourg dabei war, erklärte: "Neunzehn Tage stand ich im Kampf um die Halbinsel Cherbourg. Wir steckten in einem Hexenkessel, wie er schrecklicher nicht vorstellbar ist. Und es vergingen Tage, ohne dass der feindliche Druck nachliess. Im Gegenteil, die Materialüberlegenheit der Amerikaner wuchs stündlich an. Und nun begann unsere Stimmung in das Gefühl der Hilflosigkeit umzuschlagen. Ich musste zusehen, wie viele meiner Kameraden vom Granaten- und Bomben zerrissen wurden, ohne zum Kampf zu kommen. Nun griff Verzweiflung in der Hölle von Cherbourg um sich. Wir erkannten, dass jeder weitere Widerstand sinnlos war . . ."

G. 27

It's queer this loot question. We are usual law-abiding citizens of the Kingdom, as soldiers have always been. When an army sweats blood and guts to win a town or ground, it presumes that that town is their prize – quite forgiveable really. And also because the civvies generally have flown, and houses are open and there's no one to stop you – you loot. And as you rifle the house, murmuring 'what a shame' frequently at the shell-holes in the walls, and the general damage of the place, sympathising with the unfortunate owner, at the same time pocketing his best silver, and a couple of watches maybe. It is very unfortunate, but there it is. If we, who have lost men and sweated pints to get there, *don't* pick up a thing or two there, the base-wallahs will. A poor excuse I know – though we generally have little opportunity for skipping out of the old tin-horse and indulging in a small amount of knick-knack filching.

Die Schlacht in Kartenskizzen

Die Landung

Schon wenige Stunden nach ihrer Landung am 6. Juni hatten die Alliierten den Atlantik-Wall durchbrochen und am 13. Juni ihre Landeköpfe in einer zusammenhängenden Front vereinigt. Rommel konzentrierte seine Hauptmacht bei Caen auf dem Ostflügel. Aber die Amerikaner schlugen weiter im Westen, am Fuss der Cherbourg-Halbinsel, zu. Die deutschen Verbände auf der Halbinsel wurden durch einen raschen Vorstoss zerspalten. Die Halbinsel selbst wurde abgeschnitten. Am 26. Juni musste sich Cherbourg mit 46 000 deutschen Soldaten ergeben.

Der Durchbruch

Am 26. Juli begann die grosse Offensive. Die deutschen Panzerdivisionen und SS-Verbände wurden auf dem Ostflügel durch starke britisch-kanadische Angriffe, die inzwischen zur Eroberung von Caen geführt hatten, gebunden. Die amerikanischen Verbände auf dem Westflügel durchbrachen am 31. Juli die deutschen Stellungen bei Avranches, trieben einen Panzerkeil quer durch die Bretagne, schwenkten mit einem anderen Panzerkeil erst nach Süden, dann nach Osten und schliesslich nach Norden mit der Stossrichtung auf Argentan ab, also in den Rücken der deutschen Abwehrfront hinein.

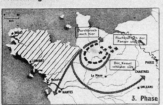

Der Kessel

Die deutsche Führung zog ihre Truppen nicht heraus, sondern setzte alle in Frankreich überhaupt verfügbaren SS- und Panzerverbände zu einer Gegenoffensive an, um den amerikanischen Panzerkeil abzuschneiden. Der Versuch misslang. Die Kanadier erstürmten Falaise, die Amerikaner eroberten Argentan, der Kessel wurde enger. Die SS- und Panzerverbände erhielten Befehl, sich herauszuschlagen. Nur wenige kamen durch, der Rest und mit ihm die Infanterie, die den Rückzug der Elite-Verbände decken sollte, wurden vernichtet. Von rund 100 000 deutschen Soldaten kamen nur 42 000 als Gefangene mit dem Leben davon.

Das Ende

Die Trümmer der geschlagenen Armee mussten nunmehr versuchen, in wilder Flucht die Seine zu erreichen. Aber ein noch weiter südlich ausholender amerikanischer Panzerkeil hatte inzwischen nach der Eroberung von Chartres und Orleans den zurückflutenden Truppen den Fluchtweg weiter östlich versperrt. Andere amerikanische Verbände überschritten die Seine und rückten an ihr entlang. Paris wurde befreit. Die Fluchtstrassen der deutschen Truppen wurden Tag und Nacht pausenlos angegriffen, Brücken über die Seine gab es nicht mehr. Die Berichte der alliierten Kriegsberichter auf dieser Seite und unsere Bilder geben ein eindrucksvolles Bild von dem Ausmass der Vernichtung.

Sie kamen nicht davon

Für die Trümmer der geschlagenen deutschen Armee, die nicht im Kessel von Falaise vernichtet worden waren, gab es kein Entrinnen. Unvorstellbare Szenen der Zerstörung und des Grauens spielten sich ab. Der britische Kriegsberichter Alan Moorehead schreibt über den Anblick der deutschen Rückzugstrassen:

„Alles ist zerfetzt und liegt offen da: Trümmer von Krafträdern, umgestürzten Lastwagen und Stabswagen in wildem Durcheinander. Geschütze mit den Mündungen in den Dreck gebohrt, der ganze Boden übersät mit Fetzen von Kleiderresten und Zeltbahnen. Deutsche Soldaten liegen da, mit dem Gesicht in den Boden gedrückt. Ueberall liegen Pferdekadaver herum. Der Magen dreht sich einem um bei dem Gestank.

Und diese Szene muss man sich verhundertfachen. Die alliierten Jagdbomber stürzen auf sie herab und zerschmettern sie, während sie in wilder Flucht ostwärts drängen. Hier kam die Infanterie, hilflos und wie blind über die Felder irrend. Einige hielten an und schossen zurück. Wie sie sich unter die Bäume warfen, wurden sie von den Geschützen zerfetzt. . . .‟

„Einer ganz oben . . .‟

Der amerikanische Kriegsberichter James Wellard schreibt:

„Es war das wildeste Gemetzel deutscher Soldaten, die grösste Materialzerstörung seit Beginn des Krieges. Mit blossem Auge ist zu sehen, wie unsere Granaten ihre Fahrzeuge treffen und sie in Rauch und Flammen aufgehen lassen, während kleine Lebewesen, deutsche Soldaten, wie die Ameisen auf dem Felde um sie herumwimmeln. Unsere Kanoniere können ihr Ziel nicht verfehlen. Während des ganzen Tages und der Nacht liefen die deutschen Kolonnen Spiessruten. Wir brachten eine erste, eine zweite, eine dritte Kolonne zum Stehen. Aber immer mehr kamen.

Schliesslich nahm dieses Schauspiel einen phantastischen Charakter an. Die eskelhafte Atmosphäre des Schlachthauses stieg auf. Einer oben, ganz oben, opferte Tausende und Abertausende von Menschenleben und die Ausrüstung einer ganzen Armee seinem Prestige zuliebe. Unseren Männern macht es keinen Spass mehr, in diese hilflose, bewegungsunfähige Masse ohne Zielen hineinzufeuern.‟

The back page, headed The Battle in Maps, **shows exactly how the Allied strategy worked with headings:** The Landing, The Encirclement, The Kill. **The column on the right is headed:** They Could Not Escape.

(Copy held in the Department of Printed Books, negative numbers HU63707/8)

On 24 August Paris fell to the Americans and French. Few British soldiers were present. Major Peter Carrington (later Lord Carrington) in 2nd Armoured Battalion Grenadier Guards:

> I and David Fraser were given 48 hours leave to spend swimming on the beach at Arromanches. We decided this would be rather boring. The Americans and French were about to liberate Paris, so we drove there in a couple of jeeps. There was still a bit of shooting going on when we arrived. We drove round to the Ritz. The Germans were going out of the back, as we drove up and booked in. The Hotel was quite unmoved by what they appeared to regard as a perfectly ordinary occurrence; one lot of visitors leaving and another lot coming in.

It would be wrong to imagine that units did not have spells out of the line at intervals throughout the campaign, or that individuals neither

Montgomery confers with his army commanders. Left to right: **Dempsey** (British 2nd Army), **Hodges** (United States 1st Army), **Crerar** (Canadian 1st Army), **Montgomery, Bradley** (12th Army Group) **all still under Montgomery's command but not for much longer. Soon after this picture was taken, Eisenhower took overall charge of all Allied armies in North-West Europe.** (B9474)

washed nor removed their boots from Bayeux to Brussels. Some spent several weeks resting, others less. Major Peter Martin:

> On 24 August we had a couple of days rest. One of the DLI battalions had a tremendous party which I attended. The medical officer was well away. Later, I was woken by one of my platoon commanders. The wife of the owner of the house in which his platoon was billeted, was about to give birth. The husband was asking for assistance. I dug out the MO, who said he would come straight away. When I asked him if he was fit, he replied that he would 'get the little bugger out even if I have to use a corkscrew'. All went well. The mother announced the child would be called Philippe Libération.

By this time, Eisenhower had taken over personal command of the land battle. Bradley's 12th US Army Group was removed from Montgomery's command. 21st Army Group, under Montgomery, now a Field Marshal, consisted of 1st Canadian Army and 2nd British Army. The wisdom or otherwise of Eisenhower taking direct control of the land battle has been debated ever since. It was undoubtedly necessary politically; the Americans had the greater proportion of forces in the field, and the disparity in numbers between them and the British would increase. Public opinion in the United States would hardly have stood for a British General continuing in overall command. Also without doubt, Eisenhower was not a success in this role. His forte was as a military statesman, not as a commander in the field, for which he had neither the experience nor temperament. As a compromiser and conference chairman he was without equal. Faced with strong-willed, battle-experienced commanders such as Patton and Montgomery, he was simply out of his depth. That said, it is difficult to see an alternative, if Allied sensibilities were to be soothed. Unless, as he offered, Montgomery placed himself under command of Bradley.

By 4 September, both Brussels and Antwerp were in British hands. Montgomery had driven his armour forward 250 miles in a week, making nonsense of the accusation by General Morgan on the staff of SHAEF, that he was a defensive General. 11th Armoured captured Antwerp before the Germans could blow the harbour sluice gates and dockside equipment.

On the day Antwerp fell, Hitler reinstated von Rundstedt as C.-in-C. West. Under him, the efficient and ruthless Model commanded Army Group B. Once dubbed by Hitler, 'the saviour of the Eastern Front', Model demanded reinforcements if he was to fulfil the order to hold a line from Antwerp, along the Albert Canal, the River Meuse, and to the Franco-Luxembourg frontier. Few troops were available. The nearest formed Army, the Fifteenth, was isolated in the Scheldt estuary and Walcheren. They would eventually escape by ferry, and across the causeway to South Beveland, taking about three weeks, and losing much equipment. Hitler scraped together men from hospitals, training regiments and officer cadet schools, but these, without mobility, were only capable of manning the fixed defences of the Siegfried Line or West Wall. At this point, Goering, like a conjuror pulling rabbits out of a hat, said he could raise a force from parachute troops under training. German parachute troops were part of the Luftwaffe, not the Army. They included: the 6th Parachute Regiment, a formation with a formidable fighting record, and reconstituted at a strength considerably greater than a normal regiment; one battalion 2nd Parachute Regiment; five new parachute battalions; and about 5,000 logistic troops. To this he would add 20,000 men from Luftwaffe aircrews, whose training had been stopped for lack of fuel, and redundant ground crews. Although all the paratroopers were not fully trained, they already possessed the elan and determination of parachute soldiers. These Luftwaffe troops formed the basis of Student's First Parachute Army. [Student had founded the German parachute formations, and led the assaults on Rotterdam and Crete.]

General Kurt Student, commander, German 1st Parachute Army.
(MH6100)

It was important for 2nd British Army to move quickly, and seize crossings over the Albert Canal. This was but the first of a series of waterways that crossed Montgomery's intended axis to the Ruhr, the last of which was the Rhine. Major Martin was told:

> When we got to Brussels, we would be there for four days. We drove to
> Brussels up exactly the same route as we had in 1940, through Tournai. The
> next evening I told the platoon commanders to go and have a really good
> time. I would hold the fort. They and most of the soldiers went off. At about
> 22.00 hours I was woken by a despatch rider from 151 Brigade HQ, with a
> complete change of orders. We were to move at 07.00 hours the next
> morning to the Albert Canal. Out of my usual 5 officers and 140 soldiers, I

had myself, one other officer and 30 soldiers. All the rest were out on the tiles in Brussels, where, we knew not. We sent all over the place scouting for our soldiers. The platoon commanders came in at about 03.00 hours. Somehow we got away at 07.00 hours. But it was a blow to morale. You think you're going to have a rest, and suddenly you're not, it's much more shattering that way.

On 8 September, Guards Armoured Division crossed the Albert Canal at Beeringen, establishing a bridgehead despite considerable opposition. By nightfall that day, 50th Division had secured a small bridgehead over the canal south-west of Gheel. Company Sergeant-Major Bill Brown, of D Company 8th DLI:

We were about to have three days' rest, when we heard we were to cross the Albert Canal that night. Assault boats were there to meet us. These were collapsible wood and canvas boats, and heavy to carry down the bank. We could see boats sinking, and blokes getting shot by German machine-guns. Later I was standing talking to a section commander in a sunken road, when the enemy opened up with a machine-gun. It looked like flashing lights going past me. I fell into the sunken road. About three men were killed, and my guts were oozing out. I said to a young officer, who had not been with us for long, 'Give us your hand, grip as tight as you can.' He took my hand. I was conscious all the time. I thought, 'If I lose consciousness, I will die.' Stretcher-bearers came up from another battalion. They put about four field dressings on me, put me on a stretcher, and the two stretcher-bearers carried me down the road.

The German machine-guns could have opened up on us, but they didn't. At the RAP I was given morphia. They wrote on my brow the time administered. The MO said it was definitely a Blighty one this time. I was put on a stretcher on a jeep, and given a cigarette. The engineers had built a bridge over the canal further along. As we drove, on the far side was a Tiger tank. The lad driving the jeep tooted his horn, and the man on the Tiger just waved. The jeep driver said, 'When we first came along, we found that tank there. The commander told me to just give a couple of toots on the horn, and we'll wave you through.' The tank must have been left behind when we crossed the canal.

The bridgehead formed by 8th DLI was out on a limb, about 1,000 yards to the right of the neighbouring bridgehead seized by 69th Brigade. Their sister battalion, 6th DLI, had also crossed and were advancing to Gheel. The Germans had shown that they were beginning to fight again with their customary aggressive skill: a portent of things to come. Major Peter Martin, now forward with his machine-gun company, after a night of confused fighting:

As the mist began to clear in the morning, the enemy tanks started to take a toll of our tanks and transport. Our anti-tank guns were having no effect on the well-concealed German armour, although a German commander who

stood up in the hatch of his tank, shouting in English, 'I want to die for
Hitler', had his wish fulfilled by one of my platoons. As the mist continued
to lift, Du Pre, one of my platoon commanders, spotted a Tiger 100 yards
away, facing in the opposite direction. He crawled to a Sherman nearby and
directed its fire onto the Tiger, brewing it up. This seemed to mark the turn
of the battle. The enemy may have sensed that they were in a very sticky
position, and began to withdraw. As soon as their tanks came out of hiding,
they were good targets for our anti-tank guns and Vickers.

Du Pre's Platoon engaged some German infantry withdrawing with a
Mark IV tank. The tank turned, advancing in a menacing way. The Platoon
Sergeant crawled on to a Sherman, directing the gun on to the Mark IV,
brewing it up. The Platoon, with their Vickers mounted on their carriers
drove in extended line straight for the enemy infantry, killing 15, wounding
20 and taking 60 prisoners.

By about 14.00 hours, the enemy were all accounted for, hardly a man,
gun or tank escaped. I found a young German hiding in a barn. I was very
angry, one of my best soldiers, Private Price, had been killed during the
night, just outside this barn. I thought this young man partly responsible.
Price had been with me right through the war. I was hopping mad, pointing
my finger at this young chap, shouting at him in fury. He was wounded. He
said he was only seventeen, and had been in the army three months. His
friends had stripped him of everything of value, including watch and
money. I took him prisoner. It was one of those times, one was so angry
that one is not in control – or hardly.

Trooper Baker also records the dangers of underestimating the Germans, and their increasing aggression and stiffening resistance after the
long 'swan':

A party of Jerry paratroops had run into the combined Al Echelons of the
Brigade, who were parked in the woods near Beeringen. During the
engagement, thirty-three lorries from the three echelons were destroyed,
mostly brewed up by bazookas or machine-gun fire, and there were quite a
lot of casualties. The RSM unfortunately got away.

Meanwhile the Canadians had been advancing along the coast clearing
the Pas de Calais of enemy except for garrisons besieged in Boulogne,
Calais and Dunkirk. On 10 September, 51st Highland and 49th Divisions
of 1st British Corps attacked Le Havre, after a bombardment by the
Navy and several attacks by Bomber Command. After 48 hours' fighting, one of the strongest fortresses of the Atlantic Wall had fallen. The
specialized armour attached from Hobart's 79th Division had played a
notable part in overcoming the concrete defences, minefields and
obstacles. By 13 September, XXX Corps had advanced to, and secured a
crossing over, the Meuse–Escaut Canal. The stage was set for Montgomery's thrust to the Rhine and beyond; Operation Market Garden.

CHAPTER FIVE

'...We stand at the door of Germany...'

OPERATION MARKET GARDEN

A British 17-pounder anti-tank gun at Nijmegen Bridge. The detachment commander, wearing an American helmet, is looking through binoculars among the crew. (B10171)

Following the fall of Antwerp, Montgomery ordered Dempsey's Second British Army to secure crossings over the obstacles in the area Grave–Nijmegen–Arnhem. Once across the Lower Rhine at Arnhem, Montgomery intended to advance east towards Osnabruck, Munster and Hamm, and from here along the eastern face of the Ruhr. Meanwhile the Canadian First Army was to clear the Scheldt estuary, in order to open Antwerp as the main supply base for the Allied Armies.

Between Second British Army on the Meuse–Escaut Canal and the far bank of the Rhine, lay three broad canals and three great rivers, from south to north: the Wilhelmina Canal, the Zuid Wilhelmina Canal, the river Maas, the Maas–Waal canal, the river Waal and the Lower Rhine. Dempsey's plan included the laying of a 'carpet' of airborne troops across the waterways, and the seizure of a bridgehead north of Arnhem. The laying of this carpet was to be the responsibility of the Commander 1st Allied Airborne Army, General Brereton, an American airman. The airborne troops were to be provided by Lieutenant-General Browning's 1st Airborne Corps, consisting of the 82nd and 101st US and 1st British Airborne Divisions. The canal crossings between Eindhoven and Veghel were allocated to the 101st, placed under XXX British Corps for the operation. The bridges over the Maas, the Waal and the Maas–Waal Canal were the objectives of the 82nd. The British 1st Airborne Division was given the most distant objective, the bridge over the Lower Rhine at Arnhem. This Division, commanded by Major-General Urquhart, consisted of four brigades: the 1st Parachute Brigade (Brigadier Lathbury), 4th Parachute Brigade (Brigadier Hackett), 1st Polish Independent Parachute Brigade (Major-General Sosabowski) and 1st Air Landing Brigade (Brigadier Hicks). Browning was also given 52nd Lowland Division, an airportable formation, to be landed in transport aircraft on Deelan airfield north of Arnhem, once it had been secured. In the van of Second Army's advance across the airborne carpet, would be Horrock's XXX Corps, consisting of Guards Armoured Division, 43rd Wessex and 50th Infantry Divisions. Horrocks would have XII Corps on his left and VIII Corps on his right. The code-name for the airborne operation was Market, and for the ground advance, Garden.

Market Garden, and the Arnhem part of the operation in particular, is one of the big 'ifs' of the Second World War. The principal reason for failure was the air plan imposed by the senior airmen for all three airborne divisions. The landings were in daylight; the DZs and LZs were too far from the objectives; no use was made of glider-borne *coup-de-main* operations; in all divisions, landings were made on one side of major water obstacles. Lack of aircraft led to the lift being carried out over three days. Surprise was lost. The enemy, who were not as some claim, sitting on, or even close to, the DZs, were given time to block the way to the key objectives, and counter-attack. In the case of British 1st Airborne Division, this resulted in the destruction of the division and the failure of the operation. The massive close air support available to the Allies, so

decisive in Normandy, was not fully exploited, particularly at Arnhem, where 1st Airborne Division were out on a limb. The Germans were able to bring reinforcements into Arnhem by road, in daylight, with impunity, an operation fraught with risk in Normandy a few weeks earlier. Sergeant Pilot John Golley:

> The Second Tactical Air Force could have destroyed the German armour. We were angry that we had to sit about, doing nothing. We regarded it as one of the biggest cock-ups of the war. It was an air force balls-up from start to finish.

Although somewhat intemperate as one might expect from a young sergeant pilot, he puts his finger on the principal reason for the failure of the operation: a flawed air plan. The airmen flying on the operation, particularly in unarmed transports, were to demonstrate that their courage and determination was undimmed. More boldness on the part of the most senior air commanders might have ensured that the efforts of the aircrew were not wasted.

Despite the reservations that both Urquhart and Browning had

British infantry crossing the Escaut Canal en route to Beeringen. (B9983)

about the plan, there was no quibbling by either. Browning, the 'father of British Airborne forces' was longing to lead his men into battle. Urquhart, and others in 1st Airborne Division, were worried, with good reason, about the morale of the Division. Between 6 June and 12 September, the Division had been stood by for sixteen operations, all of them cancelled, on four occasions when some of the aircraft were in the air. Urquhart told Montgomery's biographer, Nigel Hamilton: 'By the time we went on Market Garden, we couldn't have cared less . . . You have to visualise the euphoria which existed across the channel and in the airborne corps that the war was nearly over. Some time before he died, Urquhart repeated those words to the author of this book. Major Hibbert, the Brigade Major of 1st Parachute Brigade, told the author: 'A feeling of total exasperation and despair was felt by many of us in 1st Parachute Brigade. If we'd been asked to drop into the middle of Berlin and wait for the Russians, we would have gone quite cheerfully.'

Diary entries for early September by Lieutenant John Blackwood, commanding number 6 Platoon, 11th Parachute Battalion in Hackett's Brigade:

> *Sat 2 Sep 44:* Briefed to drop SE of Courtrai in Belgium to stop the Hun retreat across the R. Escaut. Cancelled because of the storm. Damn the storm.
> *Sun 3 Sep 44:* Fifth anniversary of the outbreak of war. Briefed to drop near Maastricht, near the Dutch border. Cancelled because the Yankee armour advancing too fast. Damn the Yanks.

Sergeant Ron Kent, a 23-year-old section commander in 21st Independent Parachute Company:

> The suspense was killing us and action was the only antidote. We were tired of fighting the Yanks in the pubs in Salisbury, Newark and Huddersfield. We were like boxers in danger of becoming overtrained and afraid of passing our peak.

Brigadier John Hackett, commanding 4th Parachute Brigade:

> Your last letters are written, you are sitting in the aircraft, somebody comes round and says: 'All right, out you get, it's all off. You can all have three days leave.' It weighed with Boy Browning. You had highly motivated, first-class troops, among the best in the army. But if you went on doing that to them, the division would fall apart.

On the first day of Market, Urquhart planned to drop Lathbury's 1st Parachute Brigade on DZ X, land Hicks's 1st Air Landing Brigade, less two companies on LZ S, and in gliders land Divisional Headquarters, most of his artillery, 21st Reconnaissance Squadron and others such as engineers and medical on LZ Z. The Reconnaissance Squadron would dash for the Arnhem road bridge in their jeeps equipped with Vickers K guns. 1st Parachute Brigade would follow on foot at best speed. Hicks would protect the LZs and DZs until the arrival of Hackett's 4th Parachute Brigade and other units on day two. Thus the air landing battalions, the best equipped and strongest in the division, were tied to protecting ground rather than going for the divisional objective, the bridge. On day three, 1st Polish Independent Parachute Brigade would drop south of the bridge on DZ K. If all went well, by the end of day three, the division, consisting of four brigades of infantry, would be formed into a three-sided box around Arnhem, with the south side resting on the river. There they would wait the arrival of XXX Corps from the south. Hackett:

> Many of the planners at Airborne Corps were highly courageous boy scouts. They hadn't fought the Germans, and didn't realise that however lightly the German army were holding a position, the moment you threatened something they regarded as vital, their reaction would be swift and violent. The people on Browning's staff planned the deployment of the airborne division without any real reference to what it was going to do when it arrived. They took little account of what the enemy would do. They were like chefs preparing a delicious dish, to which they added salt and pepper to taste. The salt and pepper were the Germans. When you are fighting people of that quality, you should take account of them first. I had fought against the Germans in North Africa and Italy.
>
> In my final briefing for the operation, I had about 100 officers present from my Brigade. I went through the plan in great detail. Our tasks were to garrison the northern approaches to Arnhem town, to hold the bridgehead already established by 1st Parachute Brigade at the Bridge. I could tell every platoon where it was going to be, and show them on beautiful maps. When it was all over, I dismissed that gathering, and kept behind the Commanding Officers and key staff. I said: 'You can forget all that. Your hardest fighting, and heaviest casualties will occur not defending the northern perimeter of Arnhem. They will be in trying to get there.' And of course we never did get there.

Sergeant Kent:

> The briefing we received on Saturday 16 September was not unlike the one we heard two weeks earlier. Most of the attention was given to the landing schedule. Information about the enemy dispositions was fragmentary and largely ignored. We were told we were going to Arnhem. The same as for the operation cancelled two weeks ago. The dropping zone was about five and a half miles west of Arnhem. If we could take and hold the bridge at Arnhem long enough, we might be in Berlin by Christmas. It was expected that the spearhead of 2nd Army would reach us within forty-eight hours of our landing. We felt it right and proper that the hardest task should be handed to the British 1st Airborne. The task of marking DZ X for the 1st Parachute Brigade fell to my platoon.

Lieutenant-Colonel John Frost, commanding 2nd Parachute Battalion:

I with 2nd Parachute Battalion was to take the three bridges over the Rhine. First the railway bridge, which was about four miles outside the town. Next a pontoon bridge, which was right inside the town, and finally the big main road bridge. I was to have part of my force on the south side of the main bridge, but the bulk on the north side. By the time we had this bridge, of course, we hoped that the rest of the brigade would have arrived in Arnhem and would be holding a perimeter north of the bridge.

We were told there was no question of any enemy armour, that they would probably consist of a few SS recruits, and a good many Dutchmen at that, who were being trained in the vicinity of Arnhem, and Luftwaffe personnel including men manning the anti-aircraft guns. We did know that there were quite a number of these. This was one of the reasons given for the inability of the air forces to land us anywhere near the main objectives. I thought that having to take three bridges was asking rather a lot. I wasn't at all happy at having my force split by the river. I would have preferred it if we had been given the task of taking the north end of the bridge, and somebody else the south end, by dropping south of the river. There was little time to raise this with Lathbury; there was a great sense of urgency. It isn't really until you look at the details of the thing that you begin to see the snags. Of course I never liked the business of dropping so far away, but even a cursory glance at a map showed there were no suitable DZs much nearer north of the river. But there was perfectly good terrain for dropping parachutists immediately south of the bridge.

Sergeant Mike Lewis, had been wounded serving in Frost's Battalion in North Africa, and joined the Airborne Section of the Army Film Unit in time to take part in the Sicily operation:

I was pessimistic about the Arnhem operation. My previous two parachute operations [Oudna in North Africa and Sicily] had been cock-ups. My task was to film the capture of the Arnhem Bridge and the relief by 2nd British Army, on both cine and still cameras.

With a camera you have a choice – unlike the continual exposure to danger and discomfort of a man with a rifle. At night you can go back and get some sleep. The next morning you can decide whether to go out, or wait until coffee time. You are in a privileged position – relatively.

The Independent Parachute Company were in the leading aircraft of those carrying 1st British Airborne Division, at the head of an air armada of 1,534 troop-carrying aircraft, and 491 gliders and tugs. They were carrying the first lift of three airborne divisions, taking off from twenty-two airfields in England. Eventually nearly 35,000 airborne soldiers would be lifted in to battle, on this and the succeeding days. That first day there were nearly 1,000 Allied fighters and fighter-bombers in the sky to protect the transport streams. Sergeant Kent:

Reveille was at some unearthly hour. 'What's the betting we'll be on a forty-eight hour pass to London tomorrow,' one voice mooted. Forty-eight-

'At Fairford we could see twelve big black Stirling bombers lined up at the end of the runway.'
SERGEANT RON KENT
21st Independent Parachute Company, 1st Airborne Division

This is number 3 Platoon. (CL1154)

Parachute soldiers checking harness before emplaning. The pregnant appearance is caused by wearing the small pack and ammunition pouches under the jumping smock to avoid the equipment snagging on the lift webs or rigging lines of the parachute as it deployed from the pack on the jumper's back. British airborne soldiers did not have reserve parachutes at the time. (K7591)

hour passes always followed an aborted operation, and we were getting a bit ashamed of it. It was time we went. We could not have the war end with 6th Airborne getting all the glory for its D-Day operations.

At Fairford, we could see twelve big black Stirling bombers lined up at the end of the runway. Stick commanders, like myself, made the acquaintance of the navigator and crew. The plan for us was to drop about twenty minutes ahead of the main body. The navigator and I compared notes over maps and air photographs taken the week before. I pointed out the roof of a farm building not far from the centre of our DZ, and asked if he could drop us within a hundred yards or so. He saw no problem.

After an hour or so in the air, I found myself looking at my watch rather too often; a sign of nervousness I had deliberately to suppress. I began to yawn wide and often, another nervous reaction. Others were yawning too. One was busy being air sick. The noise of the engines made normal conversation impossible. A thumbs-up sign to him brought a grin to his ashen face, and the OK sign of circle of thumb and forefinger. For all his discomfort – his eyes were still tear-filled from the effort of vomiting – his morale was good. He would be only too glad to jump into fresh clean air.

'Ten minutes to go,' was passed down the stick. We stood, and eased our way closer to the hole. I began to sweat. Weighed down with parachute on my back, full battle order on my chest [under the jumping smock], my helmet (the top of which was stuffed with half a pound of pipe tobacco) on my head, I waited in the queue. A red light flicked on in the roof above the aperture. We pressed forward on each others backs. Red changed to green. As if by magic the men before me disappeared, I was at the aperture, through it, and out into the slipstream. I came down in soft plough, close to the farm building. The rest of the stick were within a few hundred yards. The navigator had been as good as his word.

By the time I made contact with my Platoon Commander, the DZ letter X was out, the beacon was sited and ready, and smoke candles were in position. We had no casualties. Not so much as a sprained ankle. It was all so peaceful on that beautiful Sunday morning. The rest of the platoon were fanning out into defensive positions round the DZ. I fished out one of several pipes I had packed in my equipment, took a packet of tobacco from my helmet, filled, and lit up. It was all too perfect to be true. If this was German-held territory, where were the Germans?

Next of 1st Airborne Division to arrive were the gliders bringing Hicks's 1st Air Landing Brigade, Divisional Headquarters, some of the Artillery and other Divisional Troops. Staff Sergeant Godfrey Freeman, a glider co-pilot:

It was my first operation, I didn't know what to expect. The intercomm crackled. 'OK, tug,' said the pilot, 'leaving you any minute now. Thanks for a lovely ride.'

'Don't mention it, it was a pleasure.'

He pushed down the release lever, and we were off, slowing down to

OPERATION MARKET GARDEN

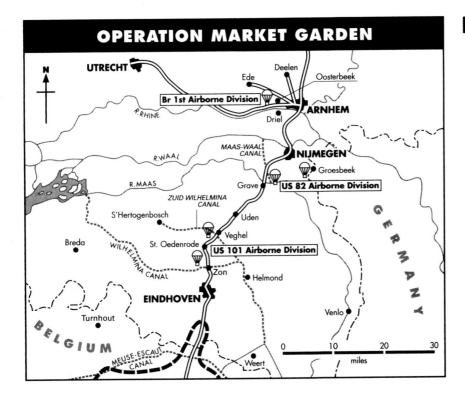

gliding speed, beginning to lose height. I kept a sharp look out for other gliders crossing our path. There were none. As we made a half circuit, I waited for the first shots to be fired at us, but none came. We swung into another turn, half flap down, the nose dipped; four hundred feet. Full flap, we were standing on our nose. Surely someone down there had his sights on us; we seemed to hang in the air. We flattened out, bump, jolt, rolling a few yards, stop. Down in one piece, we had landed unopposed. We sweated for half an hour before the load was off. Still there was no opposition.

A number of gliders flipped or crashed into trees. After a journey in a glider, which often ended with the floor awash with vomit, it was little wonder that many soldiers felt the same as Private E. W. Brown, in R Company, 1st Parachute Battalion, now coming in with 1st Parachute Brigade. Originally in an air landing battalion:

> I didn't think a lot of being in a glider regiment. Just getting a shilling a day [5p] extra for going in a plane with no engine wasn't for me. I might as well get two shillings a day for jumping out as a paratrooper, and it seemed that there was a lot more of the lads thought the same as me. So we volunteered for the Parachute Regiment.

Sergeant Ron Kent waiting for the Brigade on DZ X:

> Above us the Dakotas began disgorging the men who in North Africa had earned us the nom de guerre, 'the Red Devils'. The sky blossomed with hundreds of parachutes bearing the tough and exuberant men of the 1st, 2nd and 3rd Parachute Battalions. I had a number of old comrades with

Film still of one of the DZs to the west of Arnhem, with parachute soldiers still descending. The panel in the foreground is a DZ marker panel. The small dot below each parachutist is his kit bag. He jumped with it attached to one leg by a quick release pin, and by a long cord to his harness. As soon as possible after jumping he pulled the pin and lowered the bag to the extent of the cord.
(FLM2385)

these battalions. I saw one of them before he led his section off the DZ. We wished each other luck, and promised we would meet for a beer in Arnhem once we got to the bridge, and Second Army linked up. Watching those battalions forming up and streaming off the DZ in the direction of Arnhem, I had no reason to doubt that we would do just that in a few days' time. So far there had been no shooting, but as the battalions moved away from us, sporadic shots could be heard from about half a mile away. Our job was done, and we had orders to RV about a mile away to the north.

Model was drinking a glass of wine as a pre-lunch aperitif when the streams of aircraft passed over his Headquarters in Oosterbeek. He and his staff motored off to Doetinchem, twenty-one miles from Arnhem to find Bittrich, the commander of II SS Panzer Corps. Many of Bittrich's units (all located over twenty miles from Arnhem) were due to leave for Germany that day, and had entrained already. Some trains had left Arnhem station. Working with great speed, his staff reassembled the equipment of the two divisions. When Model arrived, he found II SS Panzer Corps already on the move. A battle group of 9th SS Panzer

Division was on its way to the DZs and LZs with orders to destroy the British landings west of Oosterbeek. The rest of 9th SS Panzer, a division in name only, was ordered to set up blocking positions west of Arnhem. Bittrich had ordered 10th SS Panzer Division to drive south to seize the Nijmegen bridge, and halt or delay the link-up forces, to give him time to destroy the British Airborne soldiers with the help of reinforcements brought in from Army Group B.

Stationed between Oosterbeek and Wolfheze was Sturmbannführer Kraft's SS Panzer Grenadier Depot and Reserve Battalion number 16. When he saw the landings he was in no doubt what he should do: drive right into it. He assessed that aggressive action was preferable to a purely defensive role. The action of this training battalion of twelve officers and 294 men, many under-age and unfit, albeit equipped with light dual-purpose flak guns, anti-tank guns, mortars and machine-guns, was to cost the British dearly.

Field Marshal Walter Model, who had relieved von Kluge as C.-in-C. West in mid August 1944. He was demoted to command Army Group B in September when Antwerp fell, when Hitler re-instated von Rundstedt, and held that appointment until March 1945, when he committed suicide rather than surrender. (MH12850)

Lathbury had ordered 2nd Parachute Battalion to move along a road running into Arnhem along the north bank of the Lower Rhine. The 3rd Battalion was also to make for the road bridge, but take a more northerly route into town. The 1st Battalion was ordered to move on the most northerly route, making for some high ground overlooking the town. By advancing on three routes simultaneously, Lathbury was left without a brigade reserve to exploit success, other than one company taken from the 1st Battalion. Brigadier Gerald Lathbury in his diary:

> The Dutch on the DZ said that there were not many Germans in Arnhem, but a few SS.
>
> Came up with 2nd Bn about one and a half miles along road. Leading company held up by minor opposition. Emphasised to Frost the need to bypass resistance, and then off to see 3rd Bn. Wireless working well. Brigade Major came through on set at about this time – 17.30 – and said the Divisional Commander thought we were being too slow. I again emphasised policy of bypassing opposition and pushing on to all COs.
>
> I was just thinking of returning to my Headquarters [with 2nd Battalion] when the enemy opened machine-gun fire on the road from the north and onto A Company who were halted in rear of the Battalion. I told A Company to clear this up, and meanwhile decided to stay put. The General then arrived in his jeep and was shot at by the machine-guns. It was decided with the CO to go into a 'Hedgehog' where it was as it was getting dark.
>
> Meanwhile we heard from the Brigade Major on the wireless that the 2nd Bn had captured the bridge. Splendid! After that all wireless communication broke down. A quiet night.

Lathbury does not mention in his diary that, at 19.30, well before nightfall, Major Hibbert the Brigade Major, who with the bulk of 1st Brigade Headquarters was following 2nd Battalion along the route by the river into Arnhem, had suggested to Lathbury that he switch the 3rd

Battalion to the southern route. He again emphasized this point, when at 21.30 he informed Lathbury that 2nd Battalion were on the main bridge. This route remained passable until the early hours of the next day. It must have been clear to Lathbury from these two radio conversations with his Brigade Major that the southern route offered the best chance of getting his whole brigade to the bridge, provided he seized the opportunity at once. If, instead of spending a quiet night, Lathbury had immediately ordered 1st and 3rd Battalions to swing south and followed Frost's route to the bridge, they might have managed to join him before the Germans blocked this last way in. As the older hands in the Brigade who had fought in North Africa could have told him, even if Lathbury had not learned from his experience in Sicily, the Germans, good as they were, did not operate well at night. They again showed this tendency at Arnhem. Failure to capitalize on this weakness was a major oversight, repeated later in the operation.

Although Frost's leading company reached the bridge at 20.00 hours, the progress of the Battalion had not been without incident. The plan required an advance through a built-up area where even a handful of riflemen can hold up many times their number; and 1st Parachute Brigade was facing more than a few riflemen. It is difficult for lightly equipped infantry to brush aside even light armour. Oosterbeek and the suburbs of Arnhem consisted of woods, detached houses and gardens. Every back garden was surrounded by a stout chest-high wire fence. When the point was held up by enemy fire, the following sections and platoons trying to outflank the opposition made painfully slow progress; every fifteen or twenty yards heavily laden soldiers had to climb a fence. The slow dawdle of troops at the rear of a battalion fighting its way forward on a one-man front can be infuriating to a commander following up behind. Hence Urquhart's impatience. To add to his problems, the mechanics of command and control were not working smoothly. Any formation after a year without action, takes time to wind up to top revs in battle, and the process was made more difficult by problems with the radios. Although communications were not as bad as some have made out since, they were far from satisfactory. The cumbersome valve wirelesses of the time, sensitive to changes of terrain, were a far cry from the robust, light-weight, military radios of today. Frost:

> For an ordinary formation advancing it's quite simple, because your sets are tuned and netted, and you just walk forward with them switched on – even if you are in radio silence. But our sets had to be loaded into aircraft at several airfields, after netting and tuning in England. On arrival, sometimes with a hefty crump, which puts the wireless off net, and in different terrain, it is understandable that they didn't work. That meant that commanders had great difficulty exercising command.

Frost had detailed his C Company to take the railway bridge. Private J. Mckernon:

Owing to the good line of approach we were able to get within 100 yards of the bridge without being seen. The Germans ran across the bridge to the south side and we fired on them. 9 Platoon charges across the bridge and halfway across they are fired on by machine-guns in a blockhouse on the south side. The bridge then blew up in a cloud of smoke. The platoon retired to the north side.

A German assault gun in Oosterbeek. A captured German photograph. (HU2128)

Unless the pontoon bridge was still in place, 2nd Battalion would have to take the southern end of the road bridge by crossing it first. The decision not to drop or land on both sides of the river was now coming home to roost. Mckernon's company never reached the Bridge, which was held by parts of 2nd Battalion, a very reduced C Company of 3rd Battalion, most of 1st Brigade HQ (less Lathbury), and parties from several other units, including engineers, drivers, divisional reconnaissance and glider pilots. The pontoon bridge was found to have been dismantled. Attempts to cross the main bridge failed.

By now the leading troops of XXX Corps, 2nd and 3rd Battalions Irish Guards, had advanced some seven out of the sixty-four miles to

Arnhem, reaching Walkenswaard, six miles short of Eindhoven, which was their objective for that day. To begin with the road to Arnhem from the Meuse–Escaut canal ran through wooded heaths and cultivated fields. But further north, it ran on a high dyke through polder. Here it was impossible to deploy vehicles off the road, and there were 20,000 of them. In places they drove two abreast, and southbound traffic was forbidden. Vehicles motoring on top of the dyke were silhouetted like sitting ducks to 88s and parties of infantry equipped with *panzerfausts*. Breakdowns, or vehicles blown up by mines, caused lengthy delays while recovery vehicles from further back struggled through rush-hour type traffic jams.

Once across the Waal, there were two other feasible routes to the Rhine within a reasonable distance from Arnhem, using minor roads to the west of the main Nijmegen–Arnhem road. In one pre-1940 paper test exercise set annually at the Dutch Army Staff College, students were required to send a force north from Nijmegen to capture the Arnhem road bridge. Any student moving his force up the main road failed the test. The school solution was to threaten an attack on the main road, while approaching the river on minor roads and attack the bridge along the south bank of the Rhine.

XXX Corps, having delayed the advance for nineteen hours after the Grenadier Guards and 82nd Airborne Division had between them captured Nijmegen road bridge, attempted to advance up the main road. Another twenty-four hours were to pass before 43rd Wessex Division began to use the minor roads to outflank 10th SS Panzer Division blocking the main road.

The two American Airborne Divisions had also landed with fewer casualties than expected. But in the 101st Division area, the Son bridge over the Wilhelmina Canal had been blown as 506th Parachute Infantry Regiment advanced towards it, en route to their objective, Eindhoven. General Williams USAAF had refused to allow a drop south of the Canal, so 506th had an eight-mile approach to their objective across a water gap. Although engineers constructed a footbridge, the Regiment stopped for the night and did not enter Eindhoven until the next morning, instead of two hours after dropping as planned. The timetable was falling behind. More serious was the loss of the Son bridge and, later, an alternative bridge over the Canal. The 101st had fifteen miles of road to keep open against German counter-attacks.

Further north, the 82nd Airborne Division had also dropped eight miles from their main objective, the Nijmegen bridge, then the largest road bridge in Europe. They did not make for it straight away, because Browning had ordered Gavin to take the Groesbeek Heights before the bridge. The Groesbeek Heights were of no tactical significance whatever. Again the drops were all on one side of a major river, this time to the south of the Waal.

Early on Monday 18 September, 1st and 3rd Parachute Battalions set

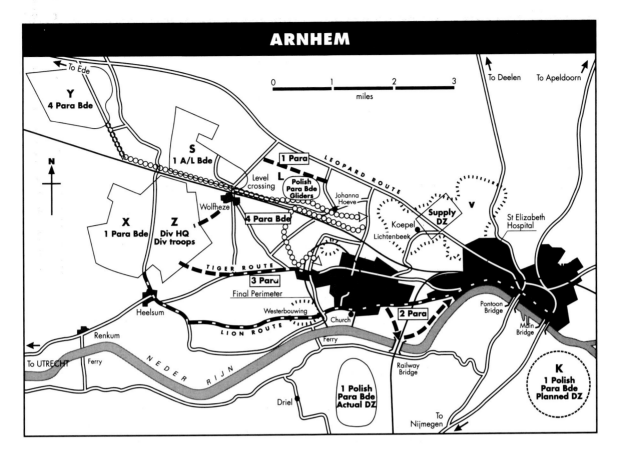

Maps labels:
To Ede · Y 4 Para Bde · To Deelen · To Apeldoorn · S 1 A/L Bde · 1 Para · LEOPARD ROUTE · N · Level crossing · L · Polish Para Bde Gliders · Johanna Hoeve · Supply DZ · V · St Elizabeth Hospital · Wolfheze · 4 Para Bde · Koepel · Lichtenbeek · X 1 Para Bde · Z Div HQ Div troops · TIGER ROUTE · 3 Para · Final Perimeter · Westerbouwing · Church · 2 Para · Pontoon Bridge · Main Bridge · Heelsum · LION ROUTE · Renkum · Ferry · NEDER RIJN · To UTRECHT · Ferry · Railway Bridge · K 1 Polish Para Bde Planned DZ · Driel · 1 Polish Para Bde Actual DZ · To Nijmegen

out to attempt to reach Frost at the Arnhem Bridge. During the night, the 1st Battalion had picked up a radio message from Frost asking for reinforcement. On his own initiative, the commanding officer decided to turn south and go to his assistance. Private Brown:

Somehow we must have become separated from the other two companies. We were going towards Arnhem and the fighting was getting a lot worse. Now we were on the outskirts of the town and there didn't seem anywhere you could go to get out of the way of the machine-gun fire and the shells bursting all round us. We came up by the side of a wall from behind which Germans were lobbing grenades at us. The Lieutenant threw two grenades over the wall, and when the Germans started screaming, he shouted, 'Right, finish the bastards off.' That was only the second time I had ever heard him use bad language, and it was to be the last. A bullet must have hit his phosphorous bomb [smoke grenade], and he went up like a ball of fire, and his American brown jumping boots went with him.

I was hit in the head with some shrapnel. For a few seconds I couldn't see anything. As I fell to the ground, I was shot in the chest. I think half the Germans in Arnhem were coming down that road towards us, and it looked as though there were only about ten of us left. There wasn't a lot we could do. One of my mates bandaged my head and chest. The Germans were all around. We were prisoners of war.

The 1st Battalion, having lost touch with one company and all its

Arnhem – Moves of Battalions 1st Parachute Brigade, Sunday 17 September 1944, and moves of 4th Parachute Brigade, Monday 18 September 1944 and Wednesday 20 September 1944.

anti-tank guns, continued advancing until it became embroiled in the same battle as the 3rd Battalion. Lathbury with 3rd Battalion describes it in his diary as a 'Hectic day'. He only knew what was happening in his immediate vicinity, and with no radios apparently working, had no control over the battle his brigade was fighting. This was becoming a matter of ever smaller groups of lightly equipped parachute soldiers desperately trying to reach the bridge, battering up against the German infantry and armour stop line. When, after ferocious fighting, or sheer cunning, they penetrated the line, they usually found themselves isolated by counter-attacks cutting in behind them. The confused fighting continued until the evening. Towards the end, Lathbury was wounded and left in a cellar. As he was being carried in, a German followed, but Urquhart shot him with his revolver. Urquhart was to spend that night hiding in a house nearby, unable to return to his divisional headquarters because a German SP gun was parked outside.

At the bridge the German attacks increased in intensity through the day. The quality of the troops they were up against became apparent. The prisoners they took were healthy, surly and contemptuous, well-trained SS Panzer Grenadiers. They were not in the least cowed by being taken prisoner. But morale was high; XXX Corps was due the next day.

After the battle for Normandy, and the swift advance across France and Belgium, the battle for Arnhem, within the 1st Airborne Division, has almost the texture of the Western Front in the First World War, before the great British advance of August–November 1918. The pre-planned programme, over which commanders in the field have no influence, rolls inexorably on, becoming less and less relevant to events on the ground, while more troops are fed into the meat grinder. Commanders involved in the fighting have little control over troops beyond their immediate vicinity. Actions decided by commanders, in response to the little information they have, take so long to lay on that they are out of date before they are implemented. The missing ingredient, as in the First World War, was good communications.

Waiting in England, unaware of their fellow parachute brigade's increasingly desperate situation, Hackett's 4th Parachute Brigade chafed at a four-hour delay in take-off. Although the majority of this brigade had seen far less fighting than 1st Parachute Brigade, one of the exceptions was Hackett, who had already won a DSO and an MC in the Western Desert, and was more experienced than either of the other two brigadiers in the Division, although at thirty-four he was the youngest. At last the order to load was given. The trip was more eventful than the previous day. Ninety enemy fighters tried to penetrate the Allied fighter screen, but failed. The flak was more effective. Lieutenant Jeffrey Noble, Machine-Gun Platoon Commander, 156 Parachute Battalion:

> My platoon was split into two sticks. My platoon sergeant took one in one aircraft, and I took the other. The flight for my platoon was catastrophic.

Healthy, surly and contemptuous, well-trained SS Panzer Grenadiers are guarded by glider pilots. British glider pilots were trained to fight as infantry so that they could contribute to the battle, instead of becoming useless mouths while awaiting evacuation for the next operation. (BU1159)

First my platoon sergeant's aircraft was hit by flak, and crashed in flames just south of Arnhem.

My aircraft was still over England when the American crew chief/jump master said to me: 'We have a bit of a problem, because one of the parachutes from the containers under the aircraft is developed so it is difficult to fly.' These containers had spare barrels and ammunition. We

Parachute soldiers attaching a container to the aircraft from which they will jump. Containers were used for weapons and equipment too heavy or bulky to be carried in the parachutist's kitbag with which he jumped. When the container is released by the pilot, the white tape static line on the right deploys the parachute. (H37727)

leant out of the Dakota door watching this parachute being shredded in the slipstream. We tried jettisoning the container. It dropped away, but the parachute had caught underneath the aircraft, so the container swung on an arc underneath, and ended up being towed behind us. This caused some consternation to the crew, because they said we couldn't land with the container hanging down. We couldn't jump either, because our parachutes would have become entangled with all this stuff flying along underneath.

Eventually we emergency-landed on what turned out to be a Flying Fortress base. We leapt out and cut off the parachute. The pilot said he could not fly with the aircraft in the condition it was in. But the engineers from the base disagreed. We watched the tail end of the air armada sailing away towards Holland. We said we'd got to go, we couldn't miss this. Then the pilot said he didn't have a navigator, he was in the lead ship. [American practice] Eventually he agreed having been on the drop the first day. Being out of formation we were able to fly a little faster, and eventually saw them in front of us. Finally we saw the DZ below us with a lot of smoke on it. Unfortunately half the stick jumped late, into woods occupied by Germans. When I got to Battalion Headquarters, I only had about a third of my platoon, and one machine-gun.

There were also German troops on the edges of the DZ, unlike the previous day. Lieutenant Blackwood, 11th Parachute Battalion:

As I struggled out of my harness after landing, I noticed that my parachute contained some bullet holes, and that a German machine-gun was blasting away about 30 yards from me, inside a wood. The Germans were ensconced in the woods which bordered the DZ on two sides, and were lacing the place with machine-gun and mortar fire. Some men were coming down dead in their harness, and others hit before they could extricate themselves. I gathered some men about me and set off for the RV.

Private R. C. Dunford, 10th Parachute Battalion:

The flak started puffing round us and other planes. Somebody shouted: 'Look, one has been hit.' I looked out of the door and saw one of our planes belching smoke, and the lads jumping out in order as if on an exercise. I don't know if they all got out. I watched the light with beating heart. The green light flashed. 'Go Go Go,' the shouting started. Number 7 in front of me stood on the edge of the door transfixed, turned his head and shouted: 'Push me'. As I went to push him, he went, and a second too soon I fell out, turning over and over. The terror of twisted rigging lines, Roman Candle [parachute not opening properly], or landing with my feet hooked up flashed through my mind. Suddenly I was straight but oscillating badly. I saw the ground rushing up to me and landed heavily just clear of a grass fire.

Major Geoffrey Powell, commanding C Company, 156th Parachute Battalion:

My drop was perfect. We were opposed by some Germans, and suffered a few casualties. But the enemy was clearly disconcerted to see 1,500 paratroopers dropping on them. As first out, I landed at the furthest part of the DZ, about 1200 yards from the RV. My finger was nicked by something in the air, otherwise I was all right. I started to trudge very heavily laden across the DZ to my company RV. There was a lot of firing, the grass was very dry, and in places the heath, the Ginkesche Heide, was on fire. I passed a subaltern, not in my Company, who had been shot in the foot coming down. I walked up to him. He said he was OK. I couldn't stop and left him. His body was discovered after the war. The heath fire had caught up with him, he couldn't move and had shot himself.

At the Company RV everything was going very smoothly indeed. We were ready to move within an hour of the first man down. There was then an unexplained delay.

When Hackett had arrived, he found that Hicks, in the absence of Urquhart, had taken over command of the Division. Hicks, although older than Hackett, was junior. Hicks had despatched two companies of the 2nd Battalion South Staffords from his own Brigade to assist 1st Parachute Brigade. Hackett now learned, to his fury, that without consulting him Hicks had ordered 11th Parachute Battalion into Arnhem to follow the South Staffords. After an altercation with Hicks, Hackett decided to follow Urquhart's original orders to him, and advance into Arnhem north of the railway line, picking up 7th Battalion King's Own Scottish Borderers (KOSB) on the way.

The 4th Brigade advance was held up as darkness was falling, and they dug in for the night. The orders for the morning were to seize the high ground occupied by the enemy north of Oosterbeek. This was part of the main German line of resistance set up after the first day to prevent reinforcements reaching the bridge. Major Geoffrey Powell:

My Company (C) was to attack first with covering fire from B Company. We were to seize the high ground to the right of the farm at Joannahoeve. The other two companies were then to pass through. We moved off in very open country. The support was totally insufficient for such an attack. Luckily the first 'bound' was not held, so we were able to make progress without any casualties. From here I overlooked the final objective. A Company attacked through woods. Here they ran into very strong opposition, losing all five officers and two-thirds of the Company. B Company were pushed in, suffering very heavy casualties. In the first two to three hours that morning, 156 Battalion was hit very hard indeed. Holding the high ground under fire from mortars, SP guns and 20mm dual-purpose flak guns, my Company suffered a steady stream of casualties, but remained quite strong. While holding that hill, we were attacked by Messerschmitts. We didn't believe it at first, thinking they were Spitfires. We had been told we had air superiority. It was a salutary lesson for us.

During that afternoon General Urquhart, who had been trapped in

Arnhem, took command of the Division again. He saw Hackett, and realised there was no hope of making any progress on that flank. Orders were given for the Brigade to move across the railway to Oosterbeek, not at this stage to form a perimeter, but with the object of attacking again towards the bridge, on another axis, to relieve Frost.

From where we were, we could see the resupply DZ about one and a half miles away, still held by the Germans. We watched the Dakotas flying through very heavy flak to drop their loads straight into enemy hands. We could not stop them. We saw the despatchers of one aircraft at the door, ready to push out the loads. This Dakota had flames coming out of one engine, and made another run over the DZ as the despatchers kept pushing out supplies.

At about that time, something went wrong with the withdrawal, and we were pushed back too quickly. To our right as we pulled back was the LZ for the anti-tank battery of the Polish Parachute Brigade. On one side were 1st KOSB, on another the Germans, on a third side ourselves, and moving through, the remnants of the 10th Battalion. Into this 'cauldron', gliders started to land. It was a horrible sight. Many were shot out of the sky. The Poles shot at everything they saw, and the KOSB shot at the Poles. Perhaps a couple of guns were driven off the LZ. I finished the day with about 8 or 9 Polish gunners attached to my Company.

There were only two places where transport could cross the high railway embankment between us and Oosterbeek: a tunnel under the railway, and the crossing at Wolfheze. We clambered up the embankment under fire. One of my platoons, and the remnants of B Company, instead of crossing with the Battalion, must have continued down the railway line to Wolfheze. They never rejoined us. When we reassembled on the other side of the embankment, I had less than half of my Company. By now it was towards the evening of 19 September. We were told to remain in that area for the night, about a mile from the centre of Oosterbeek.

Hackett's Brigade was down to about a third of its strength. Hungry and exhausted by the events of the previous thirty-six hours, 10th and 156th Battalions dug in for the night. 1st KOSB were sent to rejoin their Brigade in the Divisional perimeter that was evolving between the river and the railway line. Hackett wanted to move into the perimeter that night, but unfortunately Divisional Headquarters did not approve.

The attempt to reach the bridge, by the remnants of 1st and 3rd Battalions, the South Staffords and 11th Battalion, failed after ferocious fighting, in which all commanding officers were killed or wounded. The 1st Battalion was down to thirty-nine all ranks. Only twenty of 3rd Battalion made the RV to which their commanding officer, before he was killed, ordered them to withdraw as best they could. During the afternoon, the survivors of the four battalions drifted back towards Oosterbeek. Here they were met by Lieutenant-Colonel Thompson, commanding the Light Regiment Royal Artillery. He organized them

into a defensive position to cover his gun positions near Oosterbeek church. They were placed under command of Major Lonsdale of 11th Battalion.

The fighting at the Bridge continued for the whole of the next day, and on until the morning of the following day. Frost was wounded in both legs, and was forced to lie down. Major Gough, the commander of the Divisional Reconnaissance Squadron, took command of the force, while Major Tatham-Warter took command of the remnants of the 2nd Battalion. There were no PIAT bombs left, and ammunition of all kinds was running short.

The Germans blasted holes in the walls of the buildings, followed by phosphorous smoke shells to set the structures alight. In the cellars of the building occupied by Brigade Headquarters, where over 200 wounded lay, the doctors told Frost that these men were in imminent danger of being burned alive. A truce was arranged. Staff Sergeant Godfrey Freeman:

> Our building is on fire. We no longer have any means to put it out. In our cellar there is an all-pervading stench of blood, faeces and urine, the only latrine being an oil drum brim full, with faeces floating on top. Upstairs small arms ammunition is exploding in the fire. From time to time I caught glimpses of Colonel Frost as he lay, white as wax, issuing orders and

A photo reconnaissance shot of the road bridge at Arnhem while the northern end was still being held by a battalion-strength force consisting of part of Lieutenant-Colonel John Frost's 2nd Parachute battalion, most of 1st Parachute Brigade headquarters, with some glider pilots, engineers and other troops from 1st Airborne Division. Frost's troops occupied the houses on either side of the bridge at the top of the picture. The wrecked vehicles at the top end are German, including armoured half-tracks belonging to 9th SS Panzer Division destroyed by Frost's men on the second day of the battle. (MH2061)

**A German photograph
of captured British
soldiers of 1st
Airborne Division.**
(HU2123)

instructions. A visit from a German interpreter to enquire whether he was
prepared to surrender proved fruitless. He was sent back with a message
that Colonel Frost would accept unconditional surrender from the other
side. From then on it was only a matter of time. Some while later he
acknowledged defeat, and the bitterness in his voice was unmistakable.

Down the cellar steps comes the first SS soldier, sub-machine-gun at the
ready. In English he enquires, 'Are you British or American?' Unknown to
us, the American Airborne had sworn to avenge the massacre of their
comrades at Ste-Mère-Eglise, and were reputed [incorrectly] to have taken
no prisoners. 'We're British,' came the reply. 'Tommy,' he cried with a huge
grin of combined relief and apparent affection, 'Tommy, Tommy.' Doors
were ripped off to make stretchers. Mixed pairs of SS men and Airborne
struggled together to lug the wounded from certain death. A British medical
officer was directing operations with a vehemence that struck even the SS
with awe.

As soon as the wounded were removed, the battle restarted. Finally, house by house, from cellar to attic, in outbuildings and backyards, the remnants of Frost's force, most of them without ammunition, were overrun. As the SS Panzer Grenadiers evacuated the remaining wounded, they offered them brandy and chocolate, congratulating them on the way they had fought the battle. It was 09.00 on Thursday morning. For the first time since Sunday night the Germans could cross the bridge. The plan had called for a complete division to hold it for forty-eight hours. It had been held by a mixed force of about battalion strength for three days and four nights.

Airborne soldiers dug in waiting for the enemy. This could be 4th Parachute Brigade Headquarters. Both soldiers are equipped with the 9mm Sten sub-machine-gun. (BU1143)

By now 4th Parachute Brigade had also been destroyed. The Germans had been building up a three-sided box, first to contain 1st Airborne division at Oosterbeek, and then to squeeze it out of existence. German reinforcements were arriving hourly to assist 9th SS Panzer Division and Kraft's SS Panzer Grenadier Training and Depot Battalion.

4th Parachute Brigade had a quiet night after pulling back over the railway line. Their move into the perimeter was a nightmare. The Germans were now astride the routes in. Soon the CO and second-in-command of 156th Battalion were dead, as were all but one of Hackett's staff officers. By this time the brigade was split, the 10th Battalion having found another way into the perimeter. Powell, now in command of 156th Battalion, was sent for by Hackett, as the fighting continued round the survivors of the disastrous morning:

> The Brigadier was standing up in the middle of all this. There was nothing for it but to stand up too, I felt very exposed. He said: 'Geoffrey, you've got

C Company 1st Battalion The Border Regiment, dug in beside the Utrechtsweg in Oosterbeek. (BU1103)

the only formed body I've got left. Two hundred yards over there is a hollow full of Germans. That's our only way out. I want you to capture that hollow.'

I had no means of covering fire, and one platoon of chaps. I gathered them round. There was only one thing to do, go at it hard. We screamed and yelled firing from the hip. The Germans did not wait for us. My Sten jammed, so I picked up a German mauser, which I carried for the rest of the battle. Joined by the others, and now about one hundred strong, we held the hollow for the rest of the day. Luckily most of the German armour was pulled off.

Sometime in the afternoon, the Brigadier said: 'We can't stay here any longer. The rest of the Division is only a few yards away. I will gather you all down one end of the hollow. When I say go, you will all go. I will lead, and you, Geoffrey, will bring up the rear.'

It was a repeat on a bigger scale of what happened before. We broke straight through. I passed one German lying on the ground, screaming in terror. I came to rest in a position held by the Border Regiment, who up to then had not seen much action. They were all clean, tidy, shaved, etc.

Film still of two airborne soldiers taking cover under mortar fire at Oosterbeek. (FLM2388)

Suddenly this mob flopped down, with two day's growth of beard, bloodstained bandages and odd weapons. An officer appeared and said, 'Would you mind taking this shower out of my position.'

Then we were refitted, given ammunition, weapons for those who needed them, and a meal. The perimeter was in the process of being formed. We assumed that at any moment XXX Corps would arrive, and that for us the battle was over; we had done our share.

The battle of the perimeter was to last for another five days. Casualties suffered in the attempt to reach Frost had been high enough, but the perimeter battle was to cost the most men killed in the Arnhem operation.

By that night, Wednesday, the last night Frost's men were able to hold out, XXX Corps had reached a point eleven miles from Arnhem Bridge. The two bridges over the Waal, the road bridge at Nijmegen and a railway bridge, had been captured by the combined efforts of the Grenadier Guards of Guards Armoured Division, and 82nd US Airborne Division.

By now the guns of XXX Corps were in range and able to assist the beleaguered airborne soldiers in the perimeter in Oosterbeek. Sergeant Mike Lewis, who never reached the bridge to film:

One night I heard the sighing of shells across the trees and a terrific crash ahead of us. It was the 2nd Army artillery. At last not all of the fire was one way. It was tremendous.

On Thursday night 21/22 September, part of Sosabowski's Polish Brigade was dropped south of the Rhine, near Driel. His radios could not contact 1st Airborne Division, only two miles away on the other side of the river. No boats were available, and Sosabowski was unable to cross.

Airborne soldiers by the Hartenstein Hotel on the seventh day of the battle, displaying a parachute in an attempt to guide aircraft dropping supplies. The Hotel was Urquhart's headquarters. (BU1119)

The dogged defence of the perimeter round the Hartenstein Hotel at Oosterbeek continued, while XXX Corps, starting with Guards Armoured and then 43rd Wessex Division, attempted to relieve the 1st Airborne Division. Several times the Germans cut the one road available to XXX Corps south of Nijmegen, causing severe delays in bringing forward boats and other vital equipment, and diversion of effort from the task of relieving the 1st Airborne Division to keep the route open. Because British accounts of Market Garden have tended to concentrate on the 1st Airborne, the Guards Armoured and 43rd Wessex Divisions, the two US Airborne Divisions have received less than their due. Brereton wrote:

> In years to come everyone will remember Arnhem, but no one will remember that two American Divisions fought their hearts out in the Dutch canal country and whipped hell out of the Germans.
> quoted by Geoffrey Powell in *The Devil's Birthday*

Eventually, after hard fighting, the leading brigade of 43rd Wessex Division, by swinging to the west after crossing the Waal and moving on minor roads, reached the Rhine at Driel.

German prisoners being put to work at the Hartenstein Hotel. (BU1137)

The Sherwood Rangers Yeomanry were attached to 82nd Airborne Division, fighting to keep open the XXX Corps axis. As happens in war, unnecessary paperwork miraculously gets through, while vital supplies are held up; Leslie Skinner:

> *Saturday 23 September:* Lot bumph arrived overnight from Corps Padre – still bleating that he doesn't get Returns on time!!!
>
> Fuel shortage due to frequency with which Germans have managed to cut the 'corridor' road and likelihood that for a few days longer may occur again.

During the afternoon the 5th Dorsets had arrived at Driel, and held the southern bank of the Lower Rhine opposite Oosterbeek. Part of the Polish Parachute Brigade crossed that night. On 24 September, 4th Dorsets were ordered to cross at the Driel ferry site, to enlarge the bridgehead and get supplies across. The commanding officer, Lieutenant-Colonel Gerard Tilly, wrote to his wife the day before:

> I have got a big dose of the blues at the moment. The German is an obstinate man & I am sure he is going to fight on to the last man & the last round –

damnable waste of life as he will take an awful lot of mopping up inside Germany.

The intention was to put the whole of 4th Dorsets across. But the boats arrived late and, because of heavy fire from the opposing bank, by 02.15 the crossing was stopped. Only 17 officers, including Tilly, and 298 soldiers had crossed. Several boats were holed before crossing, some were sunk, and in others the soldiers used their shovels to augment the inadequate paddles supplied. Captain Whittle, commanding B Company:

> On the spot, the strength of B Company was 2 Officers and less than 30 soldiers. Where the trees started there was a steep bank about 100 feet high, and the enemy were well dug in on the top of it. We started an assault and met very heavy opposition; it was only too easy for the Jerries on top to roll grenades down on to us, and we eventually gained the top at the expense of 50 per cent of our strength. We were joined by the CO, and the company commander and about twenty men of C Company; they set out to the right to try to contact A Company and ran into opposition almost immediately.
>
> The CO's party advanced up the wooded slope, but was soon surrounded and forced to surrender.

The next letter Tilly's wife received was dated 14 December, from a German prison camp. Only fifteen men of 4th Dorsets, including Major Whittle, got back across the river the following night. A few more returned with the 1st Airborne Division.

Major Geoffrey Powell, commanding the remnants of 156th Parachute Battalion:

> The next day [25 September] I was called into Divisional Headquarters at first light. There I learned that we were going to be withdrawn that night. I returned to what was left of my force, about 40 people [out of a battalion of 650]. I told them. I could see their reaction on their faces. First a grin of delight, that we were going to get out that night. Everyone had lost hope of getting out of that battle alive. Next disgust, that we had been destroyed to no purpose. Their reactions mirrored mine, when I was first told.
>
> We had very detailed orders on how to pull out. We left in groups, and as we had the furthest to go we left first. We had glider pilots as guides to lead us to the river. The way was marked with white tape, and Bofors on the opposite bank fired over our heads to give us the line. We held onto the tail of the airborne smock of the man in front. The intelligence officer led, I was at the rear. About halfway to the river, we hit a German position and my column got split, and I arrived at the river with 15 men. There were no boats. The Germans were about 50 yards away. We crouched under the bank up to our knees in water. There were a few people there from other units. A sergeant, hysterical with fear, made a lot of noise. I did something I had never done before – I hit him on the mouth. That finished the noise. We moved along the river, hoping to pick up a boat. We could see some people

starting to swim. None of my party did. We passed a boat with the crew
dead around it. Then we met another boat, with a Canadian crew and
outboard. In we piled. I was last. The Corporal Coxswain said, 'We can't
take any more.' My chaps said: 'You're taking this bugger', and pulled me
in. When we got to the other side, we ran for the large embankment just
inland. I remember the feeling of relief as we climbed up and over – we were
out of this battle.

**Soldiers of 1st
Airborne Division in
Nijmegen after being
evacuated across the
Rhine.** (HU3722)

Canadian and British engineers took part in the evacuation. The Canadians reported later:

> The assault boats which the Royal Engineers are operating are not doing so
> well. The current is so swift that they are quickly carried downstream. The
> airborne fellows are too exhausted to help much in paddling them back, and
> the crews are worn out after a couple of trips.

The crossing was under constant machine-gun and mortar fire. Eventually only two Canadian boats were left functioning, which kept ferrying
until after first light. On the last trip, one boat towed another. When the

Three members of the Army Film and Photographic Unit who jumped on the first day, taken after being evacuated across the Rhine. Left to right: **Sergeants Smith, Walker and Mike Lewis.** (BU1169)

engine died, the boat being towed cast off, and the men paddled with their rifles and their hands. The machine-guns opened up, and only four out of the twenty-five passengers reached the south bank alive. The Canadians in their outboard-powered stormboats accounted for the vast majority saved from the bridgehead.

Over 300 wounded men were taken prisoner when the Germans advanced into the perimeter on Tuesday morning. Nearly 3,000 wounded were in Dutch or German hospitals in Arnhem. All the British doctors and chaplains stayed with the wounded. 2,398 withdrew across the Lower Rhine, of whom 2,183 were members of 1st Airborne Division, which had flown into battle over 10,000 strong. 1,400 were dead, and over 6,000 prisoner, including the wounded. Each parachute brigade could muster no more than a company, and the air landing brigade less than a battalion.

Was Arnhem a bridge too far? The 'island' formed by the Waal and Lower Rhine was a cul-de-sac. If Arnhem bridge was not included in the plan, there was no point in going at all. Because the bridge was not taken, part of 2nd British Army was destined to spend the winter of

1944/45 on the 'island'. Did Browning say, 'We might be going a bridge too far' to Montgomery? Unlikely, says Nigel Hamilton:

> Browning saw Dempsey, not Montgomery, on the day before the revised Comet operation, renamed Market Garden, was resurrected. For seven days [under Comet plans] Browning's airborne corps had been preparing to seize all the bridges to Arnhem with only a single British airborne division and a Polish parachute brigade; to have protested that Arnhem was a 'bridge too far', when Dempsey offered him no less than three airborne divisions plus the Polish parachute brigade, was inherently unlikely.

Geoffrey Powell:

> It was worth doing. I have never met anyone who has regrets. We [156th Parachute Battalion] had been together for three years. Most were killed, the lucky ones were wounded. I was one who did not get a serious wound.

Sergeant Mike Lewis:

> That was another cock-up.

'Complete priority over all other offensive operations . . .'

THE CLEARING OF THE SCHELDT ESTUARY AND OPENING OF THE PORT OF ANTWERP

An LCT beached by the gap in the dyke at Westkapelle, Walcheren Island, during the landing by 4th Special Service Brigade on 1 November 1944. (A26272)

By the end of September Calais, the last of the Channel ports, had fallen to the 1st Canadian Army, with two British infantry divisions under command: 49th and 51st Highland. But it was to be mid-October before all were operating, and on average they were around 150 miles from Brussels. The distance from the Normandy beaches was over twice that. Winter was approaching. Bad weather would hamper unloading at the smaller ports, and halt operations at the British Mulberry, the only survivor of the June gale, for days at a time. The long distances that supplies had to be trucked, and the inadequacies of ports already in Allied hands, aroused considerable concern about the supply situation in the British 21st Army Group, and the American 12th Army Group. The key to easing the problem of supplying both Army Groups lay in using the great port of Antwerp.

While Market Garden had been in progress, Montgomery had given little thought to the opening of the Scheldt estuary to shipping. Although Antwerp had been captured almost intact in early September, it lay idle, its seaward access held by the Germans. Blocking the mouth of the Scheldt lay the heavily fortified island of Walcheren. Along the southern shore, between Breskens and Zeebrugge, coastal batteries commanded the waterway. Walcheren could be approached by land only along the narrow isthmus and peninsula of South Beveland and thence across a narrow causeway. The Leopold canal provided a natural moat guarding the landward approaches to the batteries on the southern shore of the Scheldt. This area, known as the Breskens pocket, was defended by the battle-experienced and competent 64th Division. Much of the country was flooded. Antwerp was to be held by the Allies for a month before operations to clear the Scheldt began. It was to be 16 October, nearly six weeks after the port was seized, that Montgomery gave priority to opening it up, over all other operations.

By the end of October, in response to Montgomery's directive, the Canadians and British had closed up to the River Maas, and had cleared the northern and southern banks of the Scheldt estuary, including the Breskens Pocket, and South Beveland. The fighting in the flooded polder was savage and exhausting. Part of South Beveland had fallen to 52nd Lowland Division, which had spent the previous two years training as a mountain division in the Scottish Highlands, and had played a key part in Brigadier MacLeod's pre-Normandy deception plan. Their first experience of battle was to be in the lowest-lying land in Europe, much of it below sea level. Lieutenant D. F. Brown RNVR:

> It really looked most incongruous to see those men with their shoulder
> flashes 'Mountain', in Holland of all places.

The successful operations both north and south of the Scheldt had been greatly assisted by the use of the specialized armour of 79th Armoured Division, which in addition to the types used in Normandy, now included American tracked amphibians, Landing Vehicle Tracked

A Weasel in snow camouflage paint, designed as an amphibious over-snow vehicle for use by 52nd Lowland Division who had trained for years as a mountain division to fight in Norway. It was used in the battles to clear the Scheldt, where it proved inadequate in strong tides and mud. (H3861)

(LVT), nicknamed Buffalos. DUKWs, Weasels and Terrapins were also used in large numbers. The Buffalo was particularly useful. It could swim ashore, cross the beach and, depending on the going, motor and swim to the objective, all without having to disembark its load, unlike conventional craft which unloaded on, or close to, the waterline, the most dangerous place in any waterborne operation.

With the sides of the sea corridor to Antwerp held by the Allies, all that remained was to force the door, to allow the next important step: the sweeping of the waterway clear of mines. Then, and only then, could ships discharge their cargos at Antwerp. The door was Walcheren, a saucer-shaped island, whose rim consisted of high dunes of loose, soft sand, passable to men on foot only. The gap in the dunes, on the western edge, was filled by the Westkapelle dyke. Behind this natural and man-made rampart lay the flat polder, all reclaimed land, below sea level, strewn with farms and small villages. A pamphlet issued some six months later to all Royal Marines units to keep them informed of activities involving their Corps, entitled Royal Marine Business, described the defences of Walcheren:

> There were estimated to be some 9,000 to 10,000 German troops, together with a large number driven over the causeway linking Walcheren to South Beveland. The foundation of the Westkapelle dyke is a massive structure of unmortared blocks of basalt on enormous wooden piles. On top of the dyke sand-dunes had piled up to a height of 40 to 50 feet. These dunes were on average about 100 to 150 yards wide. The German batteries were built into the sand-dunes in massive concrete emplacements, protected on the landward side by minefield and smaller emplacements from Flushing to the extreme north of the Island.

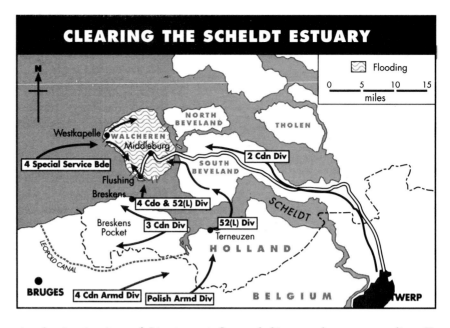

CLEARING THE SCHELDT ESTUARY

At the instigation of Lieutenant-General Simmonds, commanding II Canadian Corps, the Westkapelle dyke was breached by bombing. Simmonds had foreseen that the Germans would partially flood the saucer, leaving embanked roads and dunes above water, making the attacker's job immeasurably more difficult. His brilliant idea was to go the whole hog, and flood the saucer completely. The Germans would be denied the use of the roads and, lacking specialized vehicles, would be considerably hampered. The British, on the other hand, with amphibious vehicles and craft could penetrate the gap in the dyke and use the floodwater for mobility inside the saucer, in places attacking positions from the rear. Within a few hours of the bombing by 243 Lancasters, the North Sea had poured through the gap. After further attacks had widened the gap, and breaches made at two other points, about three-quarters of the island was under water, pinning the garrison to the saucer's rim, and Flushing, Middleburg and other smaller towns. In the west the rim was no more than 250 yards wide, between sea and flood. Fortunately the quality of the defenders was low. Lieutenant-Colonel C. F. Phillips, 47 (Royal Marines) Commando:

> The category of men serving in 70th Division at the time of the assault was not of the highest. In one report they were described as 'mostly stomach sufferers', and in another report they were called 'the white bread division', presumably with reference to their diet.

A three-pronged attack was planned. From the east, 52nd Lowland Division was to attack across the Walcheren–South Beveland causeway. Number 4 Commando was to assault Flushing under the cover of darkness, across the estuary from Breskens in LCAs, followed by 155th Infantry Brigade of 52nd Division. The 4th Special Service Brigade, under Brigadier Leicester, and consisting of 41, 47 and 48 Royal Marines Commandos, was to assault at Westkapelle after daylight. When 4

German coastal guns at Walcheren. This one was at Westkapelle, about a thousand yards north of the breach in the dyke. (BU1273)

Left to right: Montgomery, Crerar and Lieutenant-General Guy Simonds, the commander of 2nd Canadian Corps. Montgomery thought highly of Simonds, and little of Crerar. He used the opportunity of sending Crerar back to England for medical treatment to put Simonds temporarily in command of Canadian 1st Army for the Scheldt operations. (HU63664)

Commando had completed its task of clearing the town of Flushing, it was to revert to the command of 4th Special Service Brigade. In support of 4th Special Service Brigade was Captain Pugsley's Naval Force T, consisting of HMS *Warspite*, the monitors *Erebus* and *Roberts*, and twenty-five assorted landing-craft designed to provide fire support formed into the Support Squadron Eastern Flank.

The air bombardment plan included attacks on the batteries. As in Normandy, this was largely ineffective. After 2,219 sorties, including the breaching of the dykes, dropping 10,219 tons of bombs for the loss of few aircraft, only three 150mm out of twenty-five heavy guns had been

The gap in the dyke at Westkapelle, Walcheren Island, taken shortly after bombing by Lancasters. The sea pours in to flood the interior. (C4668)

put out of action. The air support on the day of the assault included dropping 500lb bombs at Westkapelle, to avoid causing craters on the landing places, and a cab-rank of Typhoons on call. Heavy bombing of Flushing had been ruled out by the senior airmen, including Harris, on humanitarian grounds. The decision was right. Apart from the casualties to Allied civilians, past experience should have demonstrated that the ensuing rubble would have slowed progress with few casualties to the enemy. As it was, 4 Commando was told that the artillery bombardment would devastate the town, burying the defenders; a repeat of the exaggerated hopes for the bombardment on 6 June.

The assault on Westkapelle was fixed for two hours after first light, allowing time for the preliminary bombardment, and transit of the difficult navigational waters by craft in daylight. Because optimum time for beaching was as soon after low water as possible, there were only two 'windows' in November which provided all the required conditions: 1st to 4th and 14th to 17th.

The problem was finding a suitable place to land 4 Commando in Flushing, and then to move quickly to seal off and protect the beach over

which 155 Infantry Brigade, including vehicles, were to land. The water-front and streets of Flushing had been fortified by the Germans. A heavily defended sea wall ran along the waterfront, about twenty to thirty feet high at low water. In most places it was unscalable. Eventually a dock and harbour, used for dumping rubbish and so accessible to vehicles, was found for 155 Brigade's landing, but it was protected by underwater stakes. It was designated Uncle beach. There were numerous enemy strong points in that area of Flushing, but provided the Commando was landed immediately after the artillery bombardment, there was a good chance that these could be rushed and overcome.

The Commando plan was for the first wave to find a suitable place for climbing the western breakwater forming one of the two arms of the dock area of Uncle beach. The second wave would carry beach-clearing troops, and men to form a beachhead. The third wave, brought in on the Commanding Officer's signal, would clear and expand the beachhead. It was an ambitious plan, the more so because it was impossible to choose the exact spot for disembarkation. As soon as Uncle beach was cleared by the Landing Craft Obstructions Clearing

Number 4 Commando embarking in LCAs for their assault on Flushing. (HU63663)

Unit (LCOCU), 4th King's Own Scottish Borderers (KOSB) would land to expand the beachhead. 5th KOSB and Headquarters 155 Brigade would follow and advance on Middleburg. Finally, the Brigade reserve, 7/9th Royal Scots, would land.

Lieutenant D. F. Brown commanding 508th LCA Flotilla, a very experienced landing-craft officer, who had seen service in Greece, Crete, Dieppe, North Africa, Sicily, Salerno and Normandy:

> In the early hours of 1 November, having loaded our troops I was first away, with eight boats of my Flotilla, making up serials one and two. We left Breskens at 04.43, and set course for Flushing. I had a good landmark – a windmill – which I managed to pick up without trouble. Soon after starting my run across, the silence was shattered as our guns opened up firing over our heads on to Flushing; a continuous, enormous, cacophony of sound.

At 05.40 the artillery lifted and the leading landing craft, two LCP and Brown's LCA, went in to land the 4 Commando reconnaissance party and the advance party of the LCOCU. The two LCPs initially touched down in the wrong place, but the LCA landed its troops on the western breakwater. Lieutenant Brown:

> We arrived off our target a little early so had to wait for our batteries to stop firing. As soon as the gunfire stopped, I took my LCA in to the beach. We did not appear to have been spotted. I had to land first, with just my own boat, and to put ashore a small army recce party and a small RN beach party. In the process of my beaching, I was unfortunate enough to manage to sit on a submerged beach obstruction which tore a hole in the bottom of my boat, and the water started to come in rather rapidly. My party however, were all safely landed, in the right place, and at just about the right time. They must have accomplished their task, because as I was pulling away from the beach I saw the letter 'G', in red, being flashed on a small signal lamp. This was the all-clear for my serials one and two to proceed in to the beach with their troops.

Sergeant Kenneth Kennett, the Signals Sergeant of 4 Commando:

> I was in the first LCA, with one officer with a fighting patrol, the Second-in-Command, the Intelligence Officer, a signaller and a naval Lieutenant. Soon after the barrage lifted, our boat touched down. We scrambled out and up the greasy mole; there was no fire. The Intelligence Officer turned, shook hands with me, saying, 'My God man, we're lucky.' The fighting patrol commander found an empty bunker, which the second-in-command decided would be a good place for Commando HQ. The naval Lieutenant went out to the end of the mole; he handed me a lamp with a red filter to shine out to sea. The next boat in had the CO on board.

The reconnaissance party had quickly cut their way through the wire taking twenty-six Germans prisoner, without the enemy firing a shot. The four craft carrying the two troops of the covering party were called in at the same place. The Germans opened fire, but the stream of tracer went overhead. Brown:

> So far all was well, some machine-gun fire had started, and I saw tracer coming from the upper floor of a house, but all my boats landed their troops, just as planned, and left the beach.

The CO called in the Commando main body, who set about clearing the Old Town, the part nearest the docks and waterfront. Brown:

> I now found that my boat was in trouble. It was rapidly filling with water a lot faster than my men were able to pump it clear, and I could only move very slowly away from the beach. Nevertheless I reckoned that if I could keep the engine room sealed, I should be able to get back all right. I soon started to have my doubts about this but fortunately, after about half an hour, another boat appeared alongside to see if I needed assistance. I did. With my crew, I transferred to this boat and took mine in tow. I need hardly have bothered, within about five minutes it sank, just about in the middle of the Scheldt estuary.
>
> I now collected as many of my boats as I could and set off again back to Breskens, as I had been ordered. On the way, there were signals for help from an LCA of 506 Flotilla. I indicated the harbour entrance to my other boats, sent them on, and went to help the other boat. It had both engines broken down and a badly wounded Sub-Lieutenant. We took him aboard, and gave him morphia. We took the boat in tow and made our way back to Breskens.

Sergeant Irving Portman, 4 Commando:

> While the rest of the Commando went on into Flushing, my Troop cleared a boatyard, in which there were three pillboxes in a row. We chucked in grenades, and the Jerries came out like rabbits. The Troop went on winkling them out ahead of us, sending the prisoners back to just three of us until we had 120 to look after. We had some trouble from a sniper in a crane cabin. The troop commander manned an anti-aircraft gun on the roof of one of the captured pillboxes. He didn't know how to use the sights properly, so he lined up on the crane by looking up the barrel. He got the sniper with the first shot.

At 07.30, 4th KOSB started to land on Uncle beach, their objective being the New Town further inland. But they were unable to make much progress. By nightfall, 4 Commando and 4th KOSB were firmly established in the Old Town, but attempts to expand the beachhead were unsuccessful. 5th KOSB crossed the Scheldt at the second attempt on 2 November. After dark, the commander of 155 Brigade, Brigadier McLaren, and 7/9th Royal Scots followed. McLaren took control of the fighting in the town.

It was to take three more days of fighting before Flushing was finally cleared of the enemy. Sergeant Jim Spearman:

The fighting was different from anything we had experienced before; it was all street fighting. We mouseholed from house to house, or used the holes made by the bombardment. Our own casualties were not so bad considering the odds. The Germans fought well in Flushing. I was picking people off with my rifle from the second floor window of a house, was blown back into the room by an explosion, and a splinter from the window hit my leg. It's still there.

Kennett:

After three days we were sent along the dunes to rejoin the Marine Commandos. We had thought we had been given the toughest job, but theirs turned out to be far worse.

The plan for the assault on Westkapelle was for 41 Commando to land on the north shoulder of the gap in the dyke, and push north; 48 Commando was to land on the south shoulder, and clear south. They were to be followed by 47 Commando, who were to push through and link up with 4 Commando advancing north from Flushing. Only 41 Commando had tank and AVRE support. As always in an amphibious operation there was concern about the weather. The west of Walcheren is exposed to the North Sea, and rough seas would prevent craft beaching successfully. Fog and low cloud would hinder bombing and spotting from the air for naval guns supporting the landing. Brigadier Leicester and Captain Pugsley, both travelling in HMS *Kingsmill*, had authority from Admiral Ramsay and General Simmonds to postpone the assault if the sea state and visibility were such that the operation was unlikely to succeed. When the force sailed from Ostend at 03.15 on 1 November, the weather was rough, but moderated during the night. Before dawn, Pugsley heard the bombardment in support of 4 Commando, followed by the success signal that they were ashore. A little later, he was told by signal that it was unlikely that the force would get any air support or air spotting because of fog over the airfields. Leicester and Pugsley agreed to go ahead, although, as Naval force commander at this stage in an amphibious operation, Pugsley had the final decision; a weighty responsibility for a Royal Naval Captain, with so much depending on the outcome. As *Warspite*, *Erebus* and *Roberts* opened fire on the German batteries, twelve Typhoons appeared overhead. It soon became obvious that the bombing had failed to silence the German batteries north and south of the gap in the dyke, when they replied to the fire. Pugsley ordered the assault to go in, sending code-word 'Nelson' to Ramsay. Royal Marine Business:

The Landing Craft of the Support Squadron Eastern Flank closed to engage the batteries. The Germans held their fire, opening up at between 3,000 and 4,000 yards with very accurate fire. As H-hour approached (09.45), three Landing-Craft (Gun) closed to 2,000 yards of an especially active battery north of the gap in the dyke, steering parallel to the beach and firing as hard as possible. Reversing course, they closed to 800 yards, bringing their Oerlikons into action as well as the main armament. Three other Landing-Craft (Gun) engaged a battery south of the gap in a similar style.

Other support landing-craft went in to attack the beach defences. They were received with heavy fire of all calibres. One was set on fire. One was hit below the waterline, but the damage control party partly plugged the hole with hammocks. At 09.45 she came under very heavy fire. She made smoke and went full ahead, but the battery had her measure. She was hit astern, a near miss filled bridge and upper deck with water, two hits forward blew away her bows and the forward magazine. Finally at 09.50 hours, she received a direct hit in the main magazine, which blew up approximately 100,000 rounds of 2-pounder and Oerlikon ammunition. Most of the crew were blown into the sea. There were 29 survivors. The enemy fired on their floats and rafts at about 1,500 yards range, so they paddled away from the beach, to be picked up 45 minutes later by another craft.

Large support landing craft closed zigzagging at top speed. They repeatedly closed the beach, engaging targets, but without much effect against the heavy concrete of the enemy pillboxes. One was hit, caught fire in the magazine, and had to be abandoned. Two were badly damaged.

Two Landing-Craft Gun beached north and south of the gap to engage pillboxes. One about 30 yards from the target which she engaged with AP. The kedge [small anchor] was dropped; this probably saved the craft from broaching-to as the tide ran at about 6 knots parallel to the beach. The craft kept up a hot fire for the next 20 minutes until both turrets were out of action, owing to small arms fire through the sighting ports. As far as could be seen no penetration of the pillbox, which had no slits facing seaward, was achieved, but it was neutralised while the first flight got ashore. It appeared that the garrison panicked, for one individual ran out into the open, to be cut down by fire. The craft was hit in several places by 150mm and 200mm shells, mostly astern, as she was so close in that the Germans guns could only just train on her. She retracted at about 10.00 hours and when about 800 yards off shore, sank by the stern. Casualties were amazingly light, two dead and four wounded. The other Landing-Craft Gun was last seen ablaze on the beach. No survivors were picked up.

Out of the twenty-five craft of the Support Squadron Eastern Flank, only four remained fit for action. Their self-sacrifice, which drew the fire of the batteries, was not in vain. Casualties among the landing-craft and commandos during the run-in of the first two waves were light. The touchdown of the leading LCIs (S) of 41 Commando north of the gap was twenty-seven minutes late, as 48 Commando landed south of the gap. These landings went well, and by nightfall both Commandos had accomplished their first day tasks, but not without losses. Time after time, they were held up by strong points and pillboxes. On at least one occasion, faults with radios slowed down the response from artillery

An LCT carrying Buffalos and Weasels lands by the gap in the dyke at Westkapelle, Walcheren Island, during the landing by 4th Special Service Brigade, 1 November 1944. A shell has just hit the LCT. (A26268)

and bombarding ships. Initial attempts, without supporting fire, by lightly armed commandos against one of the concrete emplacements ended in failure, with many casualties.

As in Normandy, the landing of 47 Commando was, through no fault of theirs, less than satisfactory, and mainly in the wrong place, north and not south of the gap in the dyke (several hundred yards of swiftly flowing water, under fire). Lieutenant-Colonel Phillips:

> The order for 47 Cdo to land was received at about 12.30 hours. By this time the Support Squadron was almost *hors de combat* and the enemy guns had turned their attention to the gap and the approaches. All four LCT carrying 47 Cdo were hit either as they beached or neared the beach.
>
> The LCT carrying B Troop lowered her ramp a short distance off the gap in the dyke at about 12.50 hours. It was intended that the amphibians (Buffalos) should swim out into the gap, and land on the south side of it, some distance in from the seaward end. Things did not work out that way. The lowering of the ramp coincided with a direct hit. The shell passed through the driving compartment of an LVT, killing the driver and the wireless operator, but not exploding until it had gone through the far side of

the LVT. Here it burst under the front Weasel on the port side, which brewed up helped by the flame thrower it carried.

The foremost LVT with the Troop Commander drove down into the water immediately the ramp was lowered. The hold of the LCT was becoming a little untidy. There was a brisk fire on the port side and imminent risk of ammunition going up. Two of the Weasels were well alight. Most of the crews and passengers of the remaining LVTs had left their vehicles and clambered up the starboard side of the LCT with a view to swimming ashore. At this critical moment, a corporal saw his vehicle catch fire. Realising that if he did not move it out of the way none of the others would be able to leave the LCT, he ordered his crew back into the LVT and drove if off the ramp. It was well alight. As soon as it got into the water, its steering gear locked. Abandoning the LVT, the men jumped out and swam ashore. B Troop's third LVT was unable to leave the LCT. The track may have been broken. Most of the men from this LVT swam ashore. One of the troop officers collected as many of B Troop as possible and started to look around for weapons for them. Two-thirds of B Troop had swum ashore, and mustered some 28 all ranks [out of 60 with which they had started]. The

Film still of a Buffalo amphibious tracked vehicle descending the ramp of an LCT before swimming ashore at Walcheren. (FLM2422)

Film still of troops of 4th Special Service Brigade, possibly 47 (Royal Marines) Commando, many of whom swam ashore at Walcheren after their Buffalos were sunk or disabled.
(FLM2421)

men in two of the three LVTs allocated to the Troop had lost their arms and equipment. Two LVTs, one of which was mine, drove out and swam ashore. I landed on the right of the gap.

Instead of deploying to starboard, as planned, the remaining LCTs carrying 47 Cdo drifted to port, towards the left-hand side of the gap, where they bunched in a disorderly fashion.

It was about 19.000 hours and nearly dark before we had concentrated in the unit assembly area on the dunes about 600 yards south of the gap. 47 Cdo had not made a very good start. Instead of being concentrated ashore by 14.00 hours at the latest, it was another five hours before we had reorganised south of the gap.

Setting off the next morning, 47 Commando had already suffered casualties before reaching their final objective, a large battery, the last between Westkapelle and Flushing. The first attack was beaten off with losses including all five rifle troop commanders in one hour.

The following day, with a new plan, and after reorganization by Major Paddy Donnell and the Adjutant Captain Paul Spencer, the Com-

mando attacked again. Captain Reg Wiltshire, commanding the LVTs in support of 47 Commando:

Wounded being transferred from a landing craft for evacuation. (A26241)

> A fair old scrap took place, and then a white flag appeared. Phillips sent his Captain interpreter forward to find out the score. The reply was that they wanted a short truce to pick up their dead and wounded. Phillips' short answer to that was that he had his Commando plus another one just behind him with a lot of naval gun support and the RAF in plenty on call, so if they wanted to die there it was up to them. After a lot of chat, they asked for an honourable surrender. This was agreed, and Phillips assembled the remains of his chaps, who were very few. At the same time he told me to bring up every available Buffalo as he reckoned we had a very difficult situation on our hands. Out came the Jerries fully armed and in hundreds, who fell in and were addressed by their commander. Phillips was most anxious to get them disarmed and hasten the proceedings. After a few 'Sieg Heils' they were eventually marched to the point to drop their arms. They realised they outnumbered us considerably and had been tricked, but it all passed off OK, and we could breathe again. I think it was one of the best spoofs of the war, and Phillips did it without batting an eyelid.

The attack on the eastern side of Walcheren had been preceded by an altercation between Major-General Foulkes commanding Canadian 2nd Corps and Hakeswell-Smith the GOC of 52nd Division. Foulkes ordered Hakewell-Smith to attack across the causeway; 1,700 yards long and a few yards wide. Three attempts by the Canadians had been beaten back. Hakewell-Smith refused, saying he would find another way. Foulkes gave him 48 hours to be in Walcheren or be sacked.

The Chief Royal Engineer of the 52nd Division, and a small engineer party after two hazardous night reconnaissance patrols, found a route across about two miles south of the causeway where a strip of saltings led to the Walcheren dyke from South Beveland. Within 48 hours, one of Hakewell-Smith's Brigades had advanced to within 1,000 yards of Middleburg. The Germans, expecting to be attacked from the east by this brigade, were surprised by the arrival of A Company 7/9th Royal Scots in Buffalos from the direction of Flushing. The Company Commander, after some tense moments, tricked the garrison of over 2,000 men to surrender. The company was isolated until early the next day, when reinforcements arrived, including Captain Wiltshire and his Buffalos:

> We were ordered to Middleburg where an Infantry platoon was trying to convince the mass of Jerries it was time to pack up. We bade our farewells to Phillips and his gallant band, and swam up the canal to Middleburg, where we climbed out of the canal and entered the Main square, much to the relief of the Feet [infantry].

The mopping up operations on Walcheren ended on 8 November, when the Germans decided to surrender just as 4th Special Service Brigade was about to put in an attack towards Vrouenpolder.

Minesweeping started before Walcheren was cleared. Lieutenant-Commander Ted Crane, the Captain of MMS78, and commanding a flotilla of six MMSs equipped with a sweep designed to clear magnetic mines, had sailed his Flotilla to Ostend. Crane had seen a great deal of service beginning with the evacuation of Dunkirk in 1940, the Mediterranean and Normandy.

> At about 13.00 we started off up stream on the flood tide. I told Cookie that he could get the midday meal going, and he was busy in the galley, when a battery of 88mm guns emplaced near the causeway between Walcheren and South Beveland opened fire on the M/Ls. They immediately stopped their sweeps and set off at about 15 knots up the river, making smoke from canisters they dropped overboard. As the wind was blowing away from the guns, it was difficult to use it for cover. The minesweeper ahead of us dropped her canisters. I managed to pick one up on my port bow, and by steering towards the guns helped not only to cover minesweeper number 78 with smoke, but also the other two of my flotilla. Only three shells were fired at us, and as the first shell fell beyond us, I was able to confuse the gunners who shortened the range each shot. The ship was completely

6th Battalion, Green Howards HQ Wireless Section in the Bocage with Private W. Wright, 'Eisenhower' the Rabbit, Corporal T. Murray and Sergeant L. Smith by Anthony Gross. (LD4480)

The platoon sergeant brings up the rations – what we wanted to know was how the damned Jerry knows? by E. Shepherd from his sketchbook on north-west Europe 1944.

The machine-gun platoon sergeant is clutching a dixie, and the man behind a container of tea or soup, while a German mortar or artillery 'stonk' falls. (LD5203)

The Commander-in-Chief, General Montgomery, in the Forêt de Cerisy, Normandy, during the battle of the 'breakthrough' by Anthony Gross.

Montgomery had his tactical headquarters in the Cerisy Forest towards the end of the battle of Normandy, during a period when he was under pressure from Eisenhower and Churchill, and being undermined by Tedder, none of whom appeared to comprehend Montgomery's plan for the battle he was fighting. (LD4483)

Rocket ships off Walcheren by Stephen Bone. (LD4707)

The crossing of the Rhine by Eric Taylor (LD5590)

Doctors attending a wounded soldier in a shattered building behind the Rhine, immediately after the crossing by Eric Taylor. (LD5279)

With the 8th Hussars in Germany – men sleeping by their tanks by Edward Ardizzone. (LD5262)

With the 8th Hussars in Germany – the evening brew by Edward Ardizzone. (LD5260)

The first Ten-Ton raid made by Bomber Command on Germany, March 1945 by Julius Stafford-Baker. (LD5407)

One of the death pits, Belsen, SS guards collecting the bodies by
Leslie Cole. (LD5105)

The front section of Lancaster F for Freddie in the Imperial War Museum. Flight Lieutenant Easton was the navigator for the sortie on the Lille Railway yards. See his log on page 16.

The gun on the left of this picture of the pair in front of the Imperial War Museum was at one time mounted as the right-hand gun in the monitor HMS Roberts.

enveloped in smoke and Cookie complained bitterly that his steak pudding would be ruined.

We all got through.

Ted Crane's Flotilla was summoned to Antwerp, to sweep the reaches of the river near the port:

> As members of the Naval Mess [in Antwerp], we were entitled to use a box at the opera and a party of us went to see *La Bohème*. We were so taken with the performance, we went to see *Carmen* and to *Bohème* a second time from seats in the 'Gods'. It was a disturbing sensation to sit up under the roof and to hear the V-1 [flying bombs] passing overhead, while the cast continued singing, and not a soul moved from their seats in the packed auditorium.

Opening the Scheldt had cost the 1st Canadian Army 12,873 dead, wounded and missing, of which 6,367 were from British, Polish, American and other Allied units under command. To this must be added the losses suffered by the naval and air forces supporting the operation. The opening of Antwerp transformed the supply situation in both the American and British Armies – not before time, for there was still much hard fighting ahead.

CHAPTER SEVEN

'Last Christmas we were in England, expectant and full of hope; this Christmas we are fighting in Germany'

THE BATTLES TO CLOSE UP TO THE RHINE, AND THE GERMAN ARDENNES OFFENSIVE

Troops of 9th Battalion the Highland Light Infantry advancing along a snow-covered road in January 1945. (BU1637)

The set-backs and delays experienced at Arnhem and in the clearing of the Scheldt gained time for the Germans to recover and prolong the War into the spring of 1945. Divisions were withdrawn, topped up with replacements, and refitted. One Army, 6th SS Panzer, was completely re-equipped. The Allied demand for Unconditional Surrender was used to good effect by Goebbels' propaganda machine to stiffen German resolve to fight to the finish. Meanwhile there was some disagreement among the Allied ground commanders over how the campaign should unfold.

Eventually Eisenhower overruled Montgomery's view that the Allied effort should be concentrated behind one or other thrust, and opted for a broad front policy. He ordered Bradley to drive for the Rhine through the Aachen gap, north of the Ardennes, while Montgomery was to clear the Reichswald and drive south between the Maas and the Rhine. Thus Eisenhower aimed to breast up to the Rhine, between Arnhem and Bonn; and cross at Düsseldorf and Cologne. In the event it was to take from mid-October 1944 to mid-March 1945 before the Allies were ready to cross the Rhine in strength, and when the time came, the crossings were to be well north of Düsseldorf, and well south of Cologne. These five months were to see some of the hardest fighting of the

Mud outside Metz: artillery of Patton's 3rd United States Army. Patton's Army suffered tens of thousands of casualties around Metz. At Metz, his bulling ahead attritional tactics reminiscent of the First World War were the antithesis of his carefully polished public image as a thrusting cavalry general. Not only were losses high, but the American line was stretched so thin that the German offensive in the Ardennes smashed through with ease. (PL43803)

campaign in north-west Europe. The cold, rain, mud and artillery bombardments sometimes produced conditions not far removed from those experienced during the First World War by many of the senior officers, and the fathers of those now serving, in the German, British, American and French Armies. Captain Freddie Graham, now commanding a company in 2nd Argylls:

> We went to the Peel country south of Helmond in Holland at the end of
> October, and stayed there closing up to the river Maas. There were mines
> everywhere, all the buildings were booby-trapped, and it never stopped
> raining. The communications were just farm tracks, which became a
> morass. It was a struggle against nature as well as the enemy. It was bloody.
> We had in two or three months the same experience as the infantry in the
> First World War endured for years. Some people got trench foot. But the
> medical support, and things like the excellent self-heating soup made life
> better, as did the logistics, the hot food and the mail.

Captain Peter Balfour of 3rd Tank Battalion, Scots Guards, wrote to his parents:

> I am getting very tired of Holland, in spite of the fact that the Dutch are a
> very nice people. It is cold and wet and you can't imagine how depressing it

A Typhoon takes off from a sodden airstrip in Holland in early 1945. (CL1961)

Company Quartermaster Sergeant Patterson 5th Coldstream Guards brewing up at Uden, September 1944.
(HU64026)

is to live in a country which is absolutely flat as a pancake and where there are no decent sized trees at all.

Battle fatigue, or in First World War terms, shell shock, also increased under these conditions, but was treated with far more understanding in this War. Graham:

Everybody breaks sooner or later. It is the job of a commander to watch out for it and send them back for a rest. That normally cures it. A really good kip in a barn, a good square meal, and their batteries are recharged. Divisions set up rest centres to which people could be sent back to recuperate. The signs to look for: some people shook, some did not register what they were being told, others were slow to react. Foul language seemed to deteriorate; irritability with a capital I. Without rest, a very small number of all ranks would just sugar off. Others would give themselves a self-inflicted wound. We had none in our Battalion, but heard of them in others.

Private Eric Codling, a mortarman in 8th Middlesex:

One morning one of our drivers was missing. After a while the story came out that he had shot himself in the arm and had been evacuated. His reason:

one of his brothers, also in the Regiment, had been killed in North Africa; another brother, serving in our Battalion, was killed at Vernon. Their mother, naturally worried to death for the safety of her third and only surviving son, had written telling of her terrible anxiety. We were asked not to reveal the truth of the matter; the cause of his wounding being attributed to an unknown, trigger-happy Yank, of whom there were plenty in the area.

There were occasionally echoes of the previous war; Private Codling, during a time when the Germans were still threatening the lines of communication in the Nijmegen area:

The supply route through Holland was constantly being cut, thereby limiting the quantities of supplies getting through. Ammunition was severely rationed, and food supplied from the German depot at Oss, which was in fact supplying both British and German troops. A kind of unofficial truce existed there, as neither side had the strength to hold the depot, each loaded rations from opposite ends.

One of the most unpleasant spots in the line was 'The Island'. Private R. H. Day, wounded with the Queen's Regiment at Salerno, and now in 1st Battalion the Leicesters:

I celebrated my 21st birthday in a Dutch Barn. All through the winter, our battalion patrolled and manned sandbagged houses and stood in flooded trenches, with the constant close companionship of shell-ridden, rotting cows, in the Nijmegen bridgehead between the rivers Waal and Rhine, known to the troops as 'The Island'.

During the bitterly cold night, when to stamp our feet to keep warm would attract the enemy, we heard footsteps on the country road beside the house.

We all thought it was the advanced guard of a Jerry patrol, and we kept a firmer grip on our bren guns and rifles waiting for the remainder of the patrol. No further sounds came, but the countryside was suddenly lit up. A trip flare had gone off, that mysterious passer-by must have been responsible for it. The expected patrol did not come. When dawn broke we quietly left the house. The enemy had blown some of the dykes. We had to splash through water nearly up to our knees. It was dangerous, for any German patrol could hear us, and pick us up easily against the lightening sky.

Major Peter Martin:

It was very monotonous on 'The Island', the slit trenches filled with water. We had to get empty 44-gallon oil drums for people to stand in to keep themselves dry. The people in the farms were very friendly. They were very upset that we left before Christmas. We were told this was because they were fattening up their cat to give us in lieu of a Christmas turkey. For that reason I was very glad we did leave.

'Not least of all, Baths'
PRIVATE CODLING
8th Middlesex

**A hotel in Brussels
used as a leave centre
by 21st Army Group.**
(BU1457)

**British troops on leave
in a hotel in Brussels.**
(BU1461)

Leave helped; Private Codling:

Next day a great bit of news – the three-day leave trips to Brussels were to begin, and I was among the first to be selected from the platoon. Setting off, in our dirty battle-dress, to company HQ, we joined the rest of the lucky blokes and were soon on our way by truck to *a hotel* with the luxury of padded chairs, soft beds with sheets, tables set with cloths and china, and not least of all BATHS. The first thing we did was to run a bath full of hot water to soak our dirty bodies, relaxing as we had never relaxed before. The last proper bath I had enjoyed was on D-Day in the public baths at Hastings. [Codling's Division had not arrived in Normandy until mid June 1944.]

Putting on newly issued shirts, pants and socks and cleaned battle-dress, we emerged new men. The transformation was completed by a visit to a nearby hairdressing saloon for an excellent haircut.

Some were lucky enough to qualify for home leave; Trooper Baker:

It was very noticeable that very few of the hundreds going on leave were actually front-line troops at all. They were mostly RASC, Signals, RAOC, various kinds of Corps HQ troops etc. Infantry and tank men were few and far between – obviously because very few of them had lasted long enough to qualify for leave.

Lieutenant-Colonel Bill Renison, who had succeeded to command of 2nd E. Yorks, the left-hand assault battalion on D-Day:

I drew the first batch of UK leave vacancies before a representative party of other ranks to see fair play. I adopted the method of drawing all who had landed on the first tide on D-Day first, and thereafter, strictly chronologically by days, which caused no ill-feeling or complaint, and was accepted by all as a fair method within the battalion. What did cause a good deal of dissatisfaction was the fact that many of the L of C units who didn't land until July or August were getting leave before some of our D-Day survivors. The Div Comd eventually wrote a letter asking for an increased percentage for the Division, but this was not possible operationally.

Captain Holdsworth, 2nd Devons went to Brussels with his brother in a jeep:

Best of all, in my view, was the prospect of a bath – several baths. In the short time I was in Antwerp, I had four, and they were among my most treasured memories of those 48 hours of leave: great steaming baths lasting an hour at a time, sweating out the aches and pains, cleansing the sores and cuts, and forcing out the dirt accumulated since D-Day. The evidence of the need for these baths was plainly to be seen after the water had drained away. They were blissful, energy-sapping, and time-consuming, they did me more good than any other diversion during those 48 hours.

Representatives of other units were there and, because we were soldiers and had shared common experiences, our conversation was almost exclusively devoted to the war, the enemy, tiger tanks, 88mm guns, the

wounded, the living, the dead, the war, and back again to the enemy. We were all the better for the exaggerations, the lies, the mock heroics, and maudlin humour, the half-admitted truths. But it was all very unreal. Reality, we knew, existed only in the slit trenches from which we had come and were going back to. We'd become attuned to their environment and, being infantrymen, enjoyed the perverted snobbery which compelled us to turn our noses up at those who had the good fortune not to share our privations and discomforts.

David Holdsworth did not return to his slit trench. His leg was crushed in an accident with a Canadian truck on the road back to Nijmegen. He was evacuated to England, and did not take any further part in the War.

Home leave could also have its problems. Sapper Alfred Lane, arriving home in Wales:

I expected and hoped that nothing had happened to change the simplicity and tranquillity of the little village – but, alas, already I could see something that disappointed and displeased me greatly. The noisy staggering figures and groups I could see were American soldiers, some with local girls, obviously the worse for drink. I was angry – my village contaminated, polluted, violated. At that moment I hated not only Americans soldiers, but all soldiers, all uniforms, and for that matter, all and everything associated with war.

As I sped homewards my anger and disappointment soon gave way to more reasonable thoughts that there were few, if any places, in Europe totally untouched by World War II – so many places destroyed, so many people killed. I had much to be thankful for. As for the Yanks, it was good to know they were on our side, since it seemed unlikely that I would have survived if they were not.

As well as similarities with the First World War during this period, there were some pointers for future wars. Lieutenant-Colonel Crawford:

> Met the General at 130 Bde Hqrs. He was going off again; 'Blast the BBC, blast the BBC. No need for the Germans to have an Intelligence service, the BBC tells them everything.' This is quite true. Both the 9 o'c news last night and the 9 o'c news this morning had a long talk on our pincer movement to the NE and SE of Geilenkirchen. And all about Gen. Dempsey's Second Army fighting on German soil, while it appears from PWs that the Hun still thought he was facing the Americans. Of course this also happened in the big rush across France. Some Hun general said the only way he and his troops could get the news was via the BBC.

Despite occasional respite in rear areas, the rests were never long, and the fighting never far away. Hewison:

> *23 October*: On the 21st we moved from Heesch into a concentration area. At dawn on the 22nd a full scale attack, after a night of intense arty preparation. Deadly ground – ditches and marshy. In the asslt we got 21 POWs, one 88mm, and our objective. Bags of brassing up all round – especially BESA. The POWs had just shot their officer, who wanted apparently to continue the fight. Dirty bastards! However they got wounded by their own mortar fire.

Taking part in these operations with 15th Scottish Division were two of the 'Desert' divisions. By now the Highland Division, under Rennie's leadership, had regained its good name. One of the other 'Desert' Divisions, 7th Armoured, had also got back into its stride, although the Divisional Commander was to be changed again before the campaign was over. One of its brigades, 22nd Armoured, was commanded by the very experienced, good-humoured, Brigadier Tony Wingfield, pro-moted from 34th Tank Brigade:

> During the previous night I had ordered the 8th Hussars Group, together with a squadron of the 11th Hussars armoured cars, to start at first light and bypass the 1st Royal Tanks Group who had by then captured Udenhout. They were to make for Loon-op-Zaand. I set off at dawn myself to see their

progress. I had not gone very far before I saw, stuck into the side of the road, a green pennant embroidered with a golden harp [8th Hussars were an Irish Regiment]. This marked the RHQ of the 8th Hussars, so I stopped my scout-car and went into a nearby house. There, to my horror, I found nearly all the officers of the 8th Hussars having breakfast at a long table covered with a white cloth and with their CO sitting at its head with a green and gold side-cap perched on his head. When I recovered from the shock of this Crimean tableau, I 'blew my top'. I asked the CO what the hell he thought he was doing here when I expected him to be in the outskirts of Loon-op-Zaand. His reply was that 11th Hussars were held up just down the road. That infuriated me even more, and I told him – in no uncertain terms – that if armoured cars could not get off the road the tanks of the 8th Hussars bloody well could and would do so at once even if they submerged in the polder. The Irish doves flew out of their dovecote pretty quick: and I remembered that the 8th Hussars had been overrun by the Germans twice in the Desert – on one occasion, I had been told, it was at breakfast time!

The 8th Hussars then – to give them their due – got past the 11th Hussars but ran into heavy opposition.

Trooper John Thorpe's last day in battle with 2nd Fife and Forfar Yeomanry, was a Sunday:

We grumble that old Monty always starts something new on Sundays. We have ten days in action and start a new action on the following Sunday. This day is different, I feel this is my last day, I'm really morose. They all tell me, 'Go on with you, it's no different than any other time.' But somehow, I know. As a matter of fact I don't tell them, but I think I'm going to be killed! In the late afternoon we begin to be mortared. One lands on Robby's periscope and blows it in. Robby and I are both wounded. Robby attempts to scramble over me to climb out through my hatch, but I try to reassure him and hold him in.

Robby's ears are bleeding beside facial cuts. I was wearing my headset so avoided concussion to my ears, but my face is opened from my eye to my mouth. I could not see with that eye. It was as if I had been hit in the face with a red-hot cricket ball. The turret boys get us up in the turret one at a time and apply field dressings. Cliff requests over the radio for us to withdraw, but permission is not granted, we must stay until stand down.

No one else can drive, and when clearance comes, Robby had passed out. So I take over. As there is no periscope, I open up and drive us back to our start. We are put in a jeep and taken back to the RAP, and to Deurne, and from there to Helmot, where a school room has been converted to a hospital. Gosh, there are female nurses here, fresh, crisp English girls, marvellous to see them, something I have missed without knowing. I could have cried with the joy of it.

The Dutch polder country and German forest in which 21st Army Group fought was ideal for defence. Fighting in these conditions needed well organized infantry/tank co-operation, and sometimes artillery. Wingfield, as his brigade continued to advance to the Maas:

I set off to join the Skins [5th Inniskilling Dragoon Guards] that morning and found them halted on a very straight and open road emerging from marshland and leading to a wood. The reason they were stuck on the road was the usual one: there were anti-tank guns firing from the edge of the wood at tanks which could not deploy off the road onto polder. However, Teddy Swetenham was making a plan to attack the wood with a carrier platoon on his motor [infantry] company which he hoped would not get bogged in the field on the left of the road.

I joined Teddy, standing up on his tank, to watch this attack go in. It was strangely like watching a point-to-point from the bonnet of a car. Unfortunately Teddy's attack was not a success. The bren-gun carrier platoon was too small for the opposition hidden in the wood, and the tank squadron was too heavy for the soggy ground. I told Teddy that I would get Pat Hobart to divert a squadron of the 1st Royal Tanks.

Soon after I had given this order to 1st Royal Tanks, Gerry Verney [GOC 7th Armoured Division] arrived. I explained the position to him. He went off to this wireless set and came back to say that the Corps Commander had laid him a bet that my pincer movement would not succeed. I told my General to go back and double his stake. In fact Pat Hobart only detached one troop to turn back towards the Skins, but it was enough. 150 Germans came out of the wood to surrender with their SP anti-tank guns.

Wingfield also recalls the innate 'bloody-mindedness' and sense of humour which makes most British troops less amenable to mindless discipline than some, and at the same time so rewarding to command:

When I was with the Rifle Brigade, I remarked to Victor Paley that I thought it was a bad idea that his riflemen always carried their side-hats tucked under a shoulder-strap rather than on their heads. I pointed out that this habit prevented them from saluting officers and that, although I was not too fussy myself, I considered it most important they should salute Dutch officers correctly.

Victor must have relayed my comments to his troops; for during our next move, I was watching the Rifle Brigade pass me at a cross-roads, where I was standing with their CO. One of their trucks contained four riflemen sitting smartly at attention. One wore a straw boater, another a homburg, the third a bowler, and the fourth an opera hat – or *chapeau mechanique*. I turned to Victor and said I had received their message.

By now the German bombardment of London by V-2 rockets, which started in mid-September, was well under way, from sites in northern Holland (not liberated until the end of March 1945). The V-1s, denied launching sites in France and Belgium by the advancing Allies, could no longer reach London. Both types could reach targets in Holland and Belgium, principally Antwerp. 3,470 Belgian civilians and 682 Allied servicemen lost their lives to these attacks. Brigadier Wingfield:

Before we left West Holland, I saw a couple of V-2s being launched somewhere in the north across the Maas, which was still in German occupation. These horribly lethal missiles were making their vertical ascent. I presumed they were destined for London, where I knew Judy was now working, and my heart trembled.

Brigadier Douglas Greenacre, Commanding 6th Guards Tank Brigade, writing to his wife on 18 October 1944:

Sorry to hear that your area has been getting doodles. I'm afraid that to a certain extent they will continue to the end of the war.

Greenacre then switches to three subjects uppermost in many soldiers minds; the progress of the war, the weather and prospects for leave:

Our battle goes on slowly, we are meeting many mines & they take time to clear. The weather has been absolutely foul & so wet that most of the ground is too soft for tanks. *[And a month later]*:

Things on the whole are progressing well I think but it is slow & wet & uncomfortable. I hope the Germans are much more so. Leave, apart from 'compassionate' or 'bowler hat' [being sacked] is not permitted to UK. Except of course for the RAF, who I gather fly out & back as they please.

Despite Montgomery's low opinion of Eisenhower, which was unknown to the soldiers at the time, the latter was usually well received by them. Greenacre, who was never sparing with criticism in letters to his wife:

We had a visit from Eisenhower and Dempsey yesterday. They stayed

about an hour & a half & were very pleasant & friendly. They chatted away to the troops & I think a good time was had by all; anyway it has done a lot of good. There is no difficulty in understanding why Ike is such a success. He has tremendous charm of manner.

General Eisenhower chatting to two British Lieutenant-Colonels. (B5570)

On 21st Army Group's right flank, XXX Corps, including 43rd Wessex Division was pushing towards Geilenkirchen and the River Roer. Sergeant Walter Caines, 4th Dorsets, relieving 5th Dorsets in a large wood, moved forward with the commanding officer's recce party:

For many weeks I had been commanding the Signal Platoon without an officer. I was happier without an officer. The Battalion's casualties since landing in Normandy had piled up, and NCOs and key men were in short supply, although reinforcements kept joining us; specialists were very short, particularly NCOs.

As soon as it became dark, Companies were sent for and positions were taken over from 5 Dorsets. Many members of rifle companies became lost while making their way through wooded country. It was a pitch black night, only lit up when gun flashes illuminated the whole area. Everything seemed to go wrong, transport failed to turn up, most of it had become stuck in the mud along the main route. Consequently ammunition and other essential supplies had to be manhandled by carrying parties. This took hours, and the whole time the Battalion area was under heavy fire from German artillery. The field behind the wood was littered with vehicles stuck in the mud. Rain fell heavily. All of us were soaked to the skin, with absolutely no cover whatsoever. Trenches taken over from 5 Dorsets were half full of water, and some were not even completed. The majority had no head cover, except the Command Post. The signals carrier with all the stores on board was lost in the woods, and there was no communication except runners. Wireless could not be relied upon, as batteries were run down, and all sets became waterlogged. I spent the night sitting in a trench half full of water, with rain trickling down my neck, it was bloody miserable. In fact the only remedy was a swig at the bottle.

22 November: Tactical Headquarters was shelled every few minutes, and we all clutched to the sides of our trenches, quietly kneeling and saying our prayers. Shells fell very close, often blowing the sides of our trenches in. Casualties were piling up, also several were reporting sick with trench feet and severe influenza.

23 November: Lines had been very badly cut up. All line parties were out, then the line to the RAP went dis. This left Private Gapper and myself to deal with it. We made our way to the RAP across swamped fields, where, while bending down to repair a break, we were sniped at, so Gapper and I had to run for it. We always seemed to have a narrow one whenever together.

25 November: A supply of water was brought up, just enough for each man to fill his mess tin for washing and shaving. None of us had washed or shaved for over five days at least. I had not changed my underwear for a long time. Some men had to be evacuated with battle exhaustion. I was now reduced to four men for line parties.

Captain Leaney, the 4th Dorset Chaplain, visiting Battalion Headquarters from the RAP:

I paid a visit each morning, my heart in my mouth. Sometimes my visit was for the purpose of burying or, later, taking away a body for burial. On several occasions I had to go forward from Bn HQ to one of the companies. When a body had to be brought back, I went up on a Weasel taking rations, and was not lightened in heart by the sight of the white, strained faces of men who normally would have eagerly rendered assistance, unable to overcome a fixed reluctance to leave their slit trenches. On more than one occasion, it was a stretcher bearer, or the Company Commander himself, who helped me lift the dead man on to the vehicle.

Sergeant Walter Caines:

26 November: Late in the afternoon, we were informed that we were being relieved by the 1st Worcesters. The Battalion was accommodated in houses and the village school. Dry blankets were found, and we were all made as comfortable as possible, no beds of course, all slept on the floor boards.

28 November: All were able to bath in the colliery at Brunssum. How grand it was to strip off and feel water again.

30 November: Orders were received to relieve the tired Wiltshires.

3 December: During the late morning, the Brigadier Commanding 130 Brigade paid a visit to the Colonel. I was sent for. I was greeted by the Colonel and introduced to the Brigadier, who said a few words to me, and then I realised that I was to jump from a three-striped sergeant to an officer in a few days' time. He told me it would take a few days to be confirmed.

Private Eric Codling, 4.2-inch mortarman, in 8th Middlesex, supporting 43rd Wessex Division was billeted in a deserted farmhouse:

Living accommodation consisted of two cellars; one under the house, which was flooded; the second a large potato store. The first cellar was made just habitable by submerging several layers of empty ammunition boxes, as this raised the level of the floor by some two feet, thereby allowing life to exist above high-water level. Our other refuge served a dual purpose in that it was possible to eat one's bed.

Major 'Banger' King, 2nd East Yorks, writing to his batman on 21 November 1944 with news of the Battalion:

We are now down to five D-day wallahs. A few have come back. Cpl Bingley came back three days ago, and now he has been hit this evening in the leg by a sniper. A nice blighty one for the second time.

The chase through Belgium really was good fun but it didn't last long enough. In Holland we had some pretty sticky jobs to do, but did them very successfully as usual. In the last big show the company got held up in a brewery. Well it was too good to miss . . . we got held up quite a time there. The next place we found ourselves was in a lunatic asylum with 1,500 lunies [sic] still inside and the Jerries only three yards away. You needn't make the obvious comment . . . I did get out!

Sorry to hear that you are still not a hundred per cent fit. Anyhow they won't send you to Burma. Please give my regards to your Mother. Herewith a Xmas present. Spend most of it on beer. Wish I could be there to help you drink it. All the best. All the old hands in the coy send you their regards.

As winter approached, reorganizations and changes affected some divisions. After being warned for an operation, Major Peter Martin's company in 2nd Cheshires:

We were then told it was cancelled, and there was a new plot for us. People began to wonder if we were going home – there were rumours from the clerks at Battalion HQ. I was told this was exactly what was going to happen. We would be reduced to 12 officers and 109 other ranks, and sent home to train surplus RAF and Naval recruits as infantry for the Rhine crossing. The reason: 50 Div had not only done its stuff, but its standard of training was getting shaky, and it was time someone else bore the burden.

This was fine, except that from my own company only myself, my 2ic and about 20 men would be left. All the rest would be dispersed round the place and retrained as infantry. This was a betrayal. We pleaded with the CO, myself and the other company commanders, to lodge an objection, to say we were quite happy to go on fighting, providing we could be kept together. We didn't want to be relieved, we didn't want to be sent back to England.

There was tremendous jubilation in the Company at the thought of going home for Christmas. Little did they know, poor chaps, what lay in wait. After leave, we who had been their company commanders had to retrain them for five weeks. One awful day in February, wearing the badges of many different units, off they went. Some went straight to battalions in the front line, some to holding units, some to the Far East. It is something I have never forgotten. The shame of the CO allowing it to happen has been with me for the rest of my life. I know that a great number got killed in the final battles of the war. That was unforgivable.

On 16 December, after the heaviest artillery barrage fired by the Germans in the whole campaign in north-west Europe in 1944–5, preceded by parties of parachutists and saboteurs in civilian clothes and Allied uniforms, three German armies under von Rundstedt, reinstated by Hitler after the fall of Antwerp, 6th SS Panzer, 5th and 7th Panzer, attacked five United States Divisions on a front of fifty miles. The German aim was to drive a wedge between the British and American armies, cross the Meuse and seize Antwerp. By 23 December the German armoured spearheads were driving for Dinant on the river Meuse, and a salient fifty miles wide at its base and forty-five miles deep had been punched in the American line. The Americans who had borne the brunt of this attack, fought with courage and tenacity, particularly at St Vith and Bastogne. Dogged resistance slowed down the German attacks, causing hold-ups of enemy traffic on the congested roads.

Meanwhile, Montgomery, realizing that Bradley was cut off from his northern armies, had suggested to Eisenhower that he should take command of the northern shoulder of the Bulge. This was agreed and control quickly established. Montgomery placed XXX Corps in a blocking position to cover the approaches to Brussels, and went to contact Hodges (1st US Army) and Simpson (9th US Army). The situation having been restored by the stout fighting of these two armies and Patton's 3rd US Army in the south, Montgomery made the mistake of giving the impression at a press conference that it was he who had saved the day. That Montgomery's swift reaction and effective control of a very dangerous situation had made Eisenhower look ineffective did nothing to improve matters. Bradley, Patton and some senior officers at Eisenhower's headquarters bayed for Montgomery's blood. Although the row was patched up, relations between Montgomery and his American Allies never recovered, and for the rest of the campaign he would pay the price.

By Christmas Day the offensive was roped off. The Allied task was to pinch off the German salient as quickly as possible before the drive across the Rhine could begin. The bulk of this task fell to the 1st and 3rd US Armies. The British contribution was a drive on the nose of the salient by XXX Corps between the two American Armies.

The Allied Air Forces also played a significant part in slowing down von Rundstedt's offensive. The low cloud and bad weather over the salient in the early days of von Rundstedt's advance made it impossible for the Allied Air Forces to give the badly needed close air support which would have made all the difference to the hard-pressed American infantry divisions. However, deep interdiction operations against the German supply lines were possible. Taking part was 582 Squadron RAF, flying Lancasters:

> The operation on 23rd December 1944 was a special mission to help in the disruption of the German offensive on the Western Front. The main supply route for the German Army lay across the Rhine at Cologne, and the Gremberg railway yards in Cologne was a vital link in this supply line. At that time the railway yard was full of supplies for von Rundstedt's advancing army.
>
> Seventeen Lancasters of 582 Squadron took part. The attack commenced just after midday. Eight Lancasters from 35 Squadron made up the third formation. There were also three Mosquitoes from 105 Squadron and one from 109 Squadron.
>
> Five Lancasters were shot down over the target area, including the leading aircraft flown by Bob Palmer, who was awarded a posthumous Victoria Cross. The 109 Mosquito was also shot down, and two 35 Squadron Lancasters were lost by collision on the outward journey.

The crew of Lancaster PB120 'P', of 582 Squadron Pathfinder Force, Little Staughton, shot down on 23 December 1944, raiding the Gremberg Railway Yards in Cologne. Left to right: **George Owen,** Wireless Operator (RAF), **Ken Austin,** Navigator (RCAF), **Bob Pearce,** Rear Gunner (RCAF), **Walt Reif,** Pilot (RCAF), **Jack MacLennan,** Mid Upper Gunner (RCAF) **and Pete Uzelman,** Bombardier (RCAF). **Only Pearce and MacLennan survived. The Flight Engineer was John Paterson** (RAF), **who was also killed.**

Page from Flight Sergeant Owen's log book, stamped Death Presumed. (From G. O. Owen papers 83/7/1, Negative number HU63700)

Lancaster PB120 'P' flown by Flight Lieutenant Walter Reif was hit by anti-aircraft fire just after making its attack, and set on fire. Attacking ME109 fighters then set upon the crippled aircraft and badly damaged the front of the plane with heavy cannon fire. This probably killed most of the crew. Walter Reif then ordered the aircraft to be abandoned and courageously tried to keep the stricken Lancaster stable so that any survivors could escape. The two gunners managed to parachute from the rear exit and then saw the blazing plane dive to the ground and explode. No other members of the crew got out.

Wingfield:

There was now circulated a ridiculous rumour that there were German Wolves in American Sheep's clothing infiltrating into our area, and we were called upon to make strict security checks causing much embarrassment to many a genuine American liaison officer.

The Reverend Skinner:

Thursday 21 December 1944: A German SS Officer captured in next village wearing a US uniform and cutting telephone wires – shot.

Sergeant Caines:

17 December: We were informed that a new German Army under von Rundstedt had broken the line in the American sector in the Ardennes. When the Dutch heard of this they became very scared, but we told them not to be afraid, as we had great confidence in Victory and that Montgomery's tactics would defeat them.

Christmas Day 1944: a sergeant carves the turkey. (B13138)

19 December: As I was moving off, Corporal Haines came running out of the signal office and said, 'Let me be the last to call you Sergeant, and the first to call you Sir,' and he handed me the signal confirming me and Sergeant Brown as commissioned officers.

As soon as we were organised, I was dragged into the Officers' Mess by the Quartermaster and the Motor Transport Officer, and between them they ripped off my stripes, and Sam gave me a couple of pips, and called his batman to find a clean shirt with a collar. I then realised I was not wearing a tie, Sam again came to the rescue. I walked into the Mess. Every member present greeted me, shook hands and called me by my Christian name, which rather surprised me.

25 December, Xmas Day: Morning tea was taken to all the men by the Officers and Sergeants. The men's Dinner Meal was issued by the Officers and Sergeants; this was always the custom in the British Army. I always enjoyed doing this. It was a splendid dinner, especially under difficult circumstances.

When the Germans attacked in the Ardennes, the 2nd Fife & Forfars were re-equipping and retraining with new tanks, near Ypres. These Comets, equipped with 77mm guns, were a considerable improvement on the Sherman, and a match for all but the super versions of the Tiger. Lieutenant Brownlie:

20 December: Bombshell, we were to move to the Ardennes soonest. Forget

Irish soldiers of the 8th Hussars on Christmas Day. The women's clothes have likely been 'liberated' from empty houses in the town. (B13135)

the Comets, leave the heavy kit behind, pick up our old Shermans in Brussels, get to the Meuse and help stop von Rundstedt.

21 December: At 6 a.m. went to the Reinforcement Unit, where Shermans of our 29 Armoured Brigade had been dumped and emptied of all ammo etc. There was no time to sort out whose tanks were whose, and the three regiments got vehicles with any old regimental sign, squadron or troop signs, which was confusing. I was lucky – my Sherman was in Ypres as a trainer, and Jock McKinnon drove it to Brussels. By midday, by a miracle of organisation, the whole Brigade were armed, rationed and fuelled. There were cheering crowds in Brussels, worried that the Germans would be back, and maybe we would stop them.

I was sent ahead in a scout-car to arrange a harbour in a suburb of Namur, and picked a street of brick-built houses, where the tanks parked. We were most welcome, and my own billet was with a delightful damsel, who was serving me a four-course meal, when her large policeman husband came in off late shift; you can't win them all.

22 December: Over the Meuse Bridge, wired for demolition, and defended by a scratch force, looking nervous and checking everyone's papers. There were latrine rumours about German parachutists disguised in captured American uniforms, but our main worry was some bloody fool would blow the bridges with us on the far side.

In early January 1945, Brownlie's squadron was supporting 13th Parachute Battalion's attack on the town of Bure, in bitter winter weather.

After supporting 13th Parachute Battalion's attack, and beating off a counter-attack, it was nightfall:

There was no wind, no more snow, but it grew colder and colder. The ground was too hard for digging, so we slept in the tank. Jock McKinnon

and MacKenzie in their seats down front; Buck Buchanan on the deck below the gun, Norman Ingram on top of the gun, self on floor with feet in one sponson, head in another. Sleep? Within ten minutes the icy cold of the metal had seeped through your clothing, and the breath froze on your lips.

After a second day of fighting, and another frozen night, Brownlie, by now the acting Squadron Leader:

> *5 January*: We were told the enemy were pulling out of Bure. Colonel Alec came up in his tank, and said we would probably be relieved by 23rd Hussars. They arrived late in the afternoon, and haggled about where they were to position themselves. I finally told them we were leaving anyway.
>
> We had been suddenly wrenched out of the comforts of Ypres at such short notice that some of the troops went in gym shoes, having no time to get their boots, never mind their bedding. My abiding memory is of the tiny black figures labouring in the white landscape, while we did our best to support them.

The 13th Parachute Battalion suffered 189 casualties, of which 66 were killed.

By the end of January preliminary clearing operations had set the scene for the Battle of the Rhineland: securing the ground between the Maas and the Rhine as a prelude to crossing the Rhine itself. For this battle, Operations Veritable and Grenade, Montgomery took Lieutenant-General Simpson's 9th US Army under command. The Rhineland was heavily defended. The Siegfried Line, consisting of concrete pillboxes, anti-tank ditches and obstacles, had been augmented by minefields. Flooding and forest, the latter in the Canadian sector, added to the already formidable problems of attacking in this sector. Montgomery's plan was for the Canadian 1st Army to debouch from the Nijmegen salient, between the Rivers Maas and Rhine, on 8 February,

Lieutenant-General Simpson, commander United States 9th Army, talks to Montgomery. 9th Army operated under Montgomery's command in the Rhineland and Reichswald battles, and for the crossing of the Rhine. (KY485064)

with XXX British Corps in the lead (Operation Veritable). Such an axis would lead behind the Siegfried Line, once the northern extremity had been breached. As the frontage widened, II Canadian Corps would come up alongside XXX Corps, both heading for Geldern and Wesel. Starting later, 9th US Army, consisting of ten divisions, was to attack from the River Roer, north of Aachen, and drive for the Rhine between Wesel and Neuss (Operation Grenade). The two armies would link up at Wesel and Geldern. The strength of 1st Canadian Army was just under half a million men. It would be wrong to imagine that 1st Canadian Army was an all Canadian affair. Austin Baker:

> The Brigade was once more attached to 43 Div which, with the rest of 30 Corps, came under the command of 1st Canadian army. This arrangement led to a lot of talk at home about the apparent lack of activity of the 2nd Army during the winter.

Clearly this talk reached high level in Whitehall. On 12 February, Montgomery received the following from the Vice Chief of the Imperial General Staff (VCIGS):

PERSONAL FOR FIELD MARSHAL MONTGOMERY FROM VCIGS.

Cabinet anxious that publicity of present operations should make it clear that high proportion of troops in Canadian Army are in fact British.

Will you do what you can at your end using your own discretion as to how far from a security aspect you can disclose relative proportion of British and Canadian troops.

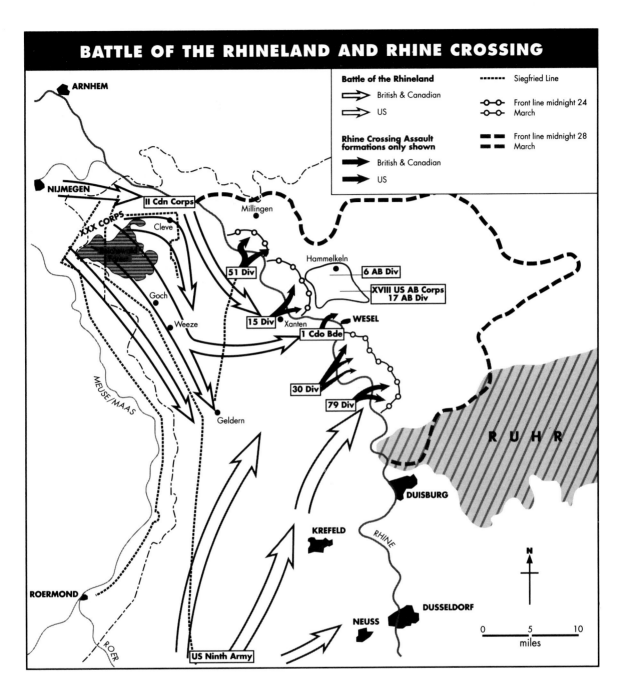

BATTLE OF THE RHINELAND AND RHINE CROSSING

Montgomery replied:

> Now I have given two more British Divisions to the Canadian army for
> Veritable there will be seven British divisions and two Canadian divisions in
> the battle. The press will be briefed accordingly tomorrow and from the
> security angle there is no objection to them disclosing that three-quarters of
> the troops engaged are British and one quarter Canadian.

Montgomery's system of thorough preparation lay behind giving
the Rhineland Battle to 1st Canadian Army. The Canadians had been

Tanks and carriers in a narrow forest track in the Reichswald. The soldier on the left is brewing up on a cooker. (BU1751)

planning for Veritable, while 2nd British Army had been engaged north of the Ardennes, and on Operation Blackcock. Similarly, 2nd British Army planned for the Rhine Crossing, during Veritable. Thus one army staff could concentrate on the current battle while the other was preparing for the next.

For the British and Canadians, the main task ahead was clearing the Reichswald, a formidable obstacle on the western end of the Siegfried Line defences, and the capture of Cleve and Goch. Captain Freddie Graham, of 2nd Argylls:

> We started Veritable just north of the forest, and 53rd Welsh Div were in the forest. As a very young officer I became aware of the question of manpower as it affected the UK. After our first battles we got our LOBS [left out of battle soldiers] as reinforcements. Then we got people from the DLI, Hampshires and others. Although we (the UK) didn't send many divisions to Normandy, within four months two were broken up to keep the remainder going. Infantry casualties were much heavier than expected. Some of our reinforcements were not even infantry. The number of people still serving who had landed with us in Normandy was quite small. So a combination of lack of trained leaders and trained manpower meant that

simple tactics had to be employed. From this time on, attacks were like the infantry assaults of World War One. White tape was laid. People formed up and walked forward at a set pace behind a barrage; halted for three minutes; coloured smoke was fired indicating that you could go on, and so on. It was very undemanding, but anything more ambitious would have been beyond us. The trained leaders and soldiers were no longer there. That was the instrument with which we had to complete the campaign.

Just east of the Reichswald were the two fortress towns of Cleve and Calcar, important strong points in the Siegfried defences. Massive air attacks by RAF Bomber Command had reduced them to rubble, but the German garrison had not abandoned them. Trooper Baker:

> The next afternoon we set off along the road to Cleve. The infantry of 214 Brigade piled on the backs of the tanks to be ferried up the line. I suppose each tank carried about ten – we even had two squatting on the turret floor. It was a nightmare journey. The Cleve road was absolutely jammed with vehicles, moving at a snail's pace. It was horribly cold and I was frozen stiff, even in a zoot suit and jerkin. I was very sorry for the infantry clinging miserably to the outsides of the tanks.

Trooper Austin Baker's tank, 'Shaggy Dog', moves up for the Reichswald battle. The tank is commanded by Sergeant le Maitre, Trooper Bert Morsley is driving (near-side front), Trooper McCarthy is co-driver, his head hidden by the gun. Trooper Baker is in the turret out of sight as is Bill Dawson. Track plates have been welded on the turret and the front of the tank for extra protection. The next tank in the column is a 17-pounder, and the barrel of another is in the foreground. The bulbous fitting on the end of the barrel is a muzzle brake to reduce recoil. (B14678[WK])

Infantry take up positions in newly captured trenches, February 1945.
(BU1719)

As a matter of fact I was sorry for myself, because the trip was made especially unpleasant for me by a bad attack of diarrhoea. Every time we stopped, I had to crawl over two infantrymen on the turret floor, squeeze past Le Maitre, get out of the hatch, and climb down by the roadside. Here I had to divest myself of leather jerkin, zoot suit, a suit of denims, and battledress; with the column about to move off at any moment.

Lieutenant Walter Caines, 4th Dorsets:
15 February: The attack commenced at approximately 10.00 hours. A and C companies reached their objectives. All went well until the last few yards, and then the German para boys opened up with all they had. Shells and mortars rained down on the attacking troops. The commanders of A and C companies were wounded. A Company had twenty-four killed, and many wounded. B Company were ordered to carry out the second phase. Very few prisoners were taken. The boys had no intentions of worrying over many.

Trooper Baker, in support of another battalion in the same battle:
While the remainder of the squadron was still on the road, it came under very heavy shelling. The shells were massive and huge geysers of earth shot up from the wide, flat fields on either side. It was obvious that a direct hit from one of them would shatter a tank, and I felt pretty nervous. I saw the infantry trudge doggedly on, hardly looking sideways at the explosions. I suppose long experience of being shelled in the open had taught them to judge quite accurately where a shell was going to fall by the noise of its approach.

As the advance continued:

> We waited in suspense, while the wireless got very busy. There were
> anti-tank guns along the edge of the wood and 1st Troop could not get
> forward without presenting ideal targets for Jerry gunners. Somebody
> suggested sending another troop around the left flank, and Bill Riley
> agreed.
>
> 'Hullo, Peter', he began (Peter was the Squadron's code letter that day).
> Then he paused, obviously wondering whether to send 2nd or 3rd Troop –
> nobody else was available. We held our breaths.
>
> 'Peter Two,' said Bill [squadron leader] at last, and I knew we'd had it.
> There was practically no cover and I was expecting every yard to be our last.
> To my surprise we got to the trees without a shot being fired at us.

The toll on tank crews continued:

> Under cover of a smoke screen, Thorniley, then 3rd Troop leader, tried to
> move his tank forward, but a Jerry tank or SP had also taken advantage of
> the screen to get into a good firing position. It brewed up both Thorniley
> and the 27 pdr. Thorniley's tank blew up instantly – nobody had time to
> bale out. Thorniley was ejected from the turret with such force that his
> webbing belt was ripped in two on some projection, but he wasn't very
> badly wounded. The rest of his crew were all killed – Cpl Sam Weaver,
> Ryan, Robinson and Barrs. Sam Weaver had just returned to the squadron
> after being wounded in Normandy. I remember him telling me that he
> believed that there was only one shot with your name on it, and if you had a
> very narrow escape then the one with your name on it had missed and you
> would be safe in future. Evidently there were two with Sam's name on.

At the end of February, Baker's regiment was switched to support 53rd
Welsh Division for their attack on Weeze. Lieutenant-Colonel Bill Renison's 2nd East Yorkshires played a key part in the battle for the bridge
over the Muhlen–Fleuth on the road leading to the town. Renison:

> Eventually the first objective was taken, but the cost was heavy: A company
> commander was killed leading a charge at close quarters, and the company
> second-in-command had received wounds from which he died in hospital.
> A platoon commander took on the remains of the company and succeeded
> in reaching his objective with only about thirty all ranks left.
>
> In the meantime D Coy were experiencing very much the same
> opposition on the right. The Boche allowed the company to get right into a
> house, and fought it out with grenades inside. The house was well alight,
> and fighting hand-to-hand was very fierce in the smoke. The company lost
> two officers killed. As they were reorganising before pushing on to the
> bridge, the Boche dropped a shell straight inside a roofless barn, where Coy
> HQ and one platoon were taking cover. Practically every man was hit,
> including the CSM who was killed. This reduced the company to little more
> than a platoon; obviously insufficient to take the bridge, if it was defended,
> and to hold it. D Coy's 18 set had gone dis [unserviceable – author's

**A Bren gunner of the
East Yorkshires firing
through a shattered
roof.** (BU1223)

comment: radio sets seem to have a knack of choosing the most
inconvenient time to do this] and my only communication with D Company
was over the tank net.

On Renison's orders, C Company rushed the bridge, taking the garrison
by surprise:
> C Company Commander put the HQ in a good solid Boche dug-out in
> Schaddenhof farm, and dug in his three platoons in a perimeter, covering
> the approaches to the bridge.

The Battalion quickly sorted itself out, Renison setting up his headquarters with A Company, while guns and mortars registered Defensive
Fire (DF) tasks to protect the battalion in the event of counter-attacks,
which the Germans were seldom slow to mount.
> Banger [Major 'Banger' King, now the second-in-command] had already
> brought up the ration carriers with a midday meal, following hot on the
> steps of the leading companies as he always did. As A Coy's carrier drew
> up, the CQMS threw up his hand with a cry of 'Char's up, chaps', and was
> immediately sniped through the wrist from the woods ahead.
>   As it was starting to get dark, C Coy reported Boche starting to infiltrate
> through the woods on their right, and a little later called down the SOS
> [artillery DF on the most critical target], accompanied by a call for more
> ammunition. The counter-attack increased in intensity as darkness fell, and
> calls for more ammunition became more insistent. Finally the company was
> reduced to drawing on the small supply in the OP tank [their gunner

A Bren gunner of the East Yorkshires advancing through back gardens. (BU1226)

observation party]. In the command post we heard a voice on the gunner net say, 'A hand will come in through the opening, fill it with .303.'

Banger, in spite of the presence of Boche between him and the bridge, set off straight away to C Coy. With his carrier going flat out down the road and in the face of a fusilade of shots, he crossed the bridge and reached Schaddenhof. It is significant of all that Banger meant to the Bn that the only message that came back over the air was 'Banger's here'. For this and many other acts during this battle, Banger received a bar to his DSO.

The next morning, all that day, and on into the night:

The Boche counter-attacks were maintaining their intensity, including tanks. The SOS continued in full intensity, and the range was shortened until it seemed to be right on top of the companies. But we left control to them on the spot. Our own anti-tank guns had been overrun, when C Coy had been forced to pull in from their first perimeter.

The culminating point was reached when the Boche actually penetrated right up to the walls of Schaddenhof itself, with infantry supported by a tank. As they passed the windows of the house, the Boche shouted at the troops inside, but were greeted with shouts of defiance, which turned the tank's gun onto the house. One shot hit the turret of the OP tank at a few yards range, but was HE and not solid shot.

At the east end of the house, a battle raged for some time between a party commanded by one of the FOOs and some Boche who had installed themselves in some of the outbuildings armed with *panzerfausts*. At one time everyone was so fully occupied, two Boche prisoners were being used to

A dead American soldier of the United States 9th Army lies on a footbridge over the river Roer, 23 February 1945, as stretcher-bearers approach. (AP55790)

The stretcher-bearers lift a wounded man over the body of the dead soldier. (AP275198)

Far left: **A British private soldier removes a swastika flag with his bayonet in Cleve.** (HU63665)

Left: **Infantry in Cleve. The soldier gesticulating on the left of Hitler's portrait is carrying a Bren gun. They are all wearing leather jerkins.** (AP275362)

hand up grenades from the cellar. However, the Boche failed to break the two companies. The effect of the continuous gunfire on the troops forming up in the woods must have been appalling. Without artillery support, it is very doubtful the two coys would have held their ground all night.

The following day, after a hectic night:

> At about four o'clock [a.m.], the counter-attacks started to ease off and we were able to drop the rate of fire of the artillery. With the coming of daylight, all efforts by the Boche to retake the bridge had ceased. The battle was over and 53 Div entered Weeze the following day. Our casualties had been heavy: four officers and twenty-nine other ranks killed, five officers wounded, one of whom died later, one hundred and eighteen other ranks wounded, and four missing.
>
> But morale was tremendous, and a visit from General Horrocks, XXX Corps Comd, was very popular as he chatted quite informally with troops by the roadside. The Div Comd gave orders to the Div Engineers to place a nameboard on the bridge bearing the Regimental Crest and the title 'Yorkshire Bridge'.

On 23 February 9th US Army crossed the Roer, the weather was fine, and the ground was drying in their sector. They made excellent progress. On 1 March the 1st Canadian and 9th US Armies linked up. Trooper Baker:

> Jock suddenly reported that he had been fired on – 'hard shot' – I think most of us got that old sinking feeling. I couldn't see Jock's tank. The troop was spread out, and he was round a corner a couple of hundred yards ahead. While we waited, some unknown person took one or two pot shots at Johnny Palmer's head with a rifle and Johnny [Baker's new tank commander] got down inside. Jock, who had got his tank behind cover,

As always, familiar names appear. A truck belonging to 4/7th Royal Dragoon Guards being directed by a military policeman of 43rd Wessex Division near Geilenkirchen. (B12092)

Captain Steel Brownlie, of the 2nd Fife and Forfar Yeomanry, is decorated with the Military Cross by Montgomery in March 1945. (B15554)

reported that a phosphorous shell had fallen near him, and this gave Bill Riley an idea. Perhaps the shot had been fired by American troops. It had.

An American Sherman column was advancing down a converging road and, after a KRRC officer had walked across 400 yards of open ground with a recognition panel, contact was established. This was the first link up between the 2nd Army and US 9th Army. [Baker understandably thinks of himself as being in 2nd British Army, although he was temporarily attached to 1st Canadian Army]

After Baker's squadron's last attack west of the Rhine, two days later they moved into a house

. . . where we cooked our dinner in the kitchen with some help from the civilians. There was rather a nice watch hanging on the dresser, and Johnny Palmer pinched it. This struck me as a bit mean and I gave him a short lecture. He put it back with very bad grace. In the evening we moved to a row of houses at the far end of the village. They were deserted and there was quite a lot of loot lying around. I collected a nice alarm clock.

The next day:

The squadron moved back to a rest area. During the reorganisation, Bill Riley asked a few of the oldest members if they would like to be retired from tanks and be sent to one of the echelons, there to spend the rest of the war travelling peacefully around on lorries. When he asked me I declined his offer. I felt that the echelon was a bit infra-dig, and I couldn't bear the

Soldiers of 5th Coldstream Guards caught 'liberating' a goose in Goch, February 1945.
(HU64077)

thought of having to play football and be pushed around by the RSM. Besides, being with the tanks was exciting in a way, in spite of the undoubted wear and tear on the nerves.

The time for the great operation was approaching fast. The CO came along himself to brief the squadron, and we all sat around him on the grass. It sounded like no end of a do, but not too bad from our angle. The 51st Highland Div was to make the assault, with the Staffs Yeomanry in DD tanks. This was to be late in the evening of March 23rd. A huge airborne drop was to follow the next morning, and then the 4/7th under command of 51st Highland, was to be ferried across the river – B Squadron first. This crossing to take place about a mile north of Rees. Preparations were rather like those for D-Day. 24-hour emergency packs were issued – two per man – and tins of self-heating soup and cocoa. Monty issued an Order of the Day, telling us how we were going to 'crack about on the plains of Northern Germany', until the enemy was done for. It sounded fun.

CHAPTER EIGHT

'And having crossed the Rhine, we will crack about in the plains of Northern Germany'

THE RHINE CROSSING AND THE ADVANCE TO HAMBURG AND THE BALTIC

United States 17th Airborne Division drop from Dakotas during operations to cross the Rhine.
(EA59634-A)

Brigadier Tony Wingfield:

> Serious planning for our part in Operation Plunder, as the entry into
> Germany was called, began with a conference at Divisional HQ on 18
> March. It was, therefore, unfortunate that I should have two Irish regiments
> in my Brigade to ensure that I would not be feeling my best after St Patrick's
> Day.
>
> My caravan was parked close to the priest's house attached to the local
> church. Shortly after I had fallen asleep I was woken by the roar of a motor
> cycle. I feared that a Despatch Rider had arrived from Divisional HQ with
> some alarming message. I soon heard footsteps approaching my caravan,
> and the voice of my BM saying: 'No. You can't wake him now.'
>
> Later that morning I learnt that the scene last night was caused by the
> parish priest wishing to complain that two of my staff officers were riding
> motor cycles up and down the aisle of his church. I tried to explain to a
> Dutchman what St Patrick's Day meant to an Irishman. I doubt whether I
> succeeded and fled to the Divisional planning conference.
>
> The strategic position in north-west Europe was that the Allied Forces
> under General Eisenhower had closed up to the west bank of the Rhine. In
> the extreme south the First French Army had fought through the Vosges
> mountains to Mulhouse and Colmar. Further north, the American Seventh
> Army was between Mainz and Mannheim. These two Armies comprised
> 6th Army Group.
>
> Further north again, General Patton's American Third Army was between
> Mannheim and Coblenz, and the American First Army, passing north of the
> Ardennes, had closed up to the Rhine between Cologne and Remagen,
> capturing the bridge at the latter intact. These two armies formed 12th Army
> Group; later to be joined by the American Ninth Army, at present part of
> Monty's 21st Army Group.
>
> Finally, the First Canadian Army, also part of 21st Army Group, had
> cleared the west bank of the Rhine, joining forces with the Americans in
> front of Wesel. The Second British Army was now concentrated behind the
> junction of those two armies for the main assault north of the Ruhr.
>
> The 21st Army Group's plan for crossing the Rhine was for the American
> Ninth Army to cross in the area of Wesel, just north of the industrial area.
> The British Second Army would cross on the Americans' immediate left in
> the area of Xanten. The initial crossings would be made by the infantry of
> VIII and XXX Corps. An Airborne 'drop' [by British 6th and US 17th
> Airborne Divisions] on the enemy gun area on the far side of the river
> would also be made. 7th Armoured Division would be the first of three
> British Armoured Divisions to cross by a pontoon bridge to be established
> near Xanten. 22nd Armoured Brigade would lead 7th Armoured Division.
> The operation was due to start on the night 23rd/24th March.

Time to prepare for assaulting the greatest water obstacle in Europe was
short. It was important to follow up the Germans quickly and so allow
them as little time as possible to reorganize, after their defeat in the

Rhineland battles, only thirteen days before the crossing. Fortunately, a great deal of thought had been given to the many problems involved in such an ambitious project, and by giving 1st Canadian Army responsibility for the Reichswald battle, 2nd British Army was free to plan and prepare for the formidable task ahead. The Rhine on the 21st Army Group front was between four and five hundred yards wide. But if the water was high, it could increase to between seven and twelve hundred yards. The current flowed at about three and a half knots [4 m.p.h.]. The river was bounded by dykes, of which the main one was around sixty feet wide at its base and ten to sixteen feet high, in itself a considerable obstacle.

Following the surprise seizure of the Remagen bridge intact by the Americans, von Rundstedt had been replaced by Field Marshal Kesselring as Commander-in-Chief West. 21st Army Group was faced by Army Group H under General Blaskowitz, consisting of 1st Parachute Army and 25th Army. On the 9th US Army sector the Germans had deployed about fifty-five batteries, and some five hundred guns faced the British crossing. The Germans could also redeploy the extensive anti-aircraft defences of the Ruhr to face airborne landings, which they clearly were expecting.

It was decided to mount the airborne operation after the assault across the river. This would enable a drop in daylight, and free all the artillery to support the river crossing. The DZs and LZs were chosen to be within artillery range of almost 2,000 Allied guns on the west bank, so that a massive weight of supporting fire would be on call to the airborne troops immediately on arrival. A link-up of airborne and ground troops was planned for the first day. Another lesson of the disaster at Arnhem had been applied in the selection of DZs and LZs: they were all as close as possible to the objectives.

The bridging, rafting, route clearance and other sapper tasks involved some 59,000 British and American engineers in 21st Army Group sector alone; Lieutenant Derrick Vernon, commanding number 2 Platoon in 24th Field Company Royal Engineers:

> On 8 March we commenced a series of dress rehearsals [on the Maas] with the 15th Scottish Division whose leading elements we were to transport across the Rhine. The Maas was in full flood, conditions were as bad as we were likely to meet and it was necessary to use RAF Balloon cables to prevent the rafts from being swept away by the fierce current.

Hobart's 79th Armoured Division was again called upon to provide specialist vehicles. Brigadier [later Field Marshal Lord] Carver's 4th Armoured Brigade was ordered to produce 44th RTR to learn how to drive DD tanks, which they had never seen before. After being pulled out of the Reichswald, tank drivers and commanders were driven off to the River Maas. As they arrived, according to 44th RTR,

> . . . a string of things like mobile hip-baths went clattering by, plunged into

**Signs to troops in the
marshalling areas by
the Rhine before the
crossing begins.**
(BU1945)

the water and proceeded to swim ashore. We the 44th RTR were to sail our
way across the Rhine. Then commenced a furious period of training lasting
10 days.

The whole Regiment concentrated in a forest just south of Xanten at about
midnight on 22nd March. On arrival, all vehicles were leapt at by a most
enthusiastic platoon of an American Camouflage Company, who in a brief
space of time had everything from the latrines upwards looking like fir
trees.

Lieutenant Vernon, Royal Engineers:

I took my sergeant to the river bank, and silently surveyed the Rhine's black
water. The Company billet was in the middle of the divisional 5.5-inch gun
area, a choking blanket of smoke covered all movement; nerves tautened in
anticipation.

On 23 March at about 17.00 hours, the artillery commenced a tremendous
barrage; according to some veterans it far exceeded Alamein.   .

Back in England, 6th Airborne Division was preparing for the Operation. James Bramwell, one of the many conscientious objector volunteers serving as medical orderlies in 224 Parachute Field Ambulance:

Code-named Varsity-Plunder; you can't imagine a more unfortunate name.
We called it Varsity-Blunder. There was no mystery about it; it was all in the
newspapers, with headlines shouting about the imminent drop. It was like
a sporting event with BBC commentators waiting to send the news back to
London. We were to drop in daylight, right on top of the enemy, which was
new to us. When Brigadier Hill briefed the brigade there was no hint of the
horrors to come:

Smoke generators laying smoke before and during the Rhine crossing. (BU1951)

Sherman tanks join the barrage across the Rhine. (NYP49678)

'No doubt you will find some Germans when you reach the ground. But you can take it from me they will be bloody frightened. Just imagine the reactions of the wretched Germans cowering in their slit trenches, when lo and behold, wave after wave of you blood-thirsty gentlemen come cascading down from the sky. What would you do in their place? But let there be no misunderstanding, if anybody does shoot at you, you will ignore him completely. You're job is to hasten to the RV and not to amuse yourself by returning his fire. And, if I find any of you gentlemen going to ground, I'll come round personally and kick his bottom. If you happen to hear a few stray bullets, you needn't think they're intended for you. That, gentlemen, is a form of egotism.'

It had a tonic effect. It gave exactly the right tone, and in such delightful turns of phrase.

By the river, the main body of 44th RTR was ready to cross:

By 05.15 hrs the Regt was complete in the inflation area and that very tricky operation commenced. The enemy shelling was luckily sporadic and not very accurate, not that it has to be, when all that is required is for one exhausted splinter to tear apart one's canvas. Only two tanks were punctured and, as dawn broke, the Regt started to move down to the water's edge. The crossing was made on a two squadron front, A Sqn right, C left, RHQ followed A Sqn and B Sqn was held back to cross by either route depending on which was the best. Both exits had been completed, and soon the river was full of tanks looking like floating baths drifting downstream. Over half of A Sqn was waterborne, when the enemy started shelling the tanks as they entered the water. One tank was hit as it left the shore and sank like a stone. The crew luckily all abandoned ship and made the shore safely. The last tank of A Sqn was hit as it was going down the runway into the water, but managed to reverse out and retired for patching. Tanks were now scrambling out of the exits in fine style. Recce officer started to lead the tanks away to the concentration area inland under the bund [raised earth bank].

By 08.15 hrs, the whole Regt was across and concentrated, only half an hour above our estimate, contact had been established with 7th Cameronians, and we were ready to go.

Lieutenant Vernon, Royal Engineers:

At about 06.00 hours, as planned, the tractors returned for our equipment. At the very moment of hitching sledges to the tractors, we were caught in the open by a sharp attack of shelling. Within a few seconds several men were killed or wounded. One of my Sappers, a young man of only 19, was killed when a splinter entered the narrow visor of my armoured car. I was dazed by a splinter furrowing my steel helmet, others had similar narrow escapes. This was a bad start, but as the shelling ceased, we heard from radio control that 1 and 3 Platoons, already on the water's edge as daylight

Infantry silhouetted against tracer and artificial moonlight ('Monty's moonlight') as the Rhine crossing begins. (BU2504 and BU2501)

broke, were under heavy mortar and small arms fire; operations had temporarily ceased and were furiously digging in to protect themselves from unnecessary losses. The infantry had unfortunately missed the Spandau nests opposite. These were eventually knocked out by direct hits from armoured cars, but not before the first two rafts had been sunk by machine-gun fire.

Having crossed, 44th RTR watched the airborne assault:

Just before 10.00 hrs the villages of Vissel and Jockern were in the bag with a suitable array of depressed Boche streaming back to the cages. At this stage an unnatural hush had fallen over the battle front, not a gun fired, and an air of expectancy and waiting was everywhere discernable. Suddenly, here they come. With a roar of engines thousands of aircraft poured across the sky and disappeared into the mists beyond. For the next hour the air seemed full, and it was only with the greatest difficulty, that one was able to concentrate on the job in hand.

Nearly 1,500 Dakotas and almost as many aircraft towing gliders brought in the 6th British and 17th US Airborne Divisions. James Bramwell:

Opposite me in the aircraft was Cranner again, now a Sergeant. The Colonel and his batman were down our end, near the door. We were silent. From the people in the front we could hear tremendous singing; 'MacNamara's Band' and 'The Call of the Canyon'. I exchanged a sickly grin with the Colonel. I thought, 'They won't be singing that for long.' I napped for a bit, until someone tapped me on the shoulder, and pointed out of the door.

Sergeant Greenley, 22nd Independent Parachute Company, 6th Airborne Division, the first British parachute soldier to drop during the Rhine crossing. (H41586)

There was an enormous fleet of gliders, hundreds of them all the way to the horizon, apparently suspended motionless above their tugs.

We stood up, hooked up, and checked each other's equipment. From my position, number three in the stick, I could see out of the door. Someone bellowed, 'The Rhine'. I had time to see a sickly, ochre-coloured ribbon. The red light came on.

The light turned green, and I was outside. We were quite high, higher than normal. It all seemed rather remote. I managed to kick out of twists, as the enormous drone of aircraft, and din of exploding shells and smell of cordite died away. I could see woods and fields as on a map. I was being drifted towards the wrong end of the DZ, where I could see a house. I could hear the sound of bullets swishing past my ears. At that moment my morale was lifted by the Brigadier's talk, remembering him saying, 'That, gentlemen, is a form of egotism'.

Managing to spill air out of my canopy, I landed heavily about 100 yards from the house. As I collapsed my parachute, there to my joy was Cranner coming towards me. Nobody shot at us. We had to go the full length of the DZ to reach the RV. There was a tremendous battle going on to our left. It was a great relief to see people one knew at the RV. The drop was absolutely accurate, but those of us at the edge of the formation were liable to go into the woods; as did half my stick. God knows what happened to them.

I saw one of the planes shot down in flames. Shortly after the gliders started coming in, some on to our DZ; the whole sky was full of them. The Germans mortared the Landing Zones. At that moment the Brigadier appeared saying, 'Come along, come along, show a little enthusiasm with those picks and shovels.' While we were digging in, a glider crashed into the wood about 30 yards from us with a rending noise of splintering wood. I was staggered to see the pilot stumbling out, apparently unhurt, with some of the people.

Hill's Parachute Brigade was on the DZ, close to their objective, in nine minutes. By the time forty minutes had elapsed the whole of 6th Airborne Division had landed on or close to their objectives. Eighteen Dakotas were destroyed by flak, or were missing; 115 had flak damage. Many glider pilots became disorientated because of the smoke obscuring their landing sites. Enemy flak was heavy and the guns were turned on to the landing zones in the ground role. Navigation problems, machine-gun and mortar fire caused many casualties among the gliders. Some were destroyed in the air, some crashed on landing, others burst into flames after skidding to a halt. The petrol in jerrycans and in jeeps was a frequent cause of disaster. Nevertheless enough of the Air Landing Brigade landed in the right places for the enemy to be rushed before surprise was lost, and the Brigade secured all its objectives within an hour of landing. Patrick Devlin, C Company, 1st Battalion Royal Ulster Rifles, in 6th Air Landing Brigade, one of thousands of Southern Irish Catholics who had crossed the border to join the British Army:

> I sat in the same seat as for D-Day. During the flight, a Belfast Protestant, Charlie McCrea, a regular soldier who had served with the Battalion on the North-West Frontier of India, said when we landed, never mind the silly war, but concentrate on the loot, at which we all laughed. About 10.30 a.m. we were cast off from the tug. I sat alert intent on getting out fast as soon as the glider landed and stopped. I was first out of the door like a jack rabbit. [Of the 66 gliders carrying 1st RUR to Landing Zone Uncle, only 16 landed undamaged]. I was in one of the undamaged ones.
>
> There was a shout that two German tanks were coming. They weren't tanks, but half-tracks. In the first, the Germans were standing up, shoulder to shoulder. As they come opposite, I let them have a burst. They all collapsed behind the armoured sides. I could not have hit them all, but there was screaming and shouting. The troops in the second were concealed behind the armour, but I sprayed it hoping to hit the driver. Both half-tracks continued on their way. It now became quiet by the glider. Our objective was about four or five hundred yards away, as we had landed on the wrong side of the field.

As Devlin's platoon was doubling to the objective, he was hit by a burst of MG 34 Spandau, which he had spotted just before it fired:

> . . . in the right forearm below the elbow, breaking the bone, along my right side and across the small of my back. I was thrown forward and lay for some seconds before I knew I was hit. It was like being hit in the back with a big stick. I found I could not move, which was just as well, as I might have

attracted more fire from them, and I had a small anti-tank mine on my small pack on my back. If they'd hit that, I'd be blown to pieces. I could feel what I thought was blood pouring along my right thigh, and thought I would bleed to death. I discovered it was two tins of carnation evaporated milk I had in a side pack, which had been ripped open by the burst. I heard a rustling noise, and saw our glider pilots crawling past me on hands and knees. I called out to them, and asked them to drag me to the ditch. But one said he was going to collect his flight and would come back for me. I damned them to hell.

After being pulled into a ditch by Rifleman McCrea and another member of his platoon, who had come back for him after securing the objective, Devlin saw two eight-wheeled armoured cars approaching:

The first tried to smash its way at speed through the glider, but the driver lost control, and it finished up in the ditch about 20 yards away. As its commander climbed out of the turret, a burst of bullets hit his helmet, and he flopped over. The second tried to level his way through the glider, and all hell broke loose, when our lads opened up with bren guns and a 6-pounder anti-tank gun, setting it and the glider on fire. A German officer slid into the ditch beside me, holding his head in his hand, in a shocked condition. Two Germans came running up the ditch, jumped over me and the officer, shouting 'kamerad'. I was wondering how I could get away from the glider, when the two boys came back, and laughed as they dragged me along, at how they had taken off and left me, but as McCrea said, when there are tanks about, you don't hang around. They helped me to the RAP.

Towards evening I was taken to a large house in its own grounds, where the Divisional Field Ambulance was in business. We were put on the ground to wait our turn. The most serious cases were being treated first. There were hundreds of wounded, both British and German. Medical orderlies from both armies were bringing round buckets of tea, they would dip in a mug and hand it to you, you took a couple of swigs and handed it to the one beside you; in my case a German. It was dusk by the time I was taken inside. A British MO looked me over, and passed me to two Germans to put a wire splint on my arm. After this I was driven in a jeep to a farm, which was already filled with wounded lying on stretchers. I was left on a stretcher covered with a blanket just inside the large barn door. Sometime during the night, a mortar bomb landed outside, and the explosion pushed the door in and my stretcher a couple of feet. I wasn't hurt. The next day we were told that ground forces had reached us, and that when the Bailey bridge across the Rhine was completed we could be evacuated back across the river. But Montgomery had ordered that there was to be one-way traffic over the bridge into Germany for 24 hours to get as many troops, armour and supplies for the advance out of his bridgehead. This meant that no wounded could be brought back, and we were left where we were. We had had no food since early Saturday, only the odd cup of tea. But I did not feel

Wounded in a barn during the battle fought by the British 6th Airborne Division after crossing the Rhine. (BU2610)

Airborne wounded being taken back to bridges across the Rhine as soon as two-way traffic was allowed. (BU2564)

An AVRE on a raft crossing the Rhine.
(BU2070)

the least bit hungry. I felt sorry for the more seriously wounded. At last, late on Monday, I was put into an ambulance and driven back over the Rhine.

On the Rhine, the rafts were in operation by about midday on the first day. Lieutenant Vernon:

Good watermanship was required to drive the raft across the wide fast-flowing river. Each platoon operated for sixteen hours non-stop. Two rafts were maintained constantly in service, signal lamps were placed for continued operation throughout the night. We fitted a public address system to broadcast the news and 'music while you work'. I had the privilege to take over Major General (Tiny) Barber, the GOC of 15th Division, 'Tiny', because he was about 6 foot 6 inches tall.

Ever anxious to be quickly on the scene of historic events, Mr Winston Churchill, accompanied by Field Marshal Sir Alan Brooke, Field Marshal Sir Bernard Montgomery and General Sir Miles Dempsey, arrived on the Rhine, not a hundred yards from our rafts. An orderly laid out a picnic on a white tablecloth for these distinguished visitors; our men muttered about camouflage, and helped themselves to a few cakes left behind.

When ordered to cease operations we were very tired. In three days, the Company had made about seven hundred round trips across a very dangerous river in flimsy craft. We suffered nine men killed in action, and twenty wounded.

Brigadier Tony Wingfield:

The crossings of XII Corps by the Commandos at Wesel and 15th Scottish

The three leading figures, left to right: Lieutenant-General Horrocks, XXX Corps Commander, Montgomery, and Major-General 'Tiny' Barber, 15th Scottish Division. (B14869)

Mr Churchill, Field Marshal Sir Alan Brooke, Chief of the Imperial General Staff, and Field Marshal Sir Bernard Montgomery picnic on the banks of the Rhine. (BU2636)

Division at Xanten had been successful. That by 51st Highland Division of VIII Corps had become a very tough fight. Luckily for me the Commandos and 15th Scottish Division had captured the village of Bislich, just beyond the east bank of the river, and a pontoon bridge was already being built over it which 7th Armoured Division was to use.

I went down with my two scout cars to Xanten bridge in the early

Number 6 Commando in Wesel. Both soldiers are armed with Thompson sub-machine-guns, with which commandos were issued from early in the war. (BU2312)

afternoon, taking one staff officer with me; but was prevented from crossing till the return of the Prime Minister's party from the far side. This was the sole exception to the one-way order. I was forced to wait till 4.30 p.m., before old Winston had satisfied his ego. He may have raised the Home morale by his escapade, but he robbed me of some vital hours of reconnaissance.

The 4/7th RDG were crossing further down the Rhine into the bridge-head seized by 51st Highland Division; Austin Baker:

Pretty soon the whole squadron was down by the river bank, and the first tanks were crossing, a slow and tedious operation. They had to be loaded one at a time on to a large raft, which was towed across the river by a balloon winch on the opposite bank. There had been two rafts working, but a misguided attempt to load two tanks at a time had sunk the other one. It was very dark by the time 'Shaggy Dog' rolled onto the raft, and we were hauled slowly across. We seemed to be afloat for hours. When we were in mid-stream, a Jerry plane started to drone around, and we saw streams of tracer from its guns as it shot up some target a mile or so along the river. Then it came over us, so low, that when the Bofors opened up at it, their shells only just cleared the opposite bank. I couldn't make up my mind whether it would be better to get inside the tank in case we got shot up, or stay outside in case we sank. I compromised by sitting on top of the turret, ready to dive off or in as the occasion might arise. Luckily we reached the other side safely.

Early the next morning, C squadron went to Millingen. It was very much

Americans crossing the Rhine in Alligators (Buffalos). (KY59434)

knocked about and there were several fires in the outskirts. It was chilly around dawn, and we warmed ourselves in the heat of burning houses.

The discovery of a shoe shop with quite good stock caused some excitement. Most of 3rd Troop fitted itself out with boots and shoes, and I found a pair of shoes that looked just the thing for tank wear – they looked like brogues, although they were actually made of canvas.

By midnight on 28 March, 21st Army Group had nine British and six American divisions, plus three brigades, across the Rhine. The stage was set for the break-out and advance to finish the war in Western Europe. During March, the German losses in prisoners alone had averaged around 10,000 a day. The Russian armies were pressing in from the East. Eisenhower, passing up the chance to capture Berlin before the Russians, ordered that the main Allied thrust was to be by the Americans towards the Elbe in the area of Magdeburg, to link up with the Russians, and cut Germany in two. As part of this plan, 9th US Army was switched from Montgomery's command back to Bradley's 12th Army Group. Montgomery ordered 21st Army Group to reach the line of the Elbe between Hamburg and Wittenburg, and take the ports of Bremen and Hamburg. 1st Canadian Army was to mop up in Holland, while the three Corps of 2nd British Army headed for the Elbe, cutting the German east–west routes, hooking in to Bremen and Hamburg from the east. In just over a month, some formations of 21st Army Group advanced nearly 300 miles. Although the Germans were disintegrating, numerous battles were fought on the way, in some cases, fierce actions

Lieutenant-General Matthew B. Ridgway, commander XVIII Airborne Corps, decorates Brigadier James Hill, 3rd Parachute Brigade, British 6th Airborne Division, after the Rhine crossing. Ridgway had 6th Airborne Division under command for the operation. Field Marshal Montgomery looks on. (BU2910)

that caused several casualties. Often small parties of fanatical troops would hold villages, woods and farmhouses until cut off or overcome. On other occasions, less determined opposition would surrender quickly at the first show of strength. Unless bypassed, street fighting in the bigger towns, was a bloody affair. Mines and booby traps on all routes were a continual hazard. The Luftwaffe even appeared on some days. For 21st Army Group, it was by no means a walk-over, until near the end when German resistance to the British and Americans in the west collapsed, while continuing to fight hard against the Russians in the east. Major Peter Carrington, 2nd Armoured Battalion Grenadier Guards, Guards Armoured Division:

> The Germans were very, very good soldiers. After the Rhine crossing, we had 15th Panzer Grenadier Division in front of us fighting a rearguard action all the way to the very end of the war; in circumstances in Germany when they must have known they were going to lose the war and didn't have much hope. They fought absolutely magnificently with great courage and skill.

Trooper Austin Baker:

> Lieut Ford came round with the encouraging news that 3rd Troop was to lead the C Squadron advance in the morning, and the leading tank was to be 'Shaggy Dog'. We were told that the operation would almost certainly develop into a swan, but most of us were rather dubious. On a road advance of this sort, the leading tank could usually be a write-off, which gave our crew considerable food for thought. One or two friends bade us tearful farewells. The prospect didn't give Rimmer, our new co-driver,

insomnia. I found him sound asleep, practically upside down in the food
bin. He had dropped off in the act of getting supper out.

Last minute instructions gave us what we thought was a reprieve.
Although 'Shaggy Dog' was to lead the squadron, it was not to be at the
front of the column. Everything was now ready for the attack [on the village
of Sinderen]. Bert Morsley started up 'Shaggy Dog's' engines and we
moved slowly up. We halted with the first house of the village immediately
to our right rear; a small modern villa. At that instant there came a
tremendous crash. It was like somebody hitting a huge anvil with a gigantic
sledgehammer. I was staring through the periscope, but out of the corner of
my eye, I thought I glimpsed a flash inside the tank. Looking across at
Johnny I saw him in agitated movement tearing off his headset and pushing
open the turret flap. He yelled, 'Bale out', through the microphone and
vanished upwards through the hole. We'd been hit by hard shot. I dived
under the gun and was pulled up sharply by my headset lead. I ripped the
thing off, and my hat came off with it. McCarthy and I rose out of the
hatchway almost simultaneously, getting in each other's way. Mac got clear
first and then, for a horrid moment, I found myself with one leg over the
side of the turret, perched up high, a perfect target for anybody interested. I
rolled across the engine covers, dropped off the back of the tank, took a
header over the low hedge, and scrambled on all fours across the garden to
the side of the house downroad from Jerry, where Mac and Johnny were
already crouching. For a moment I thought that Bert and Rimmer must have
had it, and I was wondering whether I would have the nerve to go back and
look, when they appeared intact.

We went through the side door of the house, in and behind which the
whole of the leading platoon had taken cover. They had bren-gunners and
riflemen in position in all the downstairs windows and they were getting a
small mortar into action in the back garden. Before we had much time to
think, there came a thunderous explosion from the road outside, followed
by three or four at short intervals. We hoped for a moment that Jack
Bransfield's 17-pdr had reached the house and opened fire, but we soon
realised we were hearing some more rounds crashing into poor old 'Shaggy
Dog'. The other two 3rd Troop tanks had taken cover behind the farm
buildings a hundred yards or more down the road. They couldn't move,
and neither could the rest of the infantry, because the road was commanded
by the SP and by Spandaus. We and the leading platoon were cut off in our
house and in a ticklish situation.

Somebody shouted: 'They're attacking', and the bren-gunners in the
windows opened fire. For a few minutes there was a great deal of noise –
the hammering of brens, the crack of rifles and the barking of the mortar in
the back garden. We sat tight on the floor, leaving it to the infantry and
hoping for the best. McCarthy made himself useful filling bren magazines.

After a bit Bert Morsely made the most ridiculous suggestion I have ever
heard. He thought a cup of tea would do everybody a bit of good, and he
proposed crawling out to the tank for the cooker, compo and tea powder in

the boxes welded above the exhausts. A minute later there was another massive explosion outside and Bert appeared rather quickly, looking unusually put out for him. He had apparently got as far as the hedge when a bazooka man had stuck his head up from the ditch across the road and put a bomb through the side of 'Shaggy Dog'.

An infantryman came in to say that somebody was calling us across the fields from the buildings down the road, suggesting that we should try to get across the fields to join the troop. We decided to have a go. It was a hair-raising little trip. We crawled across the fields, sometimes on all fours and sometimes flat on our stomachs, keeping well spaced out all the time. For much of the way our only cover was a slatted fence, which obstructed the view very little.

About half-way over, Bert stopped and seemed to be taking off his shoes. He said there was a stream in the way. I told him, forcibly, not to bother with his shoes, and he slipped out of sight. When I got to the place, I found there was a sunken stream about ten feet across and six feet or so below the level of the field. It was only up to our knees. We waded up it a little way, safely hidden, and then climbed out and made the final dash. All five of us safely reached the buildings which concealed 3rd Troop, and we received quite a welcome. But our troubles were by no means over. The next troop in the squadron was several hundred yards further still down the road, and that stretch was also under Jerry observation.

After a conversation with Bill Riley, Mr Ford announced that the troop was to withdraw under cover of a smoke-screen laid by the SHQ troop, which was well back out of the way.' 'Shaggy Dog's' crew was to be divided between the other two tanks. Two of us got into the turret of the 17-pdr, while the other three went as passengers with Mr Ford. I squatted under the breech-block of the gun. There isn't much room in a 17-pdr turret even for three people, let alone five. After a few minutes the smoke must have come down, because the order to move came. Pussy Youens started up and the tank moved forward a yard or two, tipped up on its nose and stopped with a jerk. The gun ran slowly backwards in its mounting and gently ejected a 17-pdr round on top of me. Pussy swore and tried to reverse, but it was no good. She was stuck fast.

We were out in the open and SHQ, having only a limited number of smoke shells, could not keep the screen going for long. There was only one thing to do. We all baled out and got onto Mr Ford's tank, which roared off down the road carrying 14 people, some inside and some clinging to the outside. It always made you feel on top of the world to have a bit of a narrow squeeze and find yourself alive and kicking. My only regret was that my new canvas shoes had started to come apart as a result of my walk down the stream.

Baker and his crew were issued with a new tank the next day. Other armoured units also took casualties in engagements with rearguards. Captain Brownlie, in his new Comet Tank:

A race to the River Weser 30 miles away. Approaching Glissen at full speed, Frank Fuller's troop was in the lead. Frank reported he was hit, then was silent. Suddenly his operator, Tpr Oxley, came on the air and said very quietly that the rest of the crew were dead, that the enemy were all around, and that he proposed to lie doggo till he could escape. He was told to do that. Glissen was taken without much trouble; more prisoners. They were from 12 SS Panzer, very young, blubbering as they ran back along the dusty road, urged by the boots of our infantry. We found bicycles and *Panzerfausts* in the ditches. Obviously the enemy were now scraping the bottom of the barrel, but they could still kill people.

At first light we took 1 Herefords on the back of the tanks. On the back of my tank I had part of Company HQ, and their Sergeant-Major. He was a hard man with a lot of service. Over the river, we motored north. This was uncleared territory, and as the enemy were sneaking about among the trees, we resumed the practice of firing at shadows and likely spots. It paid off, and at three or four places there were bicycles and *panzerfausts* left in the ditch. At one point we halted, and saw movements in the undergrowth to our right. Before I could traverse the gun round, the Sergeant-Major on the

Advancing into Germany near Munster, infantry of United States 17th Airborne Division are supported by tanks of 4th Battalion Coldstream Guards, 6th Guards Tank Brigade. (EA60915)

Captain Brownlie's Comet tank carrying men of the 1st Battalion the Herefords on the back, at Petershagen. The Comet was the first British tank to match the German tanks throughout the War, and came into service only for the last six months of the War in Europe. (BU3202)

back of my tank had picked up his rifle and dropped the German at over 200 yards.

The route followed by the Sherwood Rangers, in 8th Armoured Brigade, cut through part of Holland. The Reverend Leslie Skinner:

Thursday 5 April 1945: During the afternoon a Jewish girl of about 16 years of age was brought out of an attic a few doors down the street. For four years she had been confined to a ridiculously small space in the roof and hidden from the Germans by a Dutch family who were unrelated to her. This was the girl's first time out of the house in all that time. The lads were almost awe struck trying to realise what it meant, though they quite naturally showered her and the family with sweets and food.

Mines were a frequent hazard. Lieutenant Caines:

29 April: The Germans were using five-hundred- and one-thousand-pound bombs dug into the side of the road, and fused by a Teller Mine. When the vehicle went over the Teller Mine, it would explode the bomb, or sea mine, completely destroying the vehicle and its occupants. It was not possible to make any diversions round the mined area, as the countryside was very flat and littered with dykes and streams, and everywhere was very boggy.

Lieutenant-Colonel Bill Renison, 2nd E. Yorks outside Bremen:

At about midnight Ron Brown came through on the air from Main HQ. While returning from bringing up the rations at the wheel of my jeep, Banger had been blown up by a mine at the crossroads. Ron had been back to the Field Ambulance and had been told that Banger must certainly lose one leg, but that it was hoped that with his iron will and condition he would pull through. This was a tragedy that somehow I had never envisaged and I think that all of us had come to regard Banger as invulnerable – we could but pray that the doctors' hopes would prove true.

Early in the morning I got the news that I had been dreading; Banger had collapsed and died during the night. No words can really express what this means to the morale of the bn, and as the days and hours passed by, I realised more and more how much I had depended on him in so many things. He was buried during the afternoon.

Private E. L. Goozee, 2nd E. Yorks:

News was received that Banger King DSO and bar, had been blown up by a mine, receiving wounds from which he died later. This was the Major who ran the gauntlet supplying the Battalion with ammunition during the battle for the Bridge over the Muhlen–Fleuth.

Lieutenant Sidney Rosenbaum, Royal Artillery:

Maj. 'Banger' King of the E. Yorks had been blown up on a mine and killed; it was he who recited *Henry V* on the run-in to the Normandy beaches.

Major King was a regular soldier, with eighteen years service, including India and the Sudan. He was wounded in the Ethiopian campaign of 1941, and on returning to England from Africa, volunteered for parachuting. It was the airborne's loss, and the E. Yorks' gain that he injured his leg parachuting, and was returned to his unit. He was exactly the type that was all too often creamed off by the airborne divisions, to the detriment of 'normal' infantry. Mines took their toll of others; Rosenbaum:

Maj. Dicky Bird, with a carrier full of Ulstermen, and with no enemy in sight, was blown up on a magnetic sea mine while seeking to make contact with his opposite number in 51 Div. There were no survivors; Dicky Bird had of course, been a company commander in the RUR since Normandy.

Austin Baker's luck held:

. . . a sudden deafening explosion and a vivid flash across the periscope. 'Shaggy Dog II' stopped and lurched over sideways. I jumped over the side, and dived into a ditch crouching face-to-face with a very nervous infantryman, who said, 'What was it?' I said I thought it was a mine. It had gone off under the right-hand track, wrecking the suspension on that side, and blowing a fair-sized hole in the road.

Our new tank, immediately christened 'Shaggy Dog III', was our first 17-pdr.

As the armies penetrated into the heart of Germany some signs of the nature of the Nazi regime was being uncovered. Brigadier Wingfield:

I was able to 'swan around' and paid two visits. The first was to see a trainload of V-2 weapons, which I was delighted to see could no longer be launched on London; the other to a human stud farm, where the true Aryans were being bred to maintain the Master Race. The 'stallions' had fled, and I was not impressed by the few 'mares' who were still in the establishment.

The advancing armies began to see evidence of slave labour and concentration camps. Private Eric Codling in Bremen:

A throng of some forty or fifty Russians, dressed in their ragged prison dress, formed a tight ring outside the gates of their hutted camp. The frenzied shouting and wild gestures were enough to make us stop to investigate the cause of the riot. We were able to push through sufficiently close to see the final moments of the execution of three Kapos. The instruments employed were the three-legged stools, one of the few items of furniture provided by the Germans. Several prisoners held their former tormentors, while others beat them to death with the stools.

There was worse to come. Lieutenant-Colonel Mervin Gonin RAMC, commanding 11th Light Field Ambulance:

When the 11th Armoured Division was advancing in the direction of Belsen, the Chief of Staff of First German Para Army approached the Brigadier General Staff of 8th Corps stating that terrible conditions had arisen at Belsen and typhus was rife. He requested that the British should take the camp over. The British agreed. A neutral area was defined round the camp, the SS staff to remain, the British to do what they liked with them. The hatred of the Wehrmacht for the SS was emphasised by this act on the part of the German army. The large number of Hungarian cavalry who were in the barracks were to keep their arms.

At this time the battle was going on all round the camp, where there were approximately 50,000 people, of whom 10,000 lay dead in the huts or about the camp. Those still alive had had no food for seven days after a period of semi-starvation. For over a month the ration had consisted of one bowl of swede soup a day, and one loaf a week weighing about a pound between twelve inmates. The only water available was from filthy tanks most of which contained a body or two. Most of the inmates had either had typhus, or were suffering from it. Most other diseases except cholera were rife. Practically all the internees were abnormal mentally. The internees were

Dead and dying at Belsen. (BU3733)

eating the corpses of those that had died; the only edible portions were the kidneys, livers and hearts.

What we had was buildings, eight nurses, about 300 RAMC chaps, a regiment of Light Anti-Aircraft, at least 20,000 sick suffering from the most virulent diseases, all of whom required urgent hospital treatment, and 30,000 men, women and children who might not die if they were doctored, but would most certainly die if they were not removed from the Horror Camp.

This camp in which my men and myself were to spend the next month was as bare of vegetation as a chicken run. Corpses lay everywhere, some in huge piles, sometimes singly or in pairs where they had fallen as they shuffled along the dirt tracks. Those who died of disease usually died in the huts. When starvation was the chief cause of death, they died in the open. It is an odd characteristic of starvation that its victims seem compelled to wander till they fall and die.

Piles of corpses naked and obscene, with a woman too weak to stand propping herself up against them as she cooked the food we had given her

Women inmates of Belsen wash in a water tank. (BU3726)

over an open fire. Men and women crouching down just anywhere in the open relieving themselves of the dysentery which was scouring their bowels. A woman standing naked washing herself with some issue soap in water from a tank in which the remnants of a child floated.

In the women's compounds, the so-called hospital in the Camp. Outside a narrow path with just beyond a long pile of naked female corpses, ten or twelve deep. As you watched you might notice four figures shuffling along carrying a blanket out of which stuck the legs and arms of a corpse. The figures would suddenly slump to the ground until they had the strength to stagger on and tip their corpse onto the ever-growing pile. I saw four women do this and, as they turned away, one of the four slumped forward onto the heap of bodies to die. The other three wandered away, as if unaware of what had happened.

In an ordinary living hut, a central corridor with two rooms some sixty yards long on either side. It would have held, by British army standards, 83 soldiers. We removed 1,426 women, and that does not count the dead. Starvation without typhus or dysentery produces the most appalling diarrhoea. No inmate was allowed out of the hut after six o'clock. There was

one lavatory. One had to wear rubber boots, the floor was thick with faeces. The hut was raised a couple of feet above ground. Most of the flooring in the corridor had been pulled up and the space beneath used as a latrine, and contained in addition many corpses. They all had typhus as well as many other diseases such as TB, *cancrum oris* in which the flesh of the face rots away, syphilis, fractures in which the bones protruded through the gangrenous flesh.

One of the dead being carried to join the pile of bodies at Belsen. (BU3725)

Once the German hospital had been evacuated and the Casualty Clearing Station had set up ready to receive patients, the evacuation could begin:

The MOs and stretcher-bearers spent from 8 a.m. to 5 p.m. in those huts with the stink of the unwashed living with every disease on God's earth mixed with that of the long-unburied dead. They had to strip the living corpses of their rags, wrap them in blankets and carry them to the ambulances.

When an ambulance was loaded it did the journey of two miles to the Hospital area where it went to the human laundry, located in the cavalry

Inside the so-called hospital at Belsen most are dying. (BU3736)

stables capable of holding 150 horses. Here we had 60 tables at each of which worked two German nurses from the military hospital, two German MOs, all under the charge of the Pathologist of the Casualty Clearing Station.

The German nurses were an interesting study. At the start they laughed and joked, definitely truculent, making no effort to get ready for the job in hand; damned if they were going to work for the British. Then the first patients arrived. The nurses stood with their mouths open and gazed horror struck as those bodies were brought in. First one and then another started to sob, until almost the whole sixty were weeping. There was no more truculence after that. Those girls worked like slaves, they went down with typhus and they died, but others took their place.

Ten days after we came to Belsen, there was a noise of an unusual plane, and the rattle of machine-gun fire. The plane machine-gunned and cannoned our camp three times, killing one of my men and seriously wounding four others. Twenty ambulances, each with four large red crosses, a large red cross flag on the ground, and a red cross flag flying below the Union Jack. One of the German MOs at the 'Laundry' spoke

English. That morning I went to him in a fury (I was near shooting the fellow with my revolver). I told him exactly what had happened, and what I thought of him and everything German. 'I am so sorry, Sir,' he said, and tears ran down his cheeks.

British prisoners were also found, in better condition than the poor wretches in the Concentration Camps. Brigadier Tony Wingfield:

> The 8th Hussars Group found two Prisoner-of-War Camps containing British and American other ranks. The British had taken charge after the Germans had fled, and they welcomed the 8th Hussars with a smart guard of their own, kitted out in blancoed equipment, and posted at the main gate. An RSM of the 1st Airborne Division had assumed command and was found sitting in an office giving out orders as if he was in barracks in Aldershot. [RSM J. C. Lord, Grenadier Guards, captured at Arnhem while RSM of 3rd Parachute Battalion]

Tanks of the Guards Armoured Division advancing at Berge, Battle for Bremen, April 1945. (HU64093)

By now senior Nazi officials were being unearthed, and many prisoners were far more subdued than hitherto; Codling:

> On 26 April, the platoon was ordered to advance rapidly to an area in the north of the city where a final stand was being made in a park, the objective being the offices of the Nazi Party to apprehend the senior party official. It was a nerve-racking experience speeding through the empty, devastated streets, not knowing the dangers the ruined buildings concealed, a pitched battle going on near by. Having found the house, we rushed inside. Our arrival was too late, our quarry, his wife and Alsatian dog were found shot in a bathroom.
>
> As the day progressed, and the sounds of battle diminished, the usual stream of German prisoners appeared, being escorted to a nearby cage, in this case some tennis courts. An entirely different attitude was apparent to that displayed by prisoners taken before the crossing of the Rhine. The arrogance and spirit had gone, replaced by an acceptance of total defeat. It was clear to them that there was no one left to continue the struggle to defend their families and homes, many of which had already been engulfed by the rapidly advancing Russians, whom they feared most.

Soldiers of 5th Coldstream Guards in the ruins of Berge at night. (HU64098)

In other areas the enemy continued to resist. Lieutenant David Sheldon, a platoon commander in 4th Battalion Coldstream Guards in a letter home to his parents:

> We attacked a fairly large village, held by about 150–200 fanatical crack paratroopers. Some of the paratroopers were taken prisoner, and they were really tough-looking chaps. There must be very few indeed of such chaps left now.

Two days later:

> My platoon is down to 21 [from 36]. I have seen recently, quite honestly, boys of twelve and thirteen, particularly in one attack.

By the end of April, some towns were surrendering without a fight. Wingfield:

> A deputation of two German officers and a civilian arrived in an attempt to secure immunity from artillery fire on account of a hospital being in the centre of Harburg [just south of Hamburg]. It appeared that the civilian was the owner of The Phoenix Butter Factory, near the hospital, which gave him a vested interest in the petition – I believe he claimed to be the Lord Mayor as well. The matter was reported to the Divisional Commander. The situation developed at first into the surrender of Harburg and Hamburg, then finally into that of all parts of north-west Europe still in German hands, including Denmark and Norway. By that time, Monty himself was of course handling the negotiations.
>
> I spent the morning touring round Hamburg, and was horrified by the devastation wrought by the RAF's fire bombing. Every house in every street

A sixteen-year-old German soldier taken prisoner in Germany. (KY61457)

seemed to be gutted; and I was told that thousands of Hamburgers had been drowned in the city's large lake, in preference to being fried. But memories of watching the London blitz soon dispelled sympathy for the Germans.

During that afternoon I was ordered to move my brigade to Pinneburg, about 10 miles north of Hamburg, before marching on Denmark. Soon after our arrival at Pinneburg, we heard that a 'cease fire' had been ordered because all the German forces in north-west Europe had now officially surrendered to the 21st Army Group.

All my units went slightly mad and let off all kinds of ammunition into the air. It was strangely hard to believe that after 5 years of frequent danger one was still alive, and that it was all over. The local Germans, of course, had not heard the news and were quite staggered by our behaviour.

Captain Joe Patterson, recovered from his wounds suffered in Normandy, was back in action with 2nd Special Air Service Regiment:

5 May 45: The news came through that all fighting in NW Germany, Holland and Denmark was to stop at 08.00 hours today, 5 May. Almost at once we had a panic stand to, as one of our jeeps had just been shot up in the next village, and the four occupants wounded and taken prisoner by outposts of 400 militant SS in the immediate area. With armoured cars to support us, we went chasing up in the half light and found the jeep all shot up and full of blood. We swanned around a bit more, but only took a few prisoners, a few tough looking SS among them, but mostly boys of 15 to 16, whom we let go.

There were a lot of French POWs in the village, thirsting for the blood of a German farmer who used to beat them up. We found that he had hidden weapons too, so we burnt his farm and house. I took no part in these proceedings. Alastair MacGregor was explaining to the weeping wife how lucky she was that we were nice chivalrous English who didn't shoot people without trial, when there was a sharp burst from a tommy-gun behind the barn, and one of our tougher Poles, 'Louis' for short, came round the corner with a happy grin and announced that he had just bumped the farmer off. The name of the British Raj took a bit of set-back in the eyes of the widow after this.

8 May 45: I can't say I am much elated or excited.

Major Peter Carrington:

I did, looking back on it, commit a war crime. We commandered a house, and left tanks and jeeps in the yard. I woke up in the morning to see the son of the house putting sticks of explosive under my jeep. I thought that an unfriendly act, so I came down and said to the people in the house; 'You have half an hour to take everything out of your house, and then I'll burn it down.'

After half an hour, I asked my CSM to put some jerry cans of petrol all round the house; and I threw in a match. Believe it or not it went out. We let the son of the house go.

I did not feel sorry for the Germans; after all they had proved enormously inconvenient. This was the sixth year of the war. I don't think we behaved badly, we behaved rather well. We helped ourselves to one or two things which we shouldn't have. I found a marvellous Mercedes which in the jargon of those days, I liberated. The Divisional Commander saw me with it, and said, 'Where did you get that?' When I told him I had liberated it, he said, 'That's the most disgraceful thing I've ever heard. Send it immediately to Div HQ.' The next day I saw him riding in it.

Private James Bramwell:

In Wismar we took over a Luftwaffe hospital. One of the great troubles was the Russians trying to attack the German nurses. I was in a ward with a lot of Luftwaffe wounded. On VE night, I sat out on a balcony watching great bonfires of rejoicing. Further away in the Russian lines, there was smoke from burning buildings. The Luftwaffe wounded were detached and calm. It was not a moment for me or the Germans to rejoice; just quiet reflection.

B.A.O.K. Collection 120

disregard by their leaders of any form of decency or of honourable dealings: the same Germans whose brothers, sons and fathers were carrying out a system of mass murder and torture of defenceless civilians. You will have to remember that these same Germans are planning to make fools of you again and to escape the loathing which their actions deserve.

5. Our consciences are clear; "non-fraternisation" to us implies no revenge; we have no theory of master races. But a guilty nation must not only be convicted: it must realise its guilt. Only then can the first steps be taken to re-educate it, and bring it back into the society of decent humanity.

6. German discipline, though not our sort, is thorough. The people will judge you with no amateur eyes: and any slackness will be the cue for the resistance movements to intensify their efforts.

7. Be just; be firm; be correct; give orders, and don't argue. Last time we won the war and let the peace slip out of our hands. This time we must not ease off—we must win both the war and the peace.

B. L. Montgomery

Field-Marshal,
C-in-C 21 Army Group.

March, 1945.

PSS 1810 3.45

LETTER

BY THE

COMMANDER-IN-CHIEF

ON

NON-FRATERNISATION

TO ALL OFFICERS AND MEN OF 21 ARMY GROUP

1. Twenty-seven years ago the Allies occupied Germany: but Germany has been at war ever since. Our Army took no revenge in 1918; it was more than considerate, and before a few weeks had passed many soldiers were adopted into German households. The enemy worked hard at being amiable. They believed that the occupation was due to treachery, and that their army had never been beaten. They remained unrepentant and attached to their worship of brute force.

2. The fight was continued by the German General Staff, who concealed war criminals and equipments, built up armaments, and trained a new striking force. To evade the Armistice terms they had to find sympathisers, and "organising sympathy" became a German industry. So accommodating were the occupying forces that the Germans came to believe we would never fight them again in any cause. From that moment to this their continued aggression has brought misery or death to millions, always under the familiar smoke-screen of appeals for fair play and friendship, followed by the barrage of stark, brutal threats.

This time the Nazis have added to the experience of the last occupation; they have learned from the resistance movements of France, Belgium, Holland, and Norway. These are the type of instructions they are likely to give to their underground workers:

"Give the impression of submitting. Say you never liked the Nazis; they were the people responsible for the war. Argue that Germany has never had a fair chance. Get the soldiers arguing; they are not trained for it, and you are

"Use old folks, girls, and children, and 'play up' every case of devastation or poverty. Ask the troops to your homes; sabotage or steal equipment, petrol or rations. Get troops to sell these things, if you can. Spread stories about Americans and Russians in the British zone, and about the British to other Allies."

3. Because of these facts, I want every soldier to be clear about "non-fraternisation". Peace does not exist merely because of a surrender. The Nazi influence penetrates everywhere, even into children's schools and churches. Our occupation of Germany is an act of war of which the first object is to destroy the Nazi system. There are Allied organisations whose work it is to single out, separate and destroy the dangerous elements in German life. It is too soon for you to distinguish between "good" and "bad" Germans: you have a positive part to play in winning the peace by a definite code of behaviour. In streets, houses, cafes, cinemas, etc., you must keep clear of Germans, man, woman and child, unless you meet them in the course of duty. You must not walk out with them, or shake hands, or visit their homes, or make them gifts, or take gifts from them. You must not play games with them or share any social event with them. In short, you must not fraternise with Germans at all.

4. To refrain from fraternisation is not easy. It requires self-discipline. But in Germany you will have to remember that laughing and eating and dancing with Germans would be bitterly resented by your own families, by millions of people who have suffered under the Gestapo and under the Luftwaffe's bombs, and by every Ally that Britain possesses. You will have to remember that these are the same Germans who, a short while ago, were drunk with victory, who were boasting what they as the Master Race would do to you as their slaves, who were applauding the utter

---

The non-fraternization order issued by Montgomery in March 1945. (Held by Department of Printed Books. Negative numbers HU6398/9)

Subsequently orders were issued with examples of what constituted fraternization, which included:

The ogling of women and girls.
Shaking hands with Germans.
Small gifts to Germans, including children, e.g. a cigarette or piece of chocolate.

Later, Montgomery relented where small children were concerned, in an order issued in June 1945, ordering that: Members of British Forces in Germany will be allowed to speak to, and play with, little children.

Lieutenant-Colonel Renison:

> After dinner on 4 May, a batman came in with the news from the 9 o'clock bulletin, that the unconditional surrender had been agreed, by all the German troops facing 21st Army Group. Thus did I hear the news we had all been waiting for. It seemed an anti-climax.

Lieutenant Walter Caines, 4th Dorsets:

> I cannot express in words the joy that met our hearts on hearing the great news. I never thought to ever survive.

The Reverend Leslie Skinner:

> *Friday 4 May 1945*: Wakened to sound and sight of Very lights being fired everywhere. Sky alight like a firework display. Guessed the surrender had been announced. Too tired and cold to care. Stayed in bed. Slept miserably.
> *Friday 11 May 1945*: Cannot understand what has happened to me since war ended. I seem to have gone dry inside.

Trooper Austin Baker:

> It all seemed rather flat really. Eric Santer got drunk, but there wasn't much in the way of celebration.

Brigadier Greenacre to his wife:

> Well, we've survived the War here. Our prayers have been answered in no uncertain way and we are in good health. One cannot ask for more.
>
> However the immense problems facing a devastated Europe are such that I am staggered to know where we begin.

Private Goozee:

> We went mad with the news.

Private Eric Codling:

> Out came the rum, hoarded for this occasion, a toast to our comrades who were not there to share this moment of happiness. It seemed a lifetime since we had embarked on this adventure. Forty men drawn together by fate landed in Normandy; almost a year after, less than half of the original number were present to witness the story's end. In that space of time, almost double the initial number passed through our ranks, making it impossible to remember all their faces let alone their names.
>
> The celebrations then began and the rum flowed free. Outside it was almost as noisy as the battles of the past, signal and parachute flares soared, tracer bullets marked their graceful arcs in the sky and plastic grenades exploded. It sounded quite dangerous.

Major Peter Martin, 2nd Cheshires:

> I felt an incredible sense of anti-climax. From the age of nineteen the German war had always been there; and suddenly it disappeared. I couldn't see much point in existence any more. The whole reason for being had suddenly gone. I can remember weeping that night. I don't think I was the only person in the Division.
>
> We were told that the Battalion was to reform as a machine-gun battalion to fight the Japanese in Burma. So 'Burma When Europe's Finished' was suddenly reality.

FINAL THOUGHTS

Private James Bramwell:

>I shudder at the thought of war, but men are more evil than I had realised, and my pacifism was perhaps a little naïve.
>
>I was detailed to go in to Belsen, but this was cancelled because there were not enough people in our Field Ambulance. A major went in from our surgical team and told us about it. He had seen a woman squatting gnawing at a human thigh bone. This made me feel that Nazism was particularly evil. There was a new kind of behaviour coming. Which is why I became less worried about killing people. I began to feel that if somebody is an agent of one of these powers, I would think twice now about my status.
>
>I didn't intend to renounce my status as a pacifist at that time. But I felt rather less pacifist. I felt that men could be more evil, with propaganda brainwashing, which was still to come, and so it would be much more difficult to resist any false prophet or dictator by pacifist means. Armed resistance would have to be more active. Passive resistance would be a hopeless dream.
>
>War is the crunch of big ideas and taking sides is terribly difficult. But it has to be done; and you have to have the idea as you take your side, you're going to prevail. You have to be sure yours is the right side. They are almost religious decisions. Some pacifists have a religious feeling, I don't. If I had been a really deep pacifist I probably wouldn't have changed. Arguments about pacifism are almost always fallacious. It's not a thing you can reason about. For example how do you live on supplies imported by the state you live in and fought for by the military? You can't opt out of society.
>
>War was a kind of uplift to some people. In war you see humanity at the end of its tether, so you know what the human being is capable of. I had moments of feeling cheerful. I wasn't wasting four years of my life.

Sergeant Mike Lewis:

>The enemy, you hardly ever see them. War is mostly shell fire at a distance. Unlike the films would have you believe, where the viewer is in the position of God; one moment you see the enemy firing, and the next your side firing at the enemy, with marvellous charges led by heroic people. Battles are won by people, but you must believe in what you are doing, otherwise your weapons are just pieces of wood and iron.

Sergeant James Bellows:

>My wife will tell you I can't go to sleep with my arm round her, because in my sleep I sometimes shake and hit her. I relive parts of the war in my

sleep. You can't ever forget it. A lot of the men I lived, worked and fought with had a lot to put up with. In Sicily we had different battles nearly every day. In Sicily I was ordered to go back and put crosses on the graves of our men killed from a certain point onwards. I took some men and some wooden crosses with me. A large proportion of the graves were desecrated. The feet dug up and the boots taken off. There were all our comrades with their feet sticking up in the air. I ordered my men, 'If you see a Sicilian anywhere in the vicinity, shoot the bastard.' This is the sort of thing you see. On D plus one, we had reinforcements. One job they were given was to collect the dead for burial. One lad found his twin brother. He was shattered. Going into the attack in Normandy, we passed where the Durhams had gone in. The place was covered in Durhams' graves; CO, Adjutant, 2ic, the lot, in one field. You don't forget. Little things trigger it off. When you wake in the night, you think, 'If I'd done this, that wouldn't have happened.' Even after fifty years it's so clear.

This is where that prayer [Laurence Binyon's poem 'For the Fallen'] comes in; 'Age shall not weary them, nor the years condemn.' We're old men now. The lads I've spoken of died young. They'll always be young. But us, we become a burden to society in the end. One day it's going to be all over, and strangely you don't resent the fact, you'll welcome it when it comes.

GLOSSARY

Advanced Dressing Station, the next link in the evacuation chain behind the RAP (see below).	ADS
In north-west Europe the British had two types of anti-tank gun, the 6-pounder and the 17-pounder. Only the latter was really effective against the heavier German tanks. Anti-tank guns were issued to infantry battalions, and specialized anti-tank batteries.	Anti-tank guns
Armour Piercing shot.	AP
Armoured Personnel Carrier, an armoured tracked or wheeled vehicle designed to carry infantry into battle. Less heavily armoured than a tank.	APC
A group of armies.	Army Group
Armoured Recovery Vehicle, a turretless tank fitted with a winch to recover damaged and broken down tanks.	ARV
Armoured Vehicle Royal Engineers, a range of specialist vehicles based on a Churchill tank hull fitted with one of the following: a Petard short-range mortar, bridging equipment, a brushwood fascine bundle for bridging ditches, a carpet layer for crossing boggy ground. Not all specialist armoured vehicles were AVREs, see Crab (Flail) and Crocodile below.	AVRE
A metal tube packed with explosive, designed to be pushed into barbed wire entanglements or other obstacles in order to blow a narrow gap.	Bangalore torpedo
Infantry unit of about 36 officers and 780 NCOs and men commanded by a lieutenant-colonel. In 1944/45 a battalion consisted of four rifle companies, a headquarters company, and a support company, with organic medium mortars, assault pioneers and anti-tank guns. Each rifle company, commanded by a major or captain, consisted of a company headquarters and three platoons, each commanded by a lieutenant or second lieutenant. A platoon at full strength consisted of 36 men, divided into three sections of ten men including a bren gunner. Each section was commanded by a corporal, or sometimes a lance-sergeant. Platoon headquarters had a 2-inch mortar detachment and a PIAT crew. After arrival in the theatre of operations, and despite frequent reinforcement, infantry battalions were rarely at full strength for very long.	Battalion
The smallest, self-contained sub-unit of artillery, in field and medium regiments, normally of eight guns in two equal troops.	Battery
Bacteria carried in the colon, which spreads to the skin via the anal passage; is a possible source of infection if wounded.	B Coli
Army slang in both world wars, originally used by British troops stationed in India from the Urdu word pronounced *bilati* meaning England or home. Hence a blighty one, was a wound of sufficient seriousness to secure a return to England.	Blighty

Boase carpet	A carpet laid from a roller carried on the front of an AVRE. See photograph on page 7.
Bofors	A 40mm quick-firing anti-aircraft gun of Swedish design.
Bren	British, magazine fed, .303 inch light machine-gun.
Brigade	British formation of three infantry battalions or armoured regiments, commanded by a brigadier.
Brigade Major	Senior operations staff officer in a brigade, *de facto* chief of staff.
Browning	Most tanks were equipped with one or two Browning machine-guns in addition to their main armament. The 75mm gun Sherman had two, one ball-mounted in the hull facing forward, and fired by the co-driver; the other (known as the co-axial), in the turret alongside the main armament.
Buffalo	American Landing Vehicle Tracked, an amphibian with a water speed of 5 knots and land speed of 25 m.p.h. Propulsion in the water was provided by grousers on the tracks. The later version had a stern ramp and could lift a jeep, carrier or 25-pounder field gun. The earlier models had no ramp and could carry 25 men.
Carrier	The universal carrier, sometimes incorrectly called bren-gun carrier, was a lightly armoured, tracked vehicle, used in a variety of roles in infantry battalions, including: wireless (radio) and command vehicles, medium machine-gun and mortar carriers, and towing anti-tank guns.
CCS	Casualty Clearing Station, behind the ADS in the casualty evacuation chain (see ADS and RAP). Lightly wounded and sick could be held at the CCS before being returned to their units. More serious casualties were evacuated to Field Hospitals, and in some cases to Base Hospitals.
CGM	Conspicuous Gallantry Medal, Royal Naval decoration for sailors and Petty Officers.
Churchill tank	A heavy, but undergunned, British tank designed in 1940.
CIGS	Chief of the Imperial General Staff, the senior soldier in the British Army. In 1944/45, the position was held by Field Marshal Sir Alan Brooke, later Viscount Alanbrooke.
Concrete tetrahedra	Four-sided, dwarf, pyramids of concrete designed to impede tracked vehicles by ripping off their tracks, or hole landing-craft. Also known as dragon's teeth. See Rommel's leaflet on page 13.
Comet	British tank that came into service right at the end of 1944. The first British tank capable of defeating the best German tanks.
Corps	A formation of at least two divisions, commanded by a lieutenant-general.
COSSAC	Chief of Staff to the Supreme Allied Commander.
Coup de main	From the French, literally a blow of the hand, in military terms, a sudden, surprise attack to gain a position or valuable objective such as a bridge.
Crab	Flail Shermans (Sherman – see below) had a roller and chains fitted to the front hull, driven by the tank's engine. Flailing speed was just over one m.p.h., and

the flail would explode the current German anti-tank mine down to a depth of about six inches.

Churchill Mk VII tank fitted with a flame gun in addition to its main armament, and towing a trailer filled with 400 gallons of flame-thrower fuel.	Crocodile
British tank, with which some units were equipped.	Cromwell
Company sergeant-major.	CSM
Distinguished Conduct Medal, a decoration for gallantry for warrant officers, non-commissioned officers and soldiers.	DCM
The Duplex Drive system consisted of a boat-shaped canvas inflatable screen secured to the track guards of a Sherman tank (Sherman – see below). This gave the tank sufficient buoyancy to float. A propeller driven by the engine gave it a water speed of 4 knots. On beaching, the tracks took over the drive. As the tank drove up the beach, the screen was dropped, allowing the gun to fire.	DD Sherman
Defensive fire.	DF
Distinguished Flying Cross, Royal Air Force medal for officers.	DFC
Distinguished Flying Medal, Royal Air Force medal for non-commissioned officer air-crew.	DFM
Small lightly armoured, turretless, four-wheeled scoutcar, used by armoured commanders for command, reconnaissance and liaison, when a command tank was not suitable for the occasion.	Dingo
Formation of two or more brigades, commanded by a major-general.	Division
Distinguished Service Cross, Royal Naval decoration usually for junior officers.	DSC
Distinguished Service Medal, a Royal Naval decoration for sailors and Petty Officers.	DSM
Distinguished Service Order, a decoration for gallantry for officers of all services, usually where leadership was also displayed.	DSO
American six-wheeled amphibious truck. Initials from maker's code, pronounced 'duck'.	DUKW
Dropping Zone, area into which paratroops and/or parachuted supplies are dropped.	DZ
Slang for anti-aircraft fire, from the German *fliegerabwehrkanone*.	Flak
Tube and needle with regulating valve, for administering intravenous fluids.	Giving Set
High Explosive.	HE
The time that the first wave of craft touch down in an amphibious operation; or the leading troops cross the Start Line in a land battle.	H-Hour
Light, reconnaissance tank of American design.	Honey tank
British APC, based on Canadian-produced Sherman with turret removed. It could carry eight infantrymen.	Kangaroo

Knife rest ramps	See Rommel's leaflet on page 13. The sloping logs studded with mines, on tripod legs, are knife rest ramps.
Leaguer	An area to which armoured or mechanized units withdraw, usually at night, to rest, re-fuel and re-arm. The unit will normally be required to defend the leaguer.
LCA	Landing-Craft Assault, maximum load, an infantry platoon. Designed to be carried at a ship's lifeboat davits, and to land infantry in a beach assault. Armoured to give its passengers some protection against small arms fire and shrapnel, but not air-burst.
LCF	Landing-Craft Flak, a converted LCT (see below), to give close anti-aircraft protection to craft approaching the beach. Equipped with eight 2-pounder Bofors and four 20mm Oerlikons, or four Bofors and eight Oerlikons.
LCG	Landing-Craft Gun; a number of versions of these were produced, based on the LCT hull (see below). Their purpose was to provide close support for troops landing on a defended beach. Some had two 4.7-inch naval guns, and other lighter weapons. Others had two 17-pounder anti-tank guns.
LCI(L)	Landing-Craft Infantry (Large), designed to land follow-up infantry down gangways lowered on each side of the bow.
LCI(S)	Landing-Craft Infantry (Small), adapted from coastal forces craft. Landed infantry down gangplanks launched over rollers. Originally designed for raids, these craft proved far too vulnerable for assault against defended beaches. They had unarmoured high octane petrol tanks.
LCP(L)	Fast landing-craft (20 knots) of American design, and originally bought by the British for commando raids. They had no ramp, and a spoon bow over which troops landed by gangplank, or jumped straight into the sea. As the author can testify, the latter usually produced a very wet landing. Although some had light armour, they were unsuitable for assaulting a defended beach.
LCT	A landing-craft capable of taking six Churchills or nine Shermans, or a mix of trucks, armoured vehicles and stores, and landing them over a bow ramp on shallow beaches.
LCT(R)	An LCT converted to carry 800 to 1,000 5-inch rocket projectors, fired electrically dead ahead in a ripple salvo immediately before an assault.
LSI	Landing Ship Infantry, usually converted passenger ships, with LCAs hoisted at their davits.
LST	Landing Ship Tank, for follow-up armour and vehicles. Had bow doors and ramp, the ancestor of modern ro-ro car ferries. Could beach if required. Some carried LCAs at davits.
LVT	Landing Vehicle Tracked, *see* Buffalo.
LZ	Landing Zone, an area chosen for glider landings.
Machine-gun	In the British Army, the Vickers belt-fed, water-cooled, .303 medium machine-gun. In 1944 each infantry division had an infantry battalion designated as a specialized machine-gun battalion, consisting of three machine-gun companies,

and one heavy mortar company. Two such battalions appear in this book, 2nd Battalion the Cheshire Regiment and 8th Battalion the Middlesex Regiment. Some infantry units, notably parachute battalions and commandos, had their own machine-gun platoons, usually of only four guns.

Military Cross, a decoration for gallantry, usually for junior officers.	MC
Military Medal, a decoration for gallantry for warrant officers, non-commissioned officers and private soldiers.	MM
The British had three types of mortar in service. The 2-inch in infantry platoons, the 3-inch in infantry battalions, and a company of 4.2-inch mortars in machine-gun battalions in support of divisions. All mortars fired bombs, their high trajectory and low velocity gave little warning of incoming rounds.	Mortar
Non-commissioned officer; lance-corporal to colour sergeant (infantry and Royal Marines), Staff Sergeant (all other army units), and Flight-Sergeant RAF.	NCO
German multiple-barrel rocket launcher, sometimes referred to by British troops as a mortar.	Nebelwerfer
A 20mm quick-firing, light anti-aircraft gun of Swedish design.	Oerlikon
German tank with heavy armour and 77mm gun.	Panther
German hand-held anti-tank rocket launcher.	Panzerfaust
Naval equivalent to sergeant.	Petty Officer
Projector Infantry Anti-Tank, British hand-held anti-tank weapon. The projectile was launched by a large, strong, coiled spring.	PIAT
A self-propelled (SP) 105mm artillery piece mounted on a tracked chassis. See SP.	Priest
Regimental Aid Post, set up by the medical officer of every battalion, commando and armoured regiment in battle. The first stop in the casualty evacuation process to the rear.	RAP
In the British Army, the armoured corps equivalent of the battalion was the Regiment, consisting of three tank or 'sabre' squadrons and a headquarters squadron. Artillery batteries were also grouped into regiments.	Regiment
Rendezvous.	RV
Supreme Headquarters Allied Expeditionary Force.	SHAEF
The majority of armoured units in the British Army were equipped with several versions of this tank. It was no match in armour or hitting power for the German Tigers and Panthers. The British up-gunned some Shermans with 17-pounder guns, but even these did not redress the balance completely.	Sherman Tank
Self-propelled gun, artillery piece on tracks.	SP
Allied name for German MG34 or MG42 machine-gun.	Spandau
Beach obstacles of steel construction.	Steel hedgehogs
British 9mm calibre sub-machine-gun, a poor weapon with little stopping	Sten

power, and prone to firing accidentally, sometimes with fatal results to its owner or bystanders.

Stick   A aircraft load of parachute troops due to drop on one DZ in one run over it.

Stonk   Slang for mortar or artillery barrage.

Terrapin   Inferior British equivalent to the DUKW.

Tiger   German super-heavy tank, at 68 tons the heaviest tank in any army in the Second World War. Equipped with 88mm gun (see below).

88   The German 88mm was originally designed as an anti-aircraft gun. Early in the Second World War, the Germans began using the 88 as an anti-tank gun, while retaining large numbers as flak guns against aircraft. The 88's high velocity, flat trajectory and armour piercing capability made it a much feared weapon. The Germans first fitted it in the Tiger Mark I tank in 1942.

Typhoon   A British-designed fighter, which was originally underpowered and killed a number of pilots in crashes. With an up-rated engine, teething troubles cured, and armed with rockets, it became the most potent ground-attack aircraft in the Allied armoury. It was big, had armour plate protecting the pilot, very fast, and could take a lot of punishment.

VC   Victoria Cross, the highest award for bravery in the British services. All ranks are eligible.

Weasel   A light, unarmoured, tracked, over-snow vehicle originally issued to 52nd (Lowland) Division in their mountain role, and used by them and the commandos at Walcheren (see Chapter six). It was inadequate for the conditions it faced in the flooded, sandy terrain of Holland.

Note: The source for details of amphibious vehicles and craft is *Battle for Antwerp* by J. L. Moulton, Book Club Associates.

INDEX OF CONTRIBUTORS

This index serves two purposes: it lists those whose writings or recordings are here quoted and gives due acknowledgement to the copyright owners who have kindly allowed the publication of material held in the Museum's collections. If the copyright owner is not the contributor, their name appears in round brackets after the contributor with whom they are associated. Where the papers quoted are not contained in a collection under the contributor's own name, but form part of another collection, this is indicated in round brackets. Every effort has been made to trace copyright owners; the Museum would be grateful for any information which might help trace those whose identities or addresses are not known. The number in square brackets is the accession number in the collection.

Ranks are as they were at the time of the experiences described. Decorations are not shown.

[PP/MCR/328] (Mrs P. Lothian) 126–7, 173–4

Lieutenant Derrick Vernon [90/25/1] 233, 234, 236–7, 242

Captain V.A. Wight-Boycott RN [66/36/1] (Air Commodore Michael Wight-Boycott) 43–4

Flight Lieutenant R.H. Williams RAF [86/15/1] (Mrs D.J. Finch) 105

Captain Reg Wiltshire [94/34/1] (Donnell papers) 193, 194

Brigadier Tony Wingfield [PP/MCR/353] 109, 205–06, 207–08, 214, 232, 242–4, 252, 257, 258–9

Captain Whittle [90/20/1] (Caines collection) 174

DEPARTMENT OF SOUND RECORDS

With one exception, copyright of the contributions listed below rests with the Imperial War Museum.

Sergeant Geoffrey Barkway [10693/4] 36

Sergeant James Bellows [12913/17] 68, 263–4

Private James Bramwell [9542/20] 39–40, 103, 234, 236, 237–9, 260, 262

Company Sergeant-Major Bill Brown [9951/16] 17, 31, 48–9, 69–70, 144

Major Peter Carrington [112671] 141, 246, 260

Lieutenant-Colonel John Frost [10045/3] 151–2, 158

Sergeant John Golley [12039/4] 15–16, 130–31, 149

Captain Freddie Graham [8337/8] 86–7, 99–101, 199, 200, 220–21

Brigadier John Hackett [12022/4] 150, 151

Brigadier James Hill [12347/4] 41, 82–3

Sergeant Kenneth Kennett [10790/3] 186, 188

Sergeant Mike Lewis [4833/9] 152, 171, 177, 262

Major Peter Martin [12778/20] 18, 70–71, 89–90, 91, 94, 120, 135, 142, 143–4, 144–5, 201, 211–12, 262

Lieutenant Jeffrey Noble [10641/3] 162–4

Lieutenant-Colonel Alastair Pearson [12151/3] 41–2, 88

Brigadier Nigel Poett [11550/3] 38

Lieutenant Hugh Pond [13143/5] 39, 40

Sergeant Irving Portman [9766/5] 187

Major Geoffrey Powell [11901/3] 164–5, 165–6, 169–71, 174–5, 177

Sergeant George Self [10413/21] (Mr George Self) 16–17, 19–20, 84

Sergeant Jim Spearman [9796/8] 187–8

Major David Warren [12962/4] 10, 11, 65–6

INDEX